PSYCHOANALYTIC REFLECTIONS ON A CHANGING WORLD

PSYCHOANALYTIC REFLECTIONS ON A CHANGING WORLD

Edited by
Halina Brunning

KARNAC

First published in 2012 by
Karnac Books Ltd
118 Finchley Road
London NW3 5HT

Copyright © 2012 to Halina Brunning for the edited collection, and to the individual authors for their contributions.

The rights of the contributors to be identified as the authors of this work have been asserted in accordance with §§ 77 and 78 of the Copyright Design and Patents Act 1988.

All rights reserved. No part of this publication may be reproduced, stored in a retrieval system, or transmitted, in any form or by any means, electronic, mechanical, photocopying, recording, or otherwise, without the prior written permission of the publisher.

British Library Cataloguing in Publication Data

A C.I.P. for this book is available from the British Library

ISBN-13: 978-1-85575-886-5

Typeset by Vikatan Publishing Solutions (P) Ltd., Chennai, India

Printed in Great Britain

www.karnacbooks.com

This book is dedicated to the memory of my dear husband Robert with love forever.

CONTENTS

ACKNOWLEDGEMENTS   xi

ABOUT THE EDITOR AND CONTRIBUTORS   xiii

EDITOR'S FOREWORD   xix
Halina Brunning

INTRODUCTION   xxiii
Olya Khaleelee

PART I: PSYCHOANALYTIC REFLECTIONS ON THE WORLD OF WORK

CHAPTER ONE
Murderous mergers   3
Jinette de Gooijer

viii   CONTENTS

CHAPTER TWO
Toxicity and the unconscious experience of the body
    at the employee–customer interface   27
Mark Stein

CHAPTER THREE
Different organizations—different burnouts   51
Mathias Lohmer

PART II: PSYCHOANALYTIC REFLECTIONS ON THE FANTASTIC OBJECTS OF DESIRE

CHAPTER FOUR
Money as a phantastic object   69
Claudia Nagel

CHAPTER FIVE
With memory and desire: the function of the insurance industry
    in the world that we create   95
Matthieu Daum and Silvia Gollini

CHAPTER SIX
Psychodynamic reflections on the fashion system   113
Anna König

PART III: PSYCHOANALYTIC REFLECTIONS ON THE WORLD OF INTERCONNECTIVITY

CHAPTER SEVEN
The Twitter Revolution: how the internet has changed us   133
Philip Boxer

CHAPTER EIGHT
What are we celebrating in the celebrities?   159
Richard Morgan-Jones

CHAPTER NINE
The new unconscious: opening wider perspectives on society   179
Kenneth Eisold

PART IV: PSYCHOANALYTIC REFLECTIONS ON THE WORLD AROUND US

CHAPTER TEN
Psychoanalysis of a cityscape: a case of post-traumatic stress disorder—the city of Warsaw   197
Andrzej Leder

CHAPTER ELEVEN
Panic and pandemics: from fear of contagion to contagion of fear   213
Mario Perini

CHAPTER TWELVE
Climate change and the apocalyptic imagination   233
Paul Hoggett

CONCLUDING REMARKS
The past and present as a mirror of the future   251
James Krantz

INDEX   257

ACKNOWLEDGEMENTS

I wish to acknowledge and thank the following:

The four publishers for allowing us to reprint the original papers in this volume: Palgrave Macmillan, Res Publica, Sage Publications, Karnac Books (details in the relevant chapters).

The contributors to this volume for their professionalism, creativity, originality of thought, and generosity in their willingness to share it with me.

Olya Khaleelee and James Krantz for their willingness to act as an "impromptu reflective group" to me in my role as the sole editor, for their warm support, encouragement, and important input to this volume.

Kristof Bien and Simon Brunning for their technical support.

Daniel Brunning for his photography, which inspired the title of the book, and for letting me use three of his original photographs in this volume.

ABOUT THE EDITOR AND CONTRIBUTORS

Philip Boxer is currently completing a PhD at Middlesex University, having recently been a Senior Member of the Technical Staff at the Software Engineering Institute of Carnegie Mellon University. He consults to organizations on the challenges they face meeting unfamiliar forms of demand and the risks they face in delivering the collaborative behaviours needed to satisfy them. Philip received a BSc in electrical and electronic engineering from King's College, London University, and an MSc in business administration from the London Graduate School of Business Studies. He is a member of IEEE, INCOSE, the Institute of Business Consulting, and the Centre for Freudian Analysis and Research. His website is www.brl.com.

Halina Brunning a chartered clinical psychologist, freelance organizational consultant and executive coach. Currently an associate with LSIS, Il Nodo, and the TCS, where she is a Co-Director of the Executive Coaching Programme. She has published extensively on clinical and organizational issues and has co-edited several books, including *Executive Coaching: Systems Psychodynamic Perspective* (Karnac Books, 2006) and *Psychoanalytic Perspectives on a Turbulent World* with Mario Perini (Karnac Books, 2010). She runs training events on coaching in Europe and the UK for the HEC Paris, the iCoach Academy, Il Nodo, Rasztow, BPS, and other institutions, and is currently on the Editorial Board of the *International Journal of Coaching*. She is an Associate Fellow of the British Psychological Society, member of ISPSO, OPUS, Association of Coaching, and founder member of the BPS Coaching Psychology Forum.

Matthieu Daum was brought up in France and studied in England, where he graduated with an MSc in Group Relations at UWE, Bristol. He is founding director of Nexus, a Paris-based consultancy firm, where he consults to organizations on the issues of diversity, leadership, and strategic reorientation. Matthieu has worked on the staff of several international Group Relations conferences in France, the UK, and the US; he is a professional associate of both the Grubb Institute and the Tavistock Institute.

Jinette de Gooijer, PhD, consults to organizations on understanding the hidden aspects of organizational culture and their effects on business performance, with the view to developing work cultures that promote creativity and prosperity for the organization, the individual, and wider society. She is the Managing Director of Innovative Practice Consulting Pty Ltd; President, Group Relations Australia; Member, ISPSO; Associate and National Representative (Australia) of OPUS. Recent publications include *The Murder in Merger: A Systems Psychodynamic Exploration of a Corporate Merger* (London: Karnac, 2009), and "Drawing down the blinds on reflection: what is to be shut out or in?" in L. J. Gould, A. Lucey, & L. Stapley (Eds), *The Reflective Citizen* (London: Karnac, 2011).

Kenneth Eisold is past President of the International Society for the Psychoanalytic Study of Organizations as well as former Director of the Organizational Program at The William Alanson White Institute, where he trains consultants in working psychodynamically with organizations. He is a practising psychoanalyst as well as organizational consultant, and he has written extensively on the psychodynamics of large systems as well as on the organizational dimension of psychoanalysis. He is a Fellow of the A. K. Rice Institute. His book *What You Don't Know You Know* was published in January 2010.

Silvia Gollini, brought up and trained in Italy, graduated with a degree in Economics and a Master in psycho-socio analysis with Ariele school and ISMO. Silvia has over fifteen years' experience of consulting to organizations on HR process, change management, and increasing diversity and inclusion in the workplace, especially regarding gender diversity. She has developed her career in big consultancy firms where she has worked as consultant for a range of multinationals. She takes part in and facilitates women's circles. She is a partner and director of Nexus.

Paul Hoggett is Professor of Social Policy and Director of the Centre for Psycho-Social Studies at the University of the West of England, Bristol. He has over twenty years' experience researching welfare change and the dynamics of urban communities. He is also a psychoanalytic psychotherapist and has a strong interest in the role of emotions in organizational and political life. He has been involved in training and consultancy to public organizations and was one of the founding editors of *Organisational and Social Dynamics*. He is the author of many books, the latest being *Politics, Identity and Emotion* (Paradigm Publishers, 2009).

Olya Khaleelee is a psychoanalytic psychotherapist, corporate psychologist, and organizational consultant, with a particular interest in organizational transition and transformation. She has worked with the Tavistock Institute for over twenty-five years in developing group relations both in the UK and abroad, has been on the staff of many conferences, and was the first female Director of the Leicester Conference, which explores authority, leadership, and organization from a psychoanalytic and systemic perspective. She was for many years Director of OPUS, an Organization for Promoting Understanding in Society, and is also a past Chairwoman of the Council of the London Centre for Psychotherapy.

Anna König is a lecturer in Cultural and Historical Studies at the University of Arts, London. She completed a degree in Applied Psychology at Sussex University before studying art and design at Central Saint Martins and then fashion history at the London College of Fashion. She has contributed to a number of academic texts on fashion and the fashion media, and has written for several national newspapers and magazines. Current research interests include the ethics of fashion representation and fashion consumption.

James Krantz is an organizational consultant and researcher from New York City. He is a Principal at Worklab, an organizational constancy which concentrates on strategy implementation, team development, and work process design. He is past President of the International Society for the Psychoanalytic Study of Organizations (ISPSO); Director of the Center for Socio-Analytic Studies at the Institute for Psychoanalytic Training and Research (IPTAR); Fellow of the A. K. Rice Institute; and member of OPUS. His writing centres on the unconscious background of work life and socio-psychological challenges posed by emerging forms of organization. His PhD is in Systems Sciences from the Wharton School.

Andrzej Leder is a philosopher and a psychoanalytical psychotherapist. He works on the question of the philosophical position of psychoanalytical thought. He has four published books in Polish, including two collections of philosophical essays, one of which was awarded a literary prize in 2004. He has also published articles in English and French philosophical reviews. He is Professor at the Institute of Philosophy and Sociology of the Polish Academy of Sciences, Warsaw, Poland.

Mathias Lohmer, PhD, was trained as a clinical psychologist and psychoanalyst (IPA). He is working as organizational consultant, coach, and psychotherapist in Munich, Germany. He is a member of ISPSO (International Society for the Psychoanalytic Study of Organizations) and of IPOM (Institute for Psychodynamic Organizational Consultation Muenchen—www.ipom.net). He is on the board of an IPOM training programme for psychodynamic organizational consultation and co-director of the TFP-Institute Muenchen (Transference-Focused Psychotherapy), specializing in training and research on psychodynamic psychotherapy for severe personality disorders. He has published on a number of topics, including economic change and organizational identity, the role of the consultant, and the treatment of borderline and narcissistic patients (www.lohmer.info).

Richard Morgan-Jones is an organizational consultant and a psychoanalytic psychotherapist in Eastbourne, UK. He was educated at Cambridge, Oxford, and Exeter Universities in Anthropology, Theology, and Education, and he is a full member at the London Centre for Psychotherapy. He belongs to the Organization for Promoting the Understanding of Society (OPUS), the International Society for the Psychoanalytic Study of Organizations (ISPSO), the European Business Ethical Network (EBEN), and the Restorative Justice Consortium (RJC). He directs Work Force Health: Consulting and Research. He has written *The Body of the Organisation and Its Health* (Karnac 2010), an exploration of how organizations get under the skin. Website: www.rmjconsulting.co.uk.

Claudia Nagel holds a PhD in Organizational Psychology and an MBA. Claudia is also trained as a Jungian Analyst at ISAP (Zurich). She started her professional career as a Director of the Institute of Business Ethics. After extensive experience in management consulting (Gemini Consulting) and in different leadership positions in investment banking (Credit Suisse, Goldman Sachs), she has founded her own firm, Nagel & Company, a management consultancy focusing on her new approach to psychodynamic strategy development and the respective change processes. Claudia has worked and lived in New York, London, Paris, and Germany.

Mario Perini, MD, Director of IL NODO Group and scientific advisor of the Italian Group Relations Conferences Programme, is a psychiatrist, a psychoanalyst, and an organizational consultant, a member of the Italian Psychoanalytic Association, International Psycho-Analytic Association, and the International Society for the Psychoanalytic Study of Organizations. He works as a consultant in the public, private, and voluntary sectors, a trainer for professional and management education, a group supervisor, a psychotherapist, and a personal coach. Professor of group dynamics at the Post-Graduate School of Health Psychology, Turin University, he published the book *L'organizzazione nascosta* ("The Hidden Organization", FrancoAngeli, 2007) and co-edited with Halina Brunning *Psychoanalytic Perspectives on a Turbulent World* (Karnac Books, 2010).

Mark Stein is Professor and Chair in Leadership and Management at the University of Leicester. Previously, Mark has been a Senior Lecturer at Imperial College London, a Research Fellow at the London School of Economics and Brunel University, and a Researcher and Consultant at the Tavistock Institute. Mark has a long-standing interest in the psychoanalytic study of leadership, groups, and organizations, and has undertaken many years of research, consultancy, coaching, and teaching using these ideas. He received an Emerald Citation of Excellence for his paper on "Critical Period of Disasters" (published in *Human Relations* in 2004). He received the Richard Normann Prize for an abridged version of the paper that appears in this volume, published originally in *Organization Studies* in 2007.

EDITOR'S FOREWORD

The main purpose of this book is to look at a range of ubiquitous phenomena that make up our daily lives and to ask, not so much whether psychoanalytic thinking can add to our existing understanding of these phenomena, but what it can add. Is there another layer, below the obvious surface layer, that could be explored further? And if so, can psychoanalytic light reflect upon and illuminate some of the new contours and shapes perhaps previously not fully seen or appreciated? What interim conclusions can we reach as a result of these reflections upon our contemporary world?

This book is linked to its immediate predecessor *Psychoanalytic Perspectives on a Turbulent World* (edited by Halina Brunning and Mario Perini, Karnac Books, 2010). It was my intention to create a lighter volume that differed significantly in focus, tone, and composition from the "turbulent world" mode. This new book would no longer address the complex and troubling issues of war, conflict, the global financial crisis, and our struggle with leadership; instead, it would tend to look at the lighter side of life.

As Editor, I do not claim that this book offers a completely new way of seeing, interpreting, and analysing conscious everyday phenomena. It is my hope, however, that by linking the various elements of our lives into the famous "frieze of life", this collection of twelve essays will cumulatively form a tentative frame for noticing, exploring, hypothesizing, and reflecting upon the forces and the processes that exist beneath the surface of our interactions with each other and with our changing world.

When I started planning this book, early in 2010, I was fascinated by a number of themes that I wanted to explore: some geopolitical (such as the Iranian Revolution), some sociological (such as the growth of the Internet), some organizational (such as murderousness unleashed in mergers), some frivolous (such as money, fashion, cosmetics, and the cult of celebrities). There was no awareness, early in 2010, of what might be happening just around the corner in the Arab countries, where only a year later the revolutionary fervour was indeed fuelled by Twitter and Facebook, helping the various populations in their own demands for democratic changes to ensure that "the truth travels faster than the lies".[1] Somehow, the title given to Philip Boxer for his chapter "The Twitter Revolution: how the Internet has changed us", has been unintentionally prescient. Equally, when I asked Paul Hoggett to consider writing on the theme of climate change and the apocalyptic mindset, it was several months prior to the events surrounding the real apocalypse in Japan. When the twelve commissioned chapters started flowing in, I realized that, far from aspiring to create a light and airy volume, the book was beginning to look just as serious, heavy, and angst-ridden as its predecessor!

The book has been arranged in four parts. Each addresses a set of three linked and interconnected phenomena explored in separate chapters. A psychoanalytic lens has been applied to each one in turn and cumulatively to all four groups:

1. Psychoanalytic reflections on the world of work
2. Psychoanalytic reflections on the fantastic objects of desire
3. Psychoanalytic reflections on the world of interconnectivity
4. Psychoanalytic reflections on the world around us

Having received, read, and edited all twelve chapters, as well as the Introduction by Olya Khaleelee and the Concluding Remarks by James Krantz, I can now see that each of the four parts of the book manifests a different form of social anxiety.

In the first part, the three chapters commissioned separately deal with work issues independently of each other and yet, when read together, they spell out overwhelming social and individual anxiety arising from fast-changing organizational patterns, murderous attacks by one part of the organization upon another in the merging process, attacks of the customer upon the worker, or when all else fails, the attack of the executive upon his or her own self and body, otherwise known as "burnout".

In the second part, the three chapters dealing with "the fantastic objects of desire" independently of each other address issues of money, fashion, and insurance, yet what connects them under the surface is a narcissistic, omnipotent defence mobilized methodically in the fight against overwhelming existential anxiety.

The third part of the book on theme of "interconnectivity" features three chapters seemingly unconnected: the new unconscious, the Twitter Revolution, and the cult of celebrities. Yet when read together, they too attest to our desperate attempts to make sense of a world that is threatening to disintegrate, become meaningless, disconnected, and overwhelming.

The last part describes a world ravaged by man-made apocalypse such as the Holocaust, the epidemics and pandemics created by natural forces, and man's historical response to them. It addresses natural and man-made climate changes that could be predicting a catastrophe, at the very least a catastrophe in the mind, but also a real-life catastrophe just waiting in the wings.

The book starts with Olya Khaleelee's reflections upon these interconnected themes and what they might mean about our collective state of mind and the state of the world. The book ends with an essay by James Krantz, which critically examines the cumulative impact of the twelve chapters upon our own understanding of our changing world as he begins to outline "the future we are in".

In order to explore these and related subjects, I have invited fifteen academics, researchers, well-known and celebrated authors and experienced practitioners of psychoanalysis and related fields, to offer their creative thinking and share interim conclusions commissioned for[2] and collected in this volume. It must be said that what connects their efforts begins to look rather different from my aspirations of creating a light and a hope-filled volume.

To illustrate more accurately the newly emerging and not fully predicted essence of this volume, I have selected five black-and-white photographs which symbolize the intensity of the conclusions reached.

And so, Part One is illustrated by the dizzy heights of an escalator, able both to take you to the very top, or to trip you up and send you down onto your knees.

Part Two is symbolized by a narcissistic mirror-image of a solitary tree reflecting and contemplating itself as an object of desire.

Part Three is illustrated by an incomplete circle of the London Eye, a temporary man-made monument to the Millennium, which has become a much loved and a celebrated symbol of design in London. A true tourists' attraction, it brings people to London and has had its life extended well beyond the initial period of grace set for it by the Local Authority at the dawn of 2000. It triumphs over the recognizable landscape of the capital as a proud symbol of people-power representing their chosen object of hope, symbolism, and modernity.

The final part is illustrated by a fragment of the monument to the Heroes of the Ghetto Uprising in Warsaw, a silent cry of pain, desperation, and utter heroism in the face of destruction and obliteration.

The cover image shows a view of the City Town Hall, the London Assembly, site of London governance, a curious mass of a pregnant woman-like figure, inter-twined with its own umbilical cord, proudly bulging out, dominating the space that it is controlling and surveying.

My job is complete.

I now invite you, the reader, to reflect on and associate to this book, and to our changing world.

Halina Brunning
The Editor
31/03/2011

Notes

1. BBC *Newsnight* 8th February 2011.
2. Two of the chapters are shorter versions of previously published papers, and two chapters are reprinted with permission from other publications. Details in text.

INTRODUCTION

Olya Khaleelee

This is a sibling book, conceived through a dream with its twin: *Psychoanalytic Perspectives on a Turbulent World*. Much of its content explores through contemporary phenomena the underlying existential anxieties and consequences of loss of containment in modern society from a psychoanalytic perspective. The first three pungent and arresting titles in this new book: Murderous mergers; Toxicity and the unconscious experience of the body at the employee–customer interface; and Different organizations—different burnouts, immediately tune into these elements of our collective psyche. Murderousness, toxicity, and burnout all indicate the proximity of death and the possibility of the death instinct triumphing over life and health. These contemporary phenomena contain within them primitive and corporeal reactions and processes. All three embody assaults on the organization and on our personal boundaries, which threaten the integrity of the self and that part of the self identified with the organization.

Halina Brunning's fascinating book takes a psychoanalytic look at our lives today starting with these three very powerful inputs about the world of work. They go straight to the gut and address the most primitive needs and wants within each of us: terror, and the fight to survive the threat of invasion and of annihilation; rage, and the drive for revenge; love, and the need for the containing "mother"; desire, for attachment without merger, for deep connection, and for self-esteem.

The second section, entitled "Fantastic objects of desire", considers "Money as a phantastic object", "Psychodynamic reflections on the fashion system", and "With memory and desire: the function of the insurance industry in the world that we create". These examine the issue of survival from two perspectives: the first is the narcissistic need to find self-worth by searching elsewhere for the lost mother. Lack of identity is explored by analysing how money becomes a substitute for the mirroring mother and thus develops a perverse, fetishistic character in contemporary society, enabling the individual to find another way to hold the self together.

This is taken further through the lens of changing trends in fashion and in photography, where the "'maternal face' is described as a dominant archetype, ... characterised by ... an expression that is gently appealing ... facilitating the rediscovery of the mother's face, ... of what has been lost". This links with how fashion photography has been controlled by male-dominated, sadistic images and projections which have the effect of fragmenting the body. The author of this illuminating paper reminds us with a quote by Roland Barthes that "The photograph always serves as a reminder of death".

The second perspective, examined through the development of the insurance industry, is also about survival, in this case tracing the development of insurance as a relief against persecutory anxiety and showing how it has become more important to the individual as family and community networks have fragmented. The authors suggest that insurance defends individuals from experiencing the limits to their own potency but, in doing so, protects them from reality and therefore prevents them from experiencing themselves as fully alive.

Disappearance, obliteration, merger, being devoured, loss of all boundaries and sense of self, helplessness, loss of mind and the capacity to think, are thus explored in several of the excellent chapters in this book, leading to questions about existence, meaning, and spiritual identity for the individual in society today.

Tracing this back, it might be worth considering a thesis put forward by Eric Miller, who wondered whether the erosion of boundaries began in Europe with the loss of male authority as a dependable object through absence and death during the Second World War. The subsequent breakdown of the dependency culture of the post-war generation had the psychic effect of a related loss of a sense of personal belonging to previously dependable institutions: projections which belonged to work organizations, church, and family. These fragmenting institutions were no longer perceived to be able to provide a "holding environment" for such feelings, which had to be re-introjected by the individual in unmodified form. By the 1990s, there were clear signs of a psychological withdrawal from these institutions and heightened social anxiety. Perhaps akin to the break-up of the ice-cap—always present as an image in the collective mind, but now disappearing—like the polar bear, we are potentially threatened with extinction. It is as though we are experiencing the last vestiges of an old order, whilst in the middle of a massive revolutionary change, the outcome of which cannot be predicted. But it has a central relationship to authority and to the loss of a very significant dependency object.

This leads to the question of whether the evident loss of trust in hierarchical authority has led to a greater dependence on a horizontal "peer" authority or "sibling" attachment, evidenced in social networking and blogs, whereby any individual can comment or offer advice without having a specifically recognized expert authority to do so, or indeed any personal knowledge of or relationship with the other. Having online and personal help from unknown others to commit suicide would be one example of this "sibling" relatedness. Tens and hundreds of contacts on Facebook and Twitter provide a new "friendship" group and confirmation of personal existence and identity. It appears as though the social network supplements the "family", providing the missing mirror of mother. As the family unit fragments into ever smaller elements, so the social network expands into the hundreds.

At the same time, the signs of no longer being important to others may not be because they have necessarily said so, but because your presence is wiped off their Facebook wall, obliterated. Again, this gives rise to the question: Who am I? Do I exist? How do I survive? Where is the other, the "mirror", that will help to confirm and keep me in the world? These strands are explored in depth in the riveting chapters in the third section on the "World of interconnectivity", through the analyses of the authors of the "Twitter Revolution: how the Internet has changed us" and "What are we celebrating in the celebrities?" These contributions help us to see and understand better the primitive nature and narcissistic quality of many of the feelings expressed through these fascinating contemporary developments.

This need for the "mirror" brings to mind the film *Cast Away*, starring Tom Hanks in the title role of Chuck, a Fed-Ex systems analyst. Finding himself the only survivor, marooned and alone on an uninhabited island after a plane crash, one of the first things he does is to create an "other", in this case a literal object to which he can relate. It is a volleyball on which he draws a face with his bloodied hand, names it "Wilson", and begins talking to it as if it were a person. "Wilson" stays with him almost to the end. Four years later, Chuck escapes from the island. After some time at sea, he is hit by a storm that almost tears his raft apart. The following day, "Wilson" falls from the raft and is lost. Overwhelmed by grief and loss, Chuck abandons his attempt to find rescue. Later, he is found drifting by a passing cargo ship. He does survive, but would it have been possible without his almost constant "companion"?

These chapters on the use of fashion, the meaning of money, the analysis of the cult of celebrity in "What are we celebrating in the celebrities?" and the "Twitter Revolution", elucidate powerfully the unconscious societal dynamics operating today, linking the individual's inner world with global phenomena. Just as in space exploration, it is clear we are but a speck in a vast, ever-expanding universe, which continues to be created as we live out our own lives within it, so within our inner worlds, we are also creating other existences and universes. The IT revolution provides an escape and the means for other selves, but the question is whether and how these created identities impact on our personal sense of self. Indeed, even the boundaries of that virtual world can dissolve, so that the "real" self suffers the consequences of virtual events. For example, "virtual" infidelities within the Avatar world of Second Life may result in separation and divorce in the real world.

A recent report explains, in a piece entitled "Facebook named as third party in post-Christmas divorce risk", that there is a steep rise in divorce petitions involving Facebook and other social networking sites such as Second Life, Illicit Encounters, and Friends Reunited. Thus, there is no escape from loss and consequent existential anxiety whether in our fictional created world or in our everyday real world. We have also seen the effects of this phenomenon at a more "macro" level through the recent economic crisis. The "virtual" economy has impacted heavily on the real economy and, at the time of writing, this has led to real economic hardship for many, high unemployment, homelessness, and so on.

The loss of belief in hierarchical authority may also relate to the rise of paired leadership, not just through the present coalition government in the UK, but more generally. Paired leadership, co-directorship, partnership, distributed leadership seem to be more in focus today. Perhaps this is a manifestation of a longing in society for a different kind of leadership. It is clear that the development of horizontal authority is also a powerful force for large groups of people wishing to stand up to the prevailing hierarchical authority. Recent political events in Tunisia and Egypt are evidence of this capacity to mobilize and organize *en masse* through Twitter and Facebook in a drive for social change.

Distrust of our leaders' capacity to be truthful, confirmed through outlets like Wikileaks, leads to a questioning of reality: What is really going on? Who can we trust? What is public, what is private? Where and how do we derive meaning for our existence, or are we just specks in an ever-changing kaleidoscope of relatednesses? The more we find ourselves alongside others without relationship, the greater the isolation and inner emptiness: we "know" everyone and no-one, and the question of personal identity hangs in the air. Here, the death instinct, with the threat of implosion, struggles with the life instinct and the potential for creativity.

Sartre, in his book *Being and Nothingness* (1943), talks of expectations which are often unfulfilled, leaving the individual with a "negation", a void. He suggests that this negation allows the self to enter what he calls the "great human stream". The great human stream arises from a realization that nothingness is a state of mind in which we can become anything, within our context, that we desire. In today's world, this links directly with Second Life and Friends Reunited. Sartre argues that human existence is a state of conflict in which, on the one hand, each of us exists, for as long as we live, within an overall condition of nothingness (no thingness)—that ultimately allows for free consciousness. But on the other hand, at the same time, within our (physical existence) being, we have constantly to make conscious choices. Sartre suggests that this dichotomy causes anguish, because choice represents a limit on freedom within an otherwise free and uncontrolled range of thoughts. Subsequently, we seek to flee from this anguish through actions such as escape, visualization, visions, or dreams which are designed to lead us towards some meaningful end, our destiny, or our relationship with God.

This treatise, published during the Second World War, appears quite prophetic today when we have the possibility both of actual escape into outer space as well as into the inner virtual world. Unfortunately, wherever we go, our inner world "baggage" goes with us. This was sadly in evidence soon after the invention of the Internet, which could have been a fresh start for all of us, until it was infected by human malignance, malice, and manipulation evidenced through Internet viruses, worms, Trojans, spam, and so on. The management of aggression and the effort to maintain a balance between destructive envy and love is an ongoing battle.

Sartre goes on to discuss how the individual is bound to the conditioned, physical world—in which some form of action is always required. This leads to failed dreams of completion, as Sartre described them, because inevitably we are unable to bridge the void between the purity and spontaneity of thought and all-too-constraining action; between the being and the nothingness that inherently coincide in our self. From this perspective, Sartre suggests that we will always have to engage with our emptiness and disappointment, which sounds quite a pessimistic scenario, perhaps linked with the deathly *Zeitgeist* in which he wrote.

The last four chapters of this book link the past with the future from both pessimistic and optimistic perspectives: life and death instincts still vie with each other. On the one hand, the death instinct can be seen to operate in society through the denial of global interdependence and splitting and projection of destructive envy into other countries, which are then attacked. On the other hand, we see global acknowledgement of interdependence, with collaboration and mutual support at a time of threat of annihilation through fire, flood, and other natural disasters. Survival is therefore still the theme, but now there is the possibility of moving on and developing new insights through working across the boundaries and with the differences.

"The new unconscious: opening wider perspectives on society", an enticing, tantalizing title, does indeed open up the possibilities arising from integrating psychoanalysis and neuroscience, particularly in relation to how the individual relates to society. Self-esteem and the maintenance of inner stability, whilst feeling anxious and out of control, are by now familiar themes, but here explored in a different way. At the same time, exciting links and insights are offered which cast a different light on our economic and political institutions.

The last section of this absorbing book, entitled "Psychoanalytic reflections on the world around us", is really about life and death through catastrophe. It includes a fascinating chapter entitled "Psychoanalysis of a cityscape: the city of Warsaw". This explores in depth how its long history, near obliteration, and finally the impact of the Second World War have left the city of Warsaw, not just the people who live there, structurally in a post-traumatic state, from which, the author argues, it has not yet recovered. He offers an original and emotional argument that this history is imprinted upon and underpins its layout, in much the same way as might be hypothesized for the personality of a depressed second- or third-generation Holocaust survivor or a person suffering from symptoms of post-traumatic stress disorder. In this way, the past continues to live in the present.

The theme of catastrophe continues with "Panics and pandemics: from fear of contagion to contagion of fear", a detailed analysis of how epidemics have always been a threat to our survival and the social order. The author cogently traces how the impact of illness on a global scale generates a climate of panic, mass fear of contagion, and widespread social effects. He explores epidemics as a psychosocial process, with particular relevance to the fragmentation and lack of solidarity in modern communities. He offers a powerful and positive argument for "learning organizations, reflective spaces, and institutional containers capable of holding and transforming societal anxieties".

The author of the twelfth chapter of this book, "Climate change and the apocalyptic imagination", takes our understanding of catastrophe further by showing how historically each generation has been caught up with heightened anxieties related to the possibility of annihilation. There is almost a macro-rhythm to the escalation of anxiety about survival, which is really quite fascinating, as it shows how a collective state of mind can be writ large on the global stage and can generate a distorted sense of reality. This state of mind: "instead of attachment to life there is desperate clinging" subsumes our capacity to think about how to deal with this particular threat.

Our grasp of unconscious phenomena in contemporary society is greatly enhanced by reading these fascinating discussions, which are at the cutting edge of our understanding today. James Krantz has the final word and helps us all to reflect further on what might be possible.

Halina Brunning, the editor of this original book, leaves us with the question of whether we can envisage and create a more optimistic, life-giving future.

27 January 2011

References

Hoggett, P. (2011). *Climate Change and the Apocalyptic Imagination* (this volume).

König, A. *Psychodynamic Reflections on the Fashion System* (this volume), referring to the work of Diana Fuss (1994).

König, A. *Psychodynamic Reflections on the Fashion System* (this volume), referring to the work of Roland Barthes (1984), *Camera Lucido*. London: Flamingo.

Miller, E. J. (1986). *Making Room for Individual Autonomy in Executive Power*, Ed. Suresh Srivastra & Associates, Jossey-Bass, pp. 257–288.

The Times, 15 January 2011, p. 41.

Wikipedia entry on Jean-Paul Sartre.

PART I

PSYCHOANALYTIC REFLECTIONS ON THE WORLD OF WORK

CHAPTER ONE

Murderous mergers

Jinette de Gooijer[1]

A merger of organizations, or of business divisions within an enterprise, is a radical change to the identities of the existing enterprises. Attachments are broken and need to be reformed, experiences of loss and gain prevail. Projective processes of splitting, fears of annihilation, and anxieties about loss of loved objects are typical of some of the primitive impulses invoked by a merger. These processes are equally present for intra-organizational mergers.

Mergers and acquisitions carry the primitive hope of pairing: that the two will generate new life. The psychodynamic processes of this pairing, and the primitive impulses unleashed by them, are rarely considered by those who are charged with managing the implementation, even when popular business literature commonly cites a high failure rate of mergers. What is more often experienced in reality is that the merger is a takeover—one firm's management, systems, processes, work values, and culture dominate the other; the identity of the second firm is virtually obliterated as a result. Understandably, members of the subordinate firm are likely to feel disenfranchised or annihilated. Similar dynamics are observable on a smaller scale when organizations restructure and merge functional units or work groups.

When an enterprise engages in major change such as a merger, the importance of attending to emotional experiences and how these contribute to understanding invisible forces affecting the enterprise becomes readily apparent. Emotional forces aroused by large-scale corporate mergers and their effects upon organizational functioning are not widely understood, however.

At its most basic level, a merger radically changes and disrupts the structure and networks of role relationships, and people's identification with the enterprise. Restructures and mergers inevitably invoke realistic and neurotic anxieties about surviving changes to role and status in the organization. If the felt experiences of organizational members are not contained, their anxieties may become amplified, instinctual fears may become attached to real dangers, and primitive fears of annihilation may be aroused.

My contention is that an organizational merger is a catastrophic change for the entities involved, and depends on "killing off" parts of the former organizations for its success. The act of annihilating parts of the former organizations is experienced as disengaged and murderous by employees. This arouses persecutory anxiety of an unbearable intensity amongst organizational members, from which they defend themselves by emotionally disconnecting from the psychic reality of the organization.

Organizations are systems of meaning and symbolic objects held in the minds of members as an unconscious image, the "organization-in-the-mind" (Armstrong, 2005; Hutton, 2000). The notion of a murderous merger arises from the reality that two organizations are destroyed to create a new, third entity. Symbolically, this destruction may be experienced as a murder by organizational members. When an organization "dies", or parts of the organization are "killed off", it is a *symbolic destruction* of the "organizational object" held in the minds of members and emotionally experienced. The felt experience evokes the symbolic experience from an earlier developmental time of "the loss of a loved object from absence, injury or annihilation" (Klein, 1975a; H. F. Stein, 1996). The symbolic destruction of parts, or the whole, of the organization cannot be equated to a real, biological death, but it is linked to events in the external reality of the enterprise.

Destruction of parts of an organization will invoke feelings about members' own capacity for destruction. These feelings may be of such unbearable intensity for some individuals that they attack the "emotional link" (Bion, 1988). In the death or destruction of an organization, the same organizational object may be loved and hated, mourned and attacked.

A merger is an act of creating a new organization. As such, the new organization experiences developmental phases akin to those of an infant, the primary phase being of dealing with life and death instincts. These primary instincts, which have been worked through in early development of the individual, are re-invoked when a threatening situation to the ego occurs in adulthood (Klein, 1975b). How such anxieties are managed in the immediate aftermath of a merger is at the heart of successfully creating a new entity that can endure (Brunning, 2003). My proposition is that attending to systemic psychodynamic processes will engender more creative and healthy experiences of organizational mergers, acquisitions, and takeovers.

* * *

This chapter draws on research conducted on the nature of emotional connectedness during the first three years of a newly merged entity (de Gooijer, 2003, 2006, 2009). The focus of the research was on the dynamics of emotional connectedness experienced by employees of a multinational professional services firm who were located in the Australian offices of the company's regional operations. A high degree of disconnectedness was observed and experienced, evidence of profound disruption to emotional links caused by the recent merger of the firm. Heightened anxieties were prevalent at every level in the organization, enduring for nearly three years after the merger was implemented. Many of the staff felt under psychic attack from persecutory anxieties. While left unacknowledged and uncontained, the business suffered financial and psychic losses. Not only was the merger experienced as murderous towards the staff, but also of the enterprise itself.

The chapter is structured in three parts following this introduction. The first part presents an introduction to the organizational merger referred to above. In the second part, I consider the dynamics of a merger experienced as a catastrophic change: the persecutory anxieties invoked by the change, and the defences mobilized in response to those anxieties. The final part of the chapter discusses the containment of unconscious anxieties in organizational mergers.

Introduction to the case: the merger of two global firms[2]

The collapse of technology stocks in 2000, along with the Enron scandal and the sudden and dramatic demise of Andersen Consulting, instigated a number of mergers amongst professional services.

XYZ company was the result of one such merger between two firms that provided business consulting services. One firm was largely European-based, the other more global in its operations. The latter firm had operated in Australia for decades prior to the merger, and its global head office was located in the USA. However, the new headquarters for the merged enterprise were situated in Europe. Some of the significant changes associated with the merger included: the business structure changed from a partnership to a corporation; locally in Australia-New Zealand (A-NZ), six autonomous business units merged into one, under a regional structure; and the European firm had not previously operated in Australia.

Three months after the merger took effect, the terrorist attack on New York occurred. XYZ company began its life in an environment of fear and uncertainty.

The new enterprise employed about 57,000 people in its beginning. Of these, about 3,000 were employed in the Asia-Pacific regional offices. Within Australia and New Zealand, the focus of this chapter's discussion, some 350 people were employed at the time of the merger. Within the first year, their numbers swelled to about 800; two years later, there were fewer than 200 staff in the A-NZ offices. Two waves of redundancy occurred, each time happening before the Christmas holiday break. Staff were also "performance-managed" out of the organization based on a system of sacking those who were ranked on "the bottom 10% of the bell curve", or assessed to be "red" on the "traffic light" system of affiliation to the culture and values of the firm.

Several services and functions of the A-NZ business units were shut down at the same time. A local office manager commented that she "felt indifferent about the turnover of staff—oh, another one gone; I barely have time to get to know some and then they are gone". During this period, management continued to say they were concerned about "staff affiliation" to the firm and the "high turnover of unplanned exits".

The new structure of the A-NZ part of the organization was modelled on a matrix of service products and industry sectors. This was the stated structure. Internally, a support structure was created to replace the old partnership model of partner teams. This structure was coined "counselling families", having their primary role in managing individual performance through a role of "counsellor". This role was different from and separate to that of a project leader or manager. It was explicitly stated that no-one's work performance was to be appraised by their immediate project team leader, "because they would not be objective". An explicit desire to break the old partner relationships is evident in this structure.

However, the primary task of the organization was delivered through project teams of consultants, who formed for the duration of a project and typically worked off-site, supported by administrative support teams and a management structure. Obtaining a position on a project that offered longevity and high status was of paramount importance to a consultant. The firm's leadership expected consultants to be "self-reliant individuals" who sought out their own opportunities and prospected for project work. This engendered an informal network of personal relationships—consultants reported a dominant culture of political networking in order to get a position on high-value projects. The purported non-hierarchical matrix structure did not exist in reality; rather, there was a "real structure of hierarchy and power".

Members' experiences of connecting to the organization, connecting to their own and others' roles, and to the work of the enterprise itself, was characterized by high levels of confusion and uncertainty, chaotic processes, uncontained anxieties, feeling vulnerable and abandoned in the face of management's manic responses to a worsening business environment. The overriding quality of the work culture was distinguished by a prevalence of emotional disconnections between employees and the firm, between management and staff, and across the structure of work groups.

> Few people round here would trust this company. They may trust individuals, but not the company.
> (senior manager)

Feelings of distrust intensified with the turmoil of retrenchments and staff turnover. Many ex-partners left the firm in the first year. The regional director's role had three incumbents in eighteen months. New organizational procedures and systems, and a stronger focus on sales figures and consultants' utilization rates, were introduced. To many long-serving staff, this felt alien. Psychically, it was like an invasion by a foreign culture—a new language, a new social order, and new rules imposed by leaders who were remote and invisible. A drawing (Figure 1) made by an executive illustrates this starkly. He described it as "a representation of the need for us all to sing the one tune, in unity".

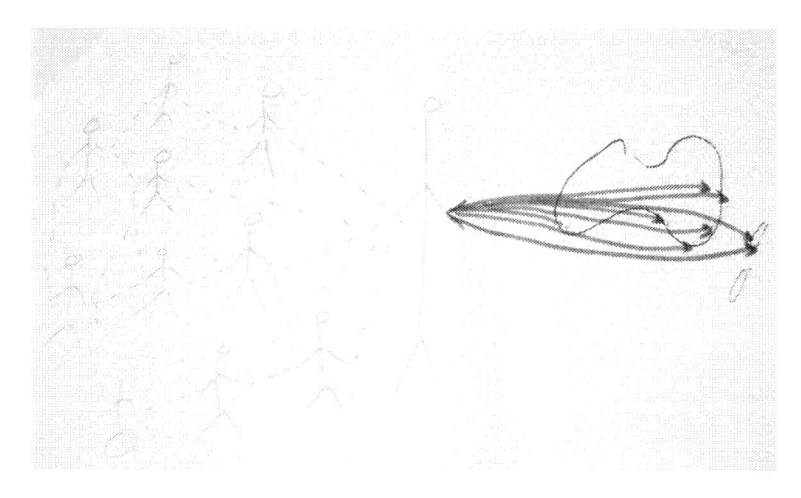

Figure 1. Merger as foreign invasion.

Yet the image suggests something more sinister. A tightly connected troop of identical figures (though one—possibly female—appears to be upside down) are arranged behind a much larger figure and appear to be advancing on Australia-New Zealand, shown as an "empty" land mass . A tall figure dominates the scene. Blue arrows emanating from this figure convey an image of the trajectories of long-range missiles. Seen in this light, the picture communicates ideas of invasion and attack.

Another drawing (Figure 2) depicts "a whole lot of people under threat of exodus from smoke stacks" (consultant). It is ambiguous in the picture as to whether people are in exodus from the smoke stacks or walking towards them, perhaps to be fed as fuel for the fire. The latter would suggest extermination. Regardless, the smoke stacks look ominous and dominate the regions in which they are located. The one near Australia is off-shore, while a solitary figure stands on the edge of the southern seaboard and faces the stack.

These feelings of being under hostile attack intensified over a period of nearly three years until a director from the company's headquarters stepped in and implemented a radical downsizing of the A-NZ operations and a return to realistic business objectives.

A post-script: Eight years later, the company has survived its tumultuous beginnings, but with a significant change—all references to the former US firm have been erased, along with the services it provided.

Figure 2. Destructive power of the merger.

There is little to suggest that XYZ company was once anything other than a smaller version of itself, a European consulting services firm.

* * *

A merger is a catastrophic change

An organizational merger implies that there is a greater chance of survival for the individual organizations if they combine resources, services, and markets. The fantasy may be that it will stave off the danger of deprivation for each organization, and that a merger will bring together the best parts of the organization; that is, only the "good objects" will merge. The unconscious fear is that perhaps only the bad parts become conjoined, and these will destroy the new entity. The envisaged change is thus filled with hope. The reality is likely to be something altogether different.

Bion (1984) uses the term "catastrophic change" to refer to a subversion of the order or system of things, felt to be a disaster by those experiencing the change. It usually occurs when a change that has taken place cannot be contained. Containment in the psychoanalytic sense is a process of transformation and growth. A catastrophic change suggests that neither transformation nor growth can take place.

The newly merged organization in the above case is characterized by a great deal of chaos, confusion, panic reactions, and an overall sense of fragmentation, suggestive of a fragmented psychic reality indicative of the experience of an "internal catastrophe" (Klein, 1975b). The capacity of an organization's management to relate to the enterprise as a whole object is destroyed by a merger, and their capacity to contain the change is impaired for a time. They may understandably experience catastrophic anxiety as a result. Managers experiencing catastrophic anxiety "fear for their survival, organizationally and individually, as they experience a radical break or cleavage from all that is past" (Lawrence & Armstrong, 1998, p. 62). Destructive impulses may then predominate, stimulating anxieties about survival. Such anxieties have their source in the known dangers of the external reality of the merger.

External and psychic realities: known dangers and unconscious anxieties

> External experiences which rouse anxiety at once activate even in normal persons anxiety derived from intrapsychic sources. The interaction between anxiety arising from external and from internal sources corresponds to the interaction between external reality and psychic reality.
>
> (Klein, 1975a, p. 40)

What are the external and internal sources of anxiety to be discerned in the case organization? Known dangers for the firm encompassed the change in legal structures, the small scale of the A-NZ operations within the overall business of XYZ company, and the global aftermath of the shocks to social, political, and business climates from the Enron scandal and terrorist attacks on New York.

For employees who experienced changes to roles, authority, role relatedness, social relationships, job security, organizational structures, processes, and procedures, their anxieties about survival had a real and realistic basis. Much, if not all, that was familiar and certain about their work life was profoundly altered.

A fear of not surviving could imaginably find purchase in these events. What is evident in the full account of my research (de Gooijer, 2006, 2009) is that organizational members' fears seemed to be greater than the real events would suggest. The merger, and in particular the reordering of roles and relationships, not only disrupted connections to loved objects, such as the local autonomous businesses, but also destroyed thriving profitable service lines particular to the A-NZ region.

Why might these events be experienced as catastrophic change in the sense that Bion and Klein use the term?

Sometimes the objective anxiety seems greater than seems proper for what is known to be the danger. In such a case, an unknown instinctual danger is attached to the known real danger (Klein, 1975b, p. 38).

While the external reality held known dangers of change and uncertainty for the firm and its employees, it is apparent that instinctual dangers became cathected to realistic dangers in its environment. And, if destruction is a necessary part of a corporate merger, then destructive impulses inevitably will be aroused. My argument is that the instinctual danger of death is aroused by the experience of an organizational merger as a catastrophic change and evokes unconscious, persecutory anxiety in organizational members.

A merger directly invokes the struggle of life and death impulses, since the intent of a merger is to create new life from the organizations that are to merge. Life and death instincts are in a perpetual struggle, and therefore fear of annihilation enters as a perpetual factor into all anxiety situations. If we assume the existence of the death instinct, we must also assume that in the deepest layers of the mind there is a response to this instinct in the form of fear of annihilation of life (Klein, 1975b, p. 29).

The equilibrium of life and death instincts are disturbed when privation (from internal and external sources) occurs and reinforces aggressive impulses. This first gives rise to greed—and hence a possible impetus for organizational merging—which in turn strengthens feelings of frustration, and in turn the aggressive impulses. It is commonly recognized that constructive and destructive elements of inter-group relations are unleashed once a merger or acquisition is embarked upon (Brunning, 2003).

In the immediate eighteen months after the merger, persecutory anxiety appears to dominate the work culture, illustrated by the two drawings reproduced at Figures 1 and 2. Furthermore, when the firm engaged in two events of drastic downsizing within two years of the merger, it was experienced by staff as an aggressive act. Symbolically, it was a further act of annihilation by the new, foreign owners. Downsizing is another form of symbolic murder in which an organization annihilates the present in order to make way for a radically different future (H. F. Stein, 1996).

In the case of XYZ company's A-NZ regional operations, the organizational system struggles to contain anxieties aroused by the merger, unable to support adequately whatever capacity exists for tolerating realistic anxiety. Organizational members seem overwhelmed by their *neurotic* anxieties about the external danger during the critical period after the merger.

At a systemic level, one possible response to the anxiety aroused by a merger is that one organization seeks to survive by annihilating the other. It follows, therefore, that a merger may be experienced as a persecutory object turned inward, invested with destructive properties that threaten to exterminate one or both organizations; and it may also mobilize a mutual desire of "I want what you have", which is the expression of envy. What may transpire from this is a dynamic of murderous rage in which destructive impulses overwhelm the life instinct. In that case, rather than creating a new, third entity from the two former organizations, one organization may seek to devour the other. In the case under discussion, organizational members feared the merger was in fact a takeover and therefore an annihilation of their existence and all that they loved (and at times hated in part). The drastic downsizing in the later stages of the post-merger period could only confirm such fears. Furthermore, the indifference towards those who were sacked, with apparent cold-heartedness, points to an absence of mourning.

Mourning is a characteristic of depressive anxiety; the inability to mourn is a critical dynamic of a psychotic kind of organization (Sievers, 1999). Persecutory feelings are also likely to be promoted when an organization cuts off the possibility for mourning to occur.

As the new organization developed, and its financial situation worsened, anxiety increased. Its culture of self-reliant individuals and idealization of autonomy led to projecting into individual consultants the survival of the firm. Individuals were endowed with the responsibility of containing the success of the firm and therefore its survival. Actions such as sacking the "bottom 10%" performers indicate the extent to which "thinking that is out of touch with reality" occurred (Lawrence, 1999). A nominal measure at the best of times, the reliance on individual performance indicators for assuring business survival does not account for systemic factors affecting any enterprise at all times.

As the merged XYZ company entered its third year of existence, profitability plummeted, and the gap between external and psychic reality widened. In the absence of facilitating structures for creating emotional connectedness, persecutory anxiety gained even more purchase.

Defence mechanisms employed to alleviate anxieties

The role of defence mechanisms in the development of individuals is primarily to defend oneself against persecutory anxiety, and hence keep the perpetual activity of the death instinct at bay. Defence mechanisms are therefore necessary for preserving the ego and the life instinct. Social defences in organizations serve a similar function: employees attempt to defend themselves against experiences of anxieties within the institution, whose sources cannot be consciously controlled. The defences so developed become institutionalized and a function of the social system (Jaques, 1955; Menzies Lyth, 1970).

For an organization and its members to survive the force of unconscious destructive impulses, it is necessary to establish both social and individual defence mechanisms. I identify five significant defences used by individuals and the system against the anxieties aroused by the creation of XYZ company through a merger. They are:

1. A social defence of multiple organizational structures
2. Splitting the sentient and technical aspects of staff performance
3. Idealization of autonomy
4. Projection of aggressive impulses
5. Regression by managers from their role.

1. A social defence of multiple organizational structures

Multiple organizational structures and their inherent complexities are a social defence against integrating and synthesizing external and psychic realities of the newly merged organization.

As described in the introduction, XYZ company employed a matrix structure for the organization of its services. What was put on paper and called "a multi-matrix structure" by management, is what I call the *stated* organizational structure (Lawrence, 1986). The existential structure, or what was *believed* to be the structure, was described by organizational members as something quite different, that XYZ was structured into two groups—a group that "sold business" and another that "delivered value". What was *experienced* in reality, the phenomenal structure as such, was a political hierarchy of status, influence, and favours.

The complexity of the multiple structures and their inter-relatedness ensured a dispersion of authority, power, leadership, and connectedness to felt experience, and limited the capacity of all members to integrate forces in the external reality with forces in the psychic reality of the organization.

2. Splitting the sentient and technical aspects of staff performance
The establishment of "counselling families" for the purpose of managing staff performance was ostensibly to help employees feel connected to the firm. In reality, they were anything but a linking mechanism. Their purpose was more akin to a "sentient group", in that the task of the counselling families had no real connection to the primary task of the firm or its project task teams. The family structure as such represented a split between the sentient and technical parts of the organization. It vividly symbolizes a defensive response to the anxiety against integrating good and bad objects of the organization's psychic reality.

3. Idealization of autonomy
The idealization of the "self-reliant individual" helps to defend organizational members, and especially management, against anxiety provoked by experiencing vulnerability, dependency needs, and destructive impulses. A denial of dependency permeates psychic reality when self-reliance is idealized. An outcome from idealizing the individual is that it ensures that social anxieties are repressed, hidden, and not available for thought. In such a way might the psychic reality of the organization itself also be denied.

4. Projection of aggressive impulses
Projection of destructive impulses into external objects is a defence mechanism to protect the individual from experiencing destructive impulses on internal objects and from connecting with the capacity for destroying loved objects. Sacking staff is a visible act of "destruction" and "killing off" of parts of the organization. While maintaining a viable level of staffing is necessary for business survival, management's concern about "high turnover" and "staff affiliation" deflects attention from their actions to employees' motivations and actions. As if the "victims" of management decisions become the perpetrators of management

anxiety. By projecting anxiety about their own destructive capacity into employees, managers are able to defend themselves from persecutory anxiety and feelings of guilt.

The turnover in the incumbents of the regional director's role is another illustration of projection of aggressive impulses. Three incumbents in as many years with the second incumbent sacked after only six months into the role. This has all the appearance of panic. At the same time, consultants reported that organizational processes were chaotic and panic-driven.

The aggression towards leadership is most visible in the appointment and sudden sacking of this second regional director. He had been appointed *because* he had a sales background, but was soon attacked for *only* being a salesman. The hope for sales was soon transformed into a hatred. Into "the salesman" was projected the paranoid anxiety about selling and survival. When it became apparent that he could not immediately secure the organization's survival, he became the *scapegoat* for persecutory anxiety.

His short-lived appointment gives an impression of the firm's owners making rapid and ruthless assessments of what was needed for a business in an environment of extreme uncertainty. Similarly to that of sacking staff, the "killing off" of a leader so soon after his appointment appears murderous, and may also be suggestive of a manic defence against the unknown dangers to the business.

Staff spoke derisively of the organization's leaders and of managers actively retreating from their role as organizational leaders. This is suggestive of projecting aggressive impulses into the leadership role. Inconsistent and changing leadership, often marked by implausible images of a sought-after future, is one characteristic of organizational change efforts stuck in a primitive mode of operating (Krantz, 2001).

Taken together, these experiences and events suggest that leadership was a "lost object" for employees. A leader represents a commonly shared object for a group which binds them together. If this object is lost or injured, the group may behave as if it has "lost its head" (Freud, 1921).

Thus, the persecutory anxiety that dominates the organization in the aftermath of the merger is defended against by killing off "other parts" of the organization or projecting aggressive impulses into leadership.

5. *Regression by managers from their role*

The roles of leadership and management were experienced as overwhelmingly painful by many role-holders. Many withdrew from these roles to where they might feel more safe and secure, seeking to manage projects instead of organizational systems. Regression is a process of retreating from a present threat or danger to a former mental state or series of actions that feels safe. When managers sought to become "consultants" to projects, rather than managers, there is evidence of regression.

Withdrawal is another form of disconnecting from perceived dangers in external reality, and a defence against the anxiety of connecting with the unconscious dangers in the psychic reality of the organization. The "thinking in touch with reality" that is a task for management is disturbed or disrupted by managers' withdrawal. Management thinking becomes disabled.

An event of significance to this discussion concerns the executive team's planning retreat during the third year of the merger. Usually at a management retreat, members engage in thinking about the organization and deciding on appropriate responses to external and internal reality. The evidence from this retreat suggested that the thinking was impeded by neurotic anxiety and resulted in symbolically flawed thoughts (Albritton, 1986).

A "retreat" itself conjures up the idea of regression, of withdrawing from the external world, or of a psychic retreat (Morgan, 1997; Steiner, 1993). During their retreat, the executive management team created a drawing of the future for the organization in which the image was of a "ship alone on the turbulent sea" carrying all that was valued about the organization on board. The image seems to be a symbol of the overwhelming anxiety experienced by management, from which they had no release. The fact that most would soon be redundant in a third round of redundancies is significant. Their anxieties about their own futures appear to be expressed in the drawing. Positive experiences of a world of work that nurtures, provides warmth and containment for the individual are absent.

Nothing suggests that the symbol of a ship all at sea is a realistic management response to "realistic anxiety". Rather, it appears to respond to management's neurotic anxieties whose sources can be found in the psychic reality of the organization. Management's retreat from role, and retreat into creating a fantasy about the future of the organization, are regressive actions and a psychic defence, in that they are resorting to previous actions that feel safe and will protect them from unconscious dangers.

Without the coherent leadership or management needed to contain and integrate the interaction between external forces and psychic reality, the organization has limited capacity to transform projective processes, or mediate aggressive forces. Persecutory anxiety will continue to prevail under such circumstances.

* * *

Containing destructive forces

Organizations undergoing major change can lose the capacity to contain primitive emotional states as social defence systems are dismantled (Krantz, 2001, p. 134).

When emotional disconnecting becomes a social defence, an organization loses important data about psychic reality and its dynamic effects. Data unavailable to employees cannot be worked through, thought about, or contained. Decision-making is likely to be impaired because only a part of organizational reality is engaged. Unprocessed anxieties continue to impinge on the firm's capacity to grow and develop.

While downsizing may have been the only viable option for XYZ company by the time it became apparent that "not surviving" was a realistic danger, it might have been avoidable if connecting to emotional experiences had been an active process in the organization. Attending to the "early warning signals" in the dynamics of emotional connectedness amongst employees would have enabled more realistic thinking about the external and psychic dangers for the organization. Emotional connectedness and availability for connection is the first step towards transforming felt experiences into "objects for thinking". The process for this transformation is the process of "containment".

Containment

The primary task of the good container is both absorption of harsh elements or soothing, and the introduction of reality even when it is painful (Albritton, 1986, p. 76).

Containment, the process by which the "good container" performs its task, was coined by Bion to describe the process of transformation undertaken by the mother to deal with the infant's primary aggression and envy. A mother with the aptitude for dealing with her infant's destructive impulses might be said to be a "good-enough container". The same aptitude is necessary within organizations, especially when organizational realities are likely to elicit aggression.

In an organizational merger, the container itself is transformed, and therefore its capacity to contain is disturbed. Physical offices may move to another location or are closed, and authority structures are disrupted or disorganized for a time. If employees experience this as catastrophic change, then their capacity to tolerate creative, innovative thinking is impinged upon. Containment in such circumstances is a paradox. "When an organization is going through change, who will serve to contain the attendant chaos?" (Smith, Miller & Kaminstein, 2004, p. 255).

How might this paradox be worked with? The hypothesis that an organizational merger necessitates killing off parts of an organization implies that *some parts remain intact*. These are, for example: a) the "internal object" of the old organization that stays with employees; b) a variety of work processes, tasks, and management systems from the former organizations; and c) continuation of some roles and groupings. Assuming this is so, then those parts of the organization become the new organizational container. The capacity of this new container to deal with the destructive impulses evoked within organizational members by the merger is untested and uncertain. The role of management is crucial for ensuring that the new container is able to deal with the catastrophic change; but management itself is under tremendous pressures, the object of projections and anxieties. Role-holders need the capability to contain these pressures and work through the projections. This is a tremendously difficult task under such circumstances.

In extremely large organizations, such as a global enterprise, the usual vehicles for containment, such as face-to-face meetings of work groups, are disturbed by the complications of geographic distance, different time zones, and national cultures. When the work of the enterprise also involves employees travelling a lot and working in temporary work structures of project teams, the usual structures of "business divisions" and "regional offices" are also inadequate containers; their boundaries do not reflect the roles and tasks within the enterprise.

One reason why a multi-network structure would appeal to a global professional services enterprise, such as the one under discussion, is that a network facilitates connections across the whole system, and might better deal with the impossibility of holding the whole system in mind. Yet, the need to be able to keep the whole system in mind remains.

More particularly, how well the "critical period" of a merger is managed illuminates how well realistic anxiety is managed. The *capacity to tolerate realistic anxiety* leads to more realistic management of the situation. When organizational structures, procedures, and technology support dealing with realistic anxiety, people's capacities to tolerate the anxiety are enhanced (M. Stein, 2004).

The new management of a merged organization must have a capacity to deal with primitive destructive impulses of murderous rage, aggression, hate, envy, and projected guilt. They need to be capable of managing their own and others' fear of annihilation. In the same way that the developing infant needs containment of its emotional life, so too does the organization. The nature of this containment process is captured by the following diagram of the dynamics of a merger.

Figure 3 depicts a process in which the merger of two organizations includes a period of chaos and fragmentation. During this time, it is not possible to say that the new organization has become "established".

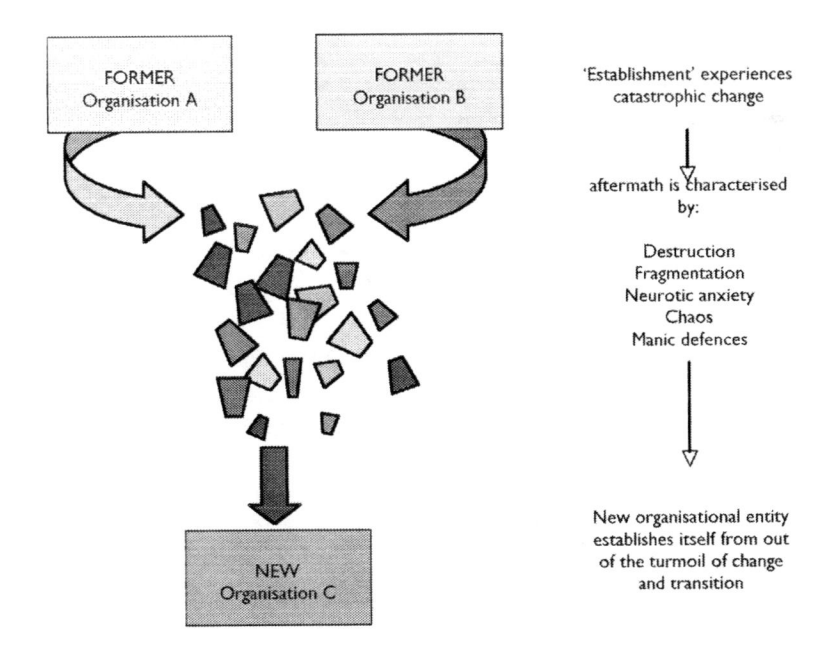

Figure 3. The "catastrophic change" of an organizational merger.

It is a time of transition, when the newly formed organization is at its most vulnerable. Not only is chaos and fragmentation evident in the disruption to routines, and losses of familiar systems, processes, services, functions, and valued people, but the psychic reality of the organization is also disorganized.

The disruptions and ruptures to established boundaries (that serve to contain anxieties) invoke neurotic anxieties amongst all employees, from which they seek protection. Various defence mechanisms are used by individuals, groups, and the organization as a whole in order to relieve the painful aspects of their experiences, or to preserve those which are cherished and loved.

After a time, and assuming the new organization survives the vicissitudes of this transition period, the entity will begin to form a new "establishment culture", one that has developed sufficient maturity and resilience to survive its environment. The model at this point makes no assumptions about the ability or capacity of the organization to deal with known or external dangers, or the unknown psychic dangers which may arise now or in the future. However, I suggest that the organization's resilience to new or future threats is dependent upon the "capacity for containment" which was developed during the transitional period.

This is what Figure 4 depicts, for it is in the period of the aftermath, when chaos reigns, that containment is most needed. It is necessary for sustaining the business and the hopes that initiated the merger in the first place. Figure 4 illuminates the dynamics of containment in an organizational merger. Here, the container, the "Establishment", comprises the two former organizations. That which is to be contained is the "New Idea", comprising the organizational merger. Each has the power to destroy the other. By this is meant that the merger may be destroyed as an idea, and in reality, if one organization acts as if it has "acquired" the other and then proceeds to destroy all vestiges of that organization—by sacking staff, shutting down services and functions, and selling off assets.

On the other hand, the merger may be impossible to realize, and the new organization fails to survive the transition. When the process of a merger necessitates "killing off" parts of the former organizations, it follows that the container–contained exists in a heightened state of vulnerability while it seeks to transform the necessary destruction into a creative process, and not become overwhelmed by destructive forces.

```
                    CONTAINER – CONTAINED
        ┌─────────────────────────────────────┐
   ┌──────────────────┐              ┌──────────────────┐
   │ 'The Establishment' │              │   'The New Idea'    │
   │      of the          │              │       of a           │
   │ former organisations │              │  corporate merger    │
   └──────────────────┘              └──────────────────┘
                    each has power to destroy the other
              ┌─────────────────────────────────────┐
              │ The process of creating a new organisation, of │
              │ necessity, involves destruction of what was    │
              │                   'before'                      │
              └─────────────────────────────────────┘
```

CONTAINMENT

of
persecutory anxieties, manic defences etc.
keeps destructive impulses at bay & enables organisational
members to
'think with one's mind' (a creative process),
rather than
'think with one's wits' (a survival response)
and
ensures individuals are emotionally supported during the
transitional period of the merger's aftermath

NEW ESTABLISHMENT

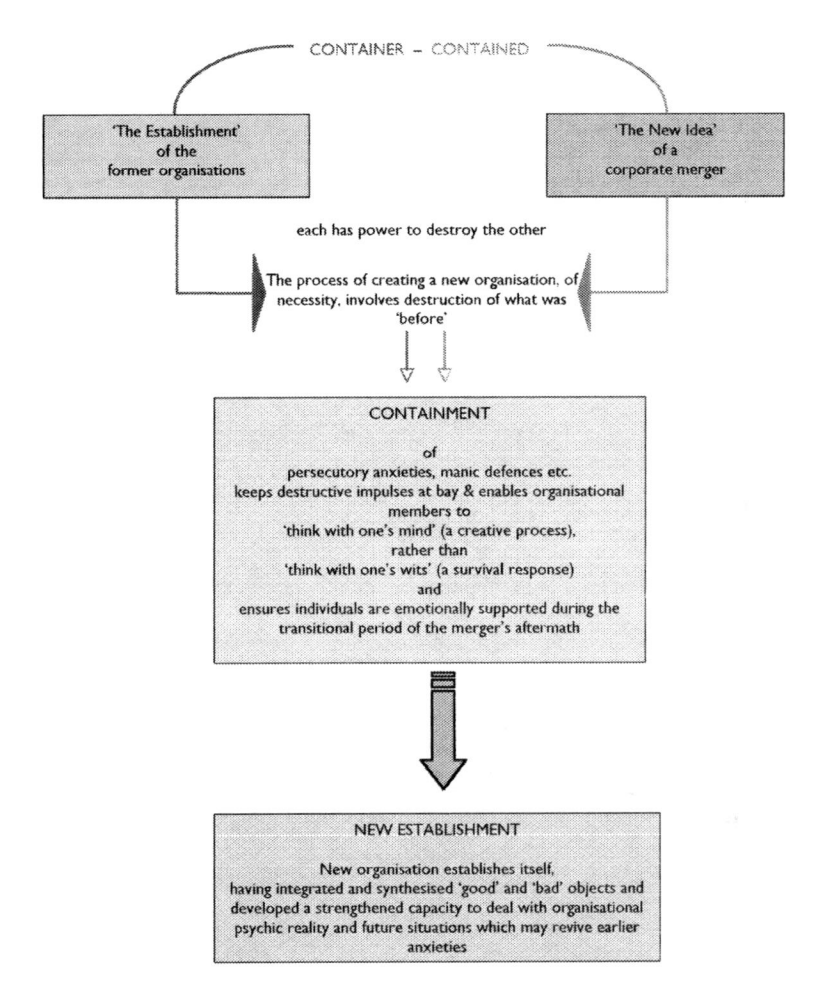

New organisation establishes itself,
having integrated and synthesised 'good' and 'bad' objects and
developed a strengthened capacity to deal with organisational
psychic reality and future situations which may revive earlier
anxieties

Figure 4. Dynamics between container–contained in an organizational merger.

The containment process needed is that which can take in the persecutory anxieties and manic defences aroused by the merger being experienced as a destructive force. If these anxieties are transformed for employees, such that they can tolerate experiences of their own and others' destructive impulses, it enables people to think creatively about the development of the new organization. "Good-enough containment" would also ensure that individuals are emotionally supported when they too are vulnerable. Practical approaches for such containment might include experiential workshops on the integration of the merging cultures (Brunning, 2003).

A successful transformation of psychic forces and emotional experiences is a developmental process for the new organization and builds the establishment of a work culture in which emotional experiences can be engaged, and with less fear. An organization that builds capacity to tolerate psychic danger develops a capability to respond more realistically to external threats and real danger, to work through the neurotic anxieties of its members, and enables them to think creatively when new situations arise which may revive earlier anxieties about organizational survival.

The practice of organizational containment—that which integrates and synthesizes experiences—is a practice applicable to organizations generally, not just those engaged in an organizational merger.

Conclusions

In this chapter, I have explored the destructive impulses that are invoked when organizations merge to form a new entity. If left unchecked and uncontained, the anxieties experienced by organizational members may invoke instinctual fears about survival. In such circumstances may a merger be experienced as murderous.

My concluding remarks concern the developmental processes that an organizational merger will go through. To witness a merger is to witness a developmental process in the creation and growth of a new organization. It is possible to think about the psychic reality of a merger as a primary process of organizational development that involves:

a. destroying "the establishment" in the former organizations;
b. killing off large parts of the former organizations;
c. splitting the organizations into fragments which are experienced as an "internal catastrophe";
d. for a time, the organization being dominated by destructive impulses, such that persecutory anxiety is excessively aroused and felt to be unbearable;
e. mobilizing defence mechanisms against the persecutory anxiety, such as splitting and denial, which generally disconnect and disengage people emotionally from the internal reality of the organization; and

f. that after a period of time, "survivors" and new employees are able to engage in the task of regeneration, and perhaps reparation, in order to generate a new organizational identity and culture.

I call this process the "primary processes of an organizational merger", during which the relatedness between external and psychic reality is developed. It marks the establishment phase of a new organizational culture. It is both a destructive and creative time of chaos, raw emotion, and vulnerability. A successful merger develops from a systemic process that acknowledges and works through the emotional experiences of its organizational members alongside the technical implementation tasks.

Notes

1. Material in this chapter is drawn from the book, de Gooijer, J. (2009). *The Murder in Merger: A Systems Psychodynamic Exploration of a Corporate Merger*. London: Karnac Books. It is reproduced with permission.
2. The full case study is available in de Gooijer, J. (2006).

References

Albritton, B. (1986). *Bion's Theory of Thinking*. Unpublished doctoral dissertation, University of Southern California, La Mirada.

Armstrong, D. (2005). *Organization in the Mind: Psychoanalysis, Group Relations, and Organizational Consultancy. Occasional Papers 1989–2003*. London: Karnac Books.

Bion, W. R. (1984). *Transformations*. London: Karnac Books.

Bion, W. R. (1988). Attacks on linking. In: E. B. Spillius (Ed.), *Melanie Klein Today: Developments in Theory and Practice*; Volume 1, *Mainly Theory*. Hove and New York: Brunner-Routledge [Reprinted 2003].

Brunning, H. (2003). Organisational merger: a dance of constructive and destructive elements. *Organisations and People*, 10(1): 2–8.

de Gooijer, J. (2003). An exploration of the dynamics of emotional connectedness in a matrix structure. *Socio-Analysis*, 5: 88–104.

de Gooijer, J. (2006). *The Murder in Merger: Developmental Processes of a Corporate Merger and the Struggle Between Life and Death Instincts*. Unpublished Doctor of Philosophy thesis, Swinburne University of Technology, Hawthorn.

de Gooijer, J. (2009). *The Murder in Merger: A Systems Psychodynamic Exploration of a Corporate Merger*. London: Karnac Books.

Freud, S. (1921). *Group Psychology and the Analysis of the Ego (Trans. J. Strachey). The Standard Edition of the Complete Psychological Works of Sigmund Freud* (Vol. 18, pp. 65–144). London: Hogarth.

Hutton, J. (2000). Working with the Concept of Organisation-in-the-Mind, Retrieved 24 June 2003, from http://www.grubb.org.uk/html/body_orgmind.html

Jaques, E. (1955). Social systems as a defense against persecutory and depressive anxiety. In: M. Klein, P. Heimann & R. Money-Kyrle (Eds.), *New Directions in Psychoanalysis* (pp. 478–498). London: Tavistock Publications.

Klein, M. (1975a). On the theory of anxiety and guilt. *The Writings of Melanie Klein: Volume 3* (pp. 25–42). London: Hogarth.

Klein, M. (1975b). Some theoretical conclusions regarding the emotional life of the infant. *The Writings of Melanie Klein: Volume 3* (pp. 61–93). London: Hogarth.

Krantz, J. (2001). Dilemmas of organizational change: a systems psychodynamic perspective. In: L. J. Gould, L. F. Stapley & M. Stein (Eds.), *The Systems Psychodynamics of Organizations: Integrating the Group Relations Approach, Psychoanalytic and Open Systems Perspectives* (pp. 134–156). New York, London: Karnac Books.

Lawrence, W. G. (1986). The issue of psychic and political relatedness in organisations. In: G. P. Chattopadhyay, Z. H. Gangjee, M. L. Hunt & W. G. Lawrence (Eds.), *When the Twain Meet: Western Theory and Eastern Insights in Exploring Indian Organisations* (pp. 49–65). London: A. H. Wheeler.

Lawrence, W. G. (1999). Centring of the Sphinx for the psychoanalytic study of organisations. *Socio-Analysis*, 1(2): 99–126.

Lawrence, W. G. & Armstrong, D. (1998). Destructiveness and creativity in organizational life: experiencing the psychotic edge. In: P. B. Talamo, F. Borgogno & S. A. Merciai (Eds.), *Bion's Legacy to Groups* (pp. 53–68). London: Karnac Books.

Menzies Lyth, I. (1970). *The Functioning of Social Systems as a Defence against Anxiety: A Report on a Study of the Nursing Service of a General Hospital.* London: Tavistock Institute of Human Relations.

Morgan, G. (1997). *Images of Organization* (2nd ed.). Thousand Oaks, CA: Sage Publications.

Sievers, B. (1999). Psychotic organisation as metaphoric frame for the socioanalysis of organizational and interorganizational dynamics. *Administration and Society*, 31(5): 588–616.

Smith, K. K., Miller, R. & Kaminstein, D. (2004). Consultant as container: assisting organizational rebirth in Mandela's South Africa. In: S. Cytrynbaum & D. A. Noumair (Eds.), *Group Dynamics, Organizational*

Irrationality, and Social Complexity (pp. 243–266). Jupiter, FL: A. K. Rice Institute.

Stein, H. F. (1996). Death imagery and the experience of organizational downsizing: or, is your name on Schindler's list? Paper presented at the International Society for the Psychoanalytic Study of Organizations, 1996 Conference, New York.

Stein, M. (2004). The critical period of disasters: insights from sense-making and psychoanalytic theory. *Human Relations*, 57(10): 1243–1261.

Steiner, J. (1993). *Psychic Retreats: Pathological Organisations of the Personality in Psychotic, Neurotic and Borderline Patients*. London and New York: Routledge.

CHAPTER TWO

Toxicity and the unconscious experience of the body at the employee–customer interface[1,2]

Mark Stein

This chapter focuses on the images used to understand employee experiences in a major part of the post-industrial economy, that of front-line service work. As front-line employees may have a wide variety of experiences and a range of possible relationships with customers, their work may be appropriately represented by a variety of images. While the images currently in use illuminate certain dimensions of the interchanges between staff and customers, I argue that they do not capture some of the more painful and problematic aspects. I therefore introduce a different image, one derived from certain of the words and phrases used by front-line service workers themselves; these words and phrases suggest that employees feel that they have been poisoned by toxic substances. Ideas from psychoanalysis and its application to organizational dynamics are then used to explore this image.

The aims of this chapter are to deepen our understanding of the specific nature of the employee–customer relationship and to contribute to the wider debates on theories of organizational images. The key contribution of this chapter is to articulate and give expression to aspects of the employee–customer interface—that of the employee experience of toxicity—that are missed by the existing literature on organizational images, and also to use such ideas in an explanatory way by showing the underlying processes and mechanisms involved in the production of their experiences.

The introduction of the new theme of toxicity needs to be set in the context of the wider debates on organizational images. While authors such as Boulding (1956) have noted the ubiquitous use of images in a range of natural and social sciences, Morgan (1986, 1997)—in his classic book *Images of Organizations*—has most clearly established the area as a legitimate focus within organization studies. Morgan (1980, 1986, 1997) and Weick (1989) have argued that metaphors (a type of image) are central to theory and theory development, with Cornelissen (2004, 2005, 2006) adding that they are especially valuable in generating new meanings beyond a previously existing similarity. Tsoukas has shown further that they may help unearth the mechanisms that underpin the phenomena of organizations (1991, p. 572): this relates to a central quest of organization theory, the search for "mechanisms or processes" (Hammersley & Atkinson, 1983, p. 20), or "motors" (Pentland, 1999; Van de Ven & Poole, 1995) that drive organizational phenomena.

Connected to this are debates about the relation between literal and metaphorical language and the role of metaphors in our thinking. Tsoukas (1993) has argued that the distinction between literal and metaphorical language is much overstated, while Foucault has called into question whether such a distinction exists at all (Foucault, 1970; White, 1979, p. 93). Whatever the status of the distinction, Morgan (1983)—following the tradition of Jakobson (1962), Ortony (1975), and Lackoff & Johnson (1980)—has argued that metaphors are unavoidably part of everyday life and our attempts to conceptualize it. Such "metaphors we live by" (Lackoff & Johnson, 1980), especially those that have unconscious framings (Marshak, 2003), are of particular interest in this chapter.

The empirical part of this study draws on a wide range of secondary data source articles (such as Hall, 1993; Hochschild, 1983; Korczynski, 2003; Spradley & Mann, 1975; Van Maanen, 1991); many secondary data verbatim accounts from workers contained in Bowe, Bowe & Streeter (2000) and Terkel (2004); and my own primary data (Stein, 1995, 2000). The chapter explores the toxicity image in a variety of employee–customer situations, where the term "customer" is used in a broad sense to refer to anyone who is a recipient of a service of any kind, be it one delivered by private-, public-, or voluntary-sector organizations.

I present my argument in the following sequence. I begin with a discussion of some of the images from the existing literature that help us understand the nature of the employee–customer interface. While the contribution of these images is acknowledged, it is argued here that aspects of the experience of customer service workers are not captured by them. This genre is then added to by introducing and outlining the toxicity image. Following this, the chapter explores a variety of types of situations in which this image may be applied: these are where customer activities and words are experienced as toxic; where employees respond to experiences of toxicity by engaging in revenge of some kind; and where feelings related to toxicity are so pervasive that one may reasonably speak of these employees experiencing a "toxic environment" in the workplace. This is followed by a discussion and conclusions.

Images illuminating the employee–customer interface

Three images currently in use are particularly helpful in illuminating certain aspects of the employee–customer relationship. Part of the long tradition of dramaturgical approaches to the study of social and organizational phenomena (Goffman, 1967, 1971; Hochschild, 1983; Mangham, 2005; Schreyogg & Hopfl, 2004), one image depicts the employee–customer interface as a theatre in which workers are paid to perform in the presence of customers. Hochschild (1983), in particular, elaborates this dramaturgical image by exploring the various techniques employees are trained to use in the production of good theatre; these workers focus on, rehearse, and perform in order to facilitate "moments of truth" (Carlzon, 1987) that have a pivotal influence on customer experience and decision-making. Mangham & Overington (1987) argue that this image highlights the ritual aspects of organizations; Vera & Crossan (2004) believe it encapsulates the improvisational aspects; while Cornelissen (2004) suggests that it highlights the creative and emergent dimensions of organizational life. Such themes have been used to analyse the work of a diversity of front-line employees, including workers at Walt Disney Enterprises (Van Maanen, 1991, p. 66), university teachers (Ogbonna & Harris, 2004), and organizational consultants (Clark & Salaman, 1998).

In some instances, the dramaturgical image may have a positive connotation: one waitress, for example, conveyed the view that being on stage was central to the pleasure she gained from the job. She declared: "I'm on stage. I tell everyone I'm a waitress and I'm proud" (Terkel, 2004, p. 297). However, in other cases, it may involve a more oppressive dimension, with the customer acting as an "emotional vampire [and] a ... thief of identity" (Rosenthal et al., 2001, p. 21—italics in original), forcing employees to act in ways that are not consistent with their inner feelings and self-perceptions.

A second, rather different image is that of the panopticon (Foucault, 1977). While the architecture of Jeremy Bentham's panopticon—a prison built round a central observation tower from which inmates are observed—was found to be replicated in a range of eighteenth-century hospitals, factories, and schools, it is seen to be present in modern organizations in a less literal sense (Burrell, 1988, p. 226). In these organizations, core management techniques, technologies, and procedures are used in the observation, disciplining, and control of employees. In particular, the modern service orientation seeks to bring customers into the organization in a central role as "partial employees" (Mills et al., 1983), "co-producers" (Normann, 1984), or "prosumers" (Toffler, 1980) working on behalf of management. In doing so, the customer may be required to act as a "spy" (Rosenthal et al., 2001, p. 26) who observes and critically evaluates employee performance.

There are some occasions in which the panopticon theme has positive connotations for employees: in response to good audit results based on "mystery-shopper" visits, for example, one print shop worker related that colleagues would enthusiastically jump around saying "I got a ninety-five [per cent] on my audit!" (Bowe, Bowe & Streeter, 2000, p. 73). More often than not, however, this notion has a pejorative meaning that conveys the idea of employees feeling intruded upon, observed, and judged. The panopticon image is therefore valuable because it emphasizes the continuing presence of the customer as observer, spy, or judge, where customers' feelings and views have a critical impact on the working lives of employees.

A third image portrays the employee as a whore or prostitute and the customer as a "consumer of sexuality" (Rosenthal et al., 2001, p. 22—italics in original). In some cases, such as prostitution work, the sexual aspects of the exchange may be entirely explicit; further, such relations may sometimes have an aggressive as well as a sexual component. However, in other work settings, there may be a more implicit, albeit widely acknowledged, sexual dimension. In Spradley & Mann's (1975) study of "Brady's Bar", for example, it is evident that male customers flirted a great deal with waitresses, and that, for some waitresses, such flirting constituted an important part of their enjoyment of the job.

In a different study, Hall (1993) cites the example of one waitress who said "[t]here's always that sexual attraction ... there's ... a little bit of a flirting thing" (Hall, 1993, p. 464), and another who liked joining certain male customers at their table so that they could share risqué jokes (Hall, 1993, p. 464). Indeed, and perhaps unsurprisingly, Hall's research (1993) shows flirting to be a central part of the waitresses' work in restaurants.

There are, however, other occasions on which the sexualization of the employee–customer relationship has an abusive quality. On the basis of interviews with female front-line workers, Folgero & Fjeldstad (1995) argue that service organizations are prime breeding-grounds for sexual harassment. Similarly, in her study Hall goes on to show that waitresses are sometimes sexually demeaned and harassed by male customers, with, for example, one waitress having reported an occasion when male customers greeted her insultingly by saying "here comes dessert" (1993, p. 464). Although waitresses have some discretion over what they are prepared to tolerate, this is limited by the nature of the work and the context: as Hopfl (2002) argues, following Diderot, the employee may be required to be like "the whore who feels nothing for the man she is with, but lets herself go into his arms anyway as a demonstration of her professional competence" (2002, p. 258).

Although other images are used in organization studies, the three above have been selected because of their prominence in the literature and because they further our understanding of a variety of dimensions of the employee–customer relationship. Despite the value of these images, however, I argue that various issues within this relationship are not conveyed by them. While in practice images overlap and are by no means mutually exclusive, these concern problems in the relationship that have less to do with being observed, abused, or losing a sense of identity; instead, they are more concerned with the employee's experience of being "poisoned" and "polluted" so that, not only is the immediate task made more problematic, but the damage is transferred to other areas of the employee's work and relationships. The new image of toxicity is thus introduced in this chapter to address this lacuna.

The toxicity image

While the concept of toxicity has thus far not had a place in the literature on the employee–customer interface, it is on occasion to be found elsewhere. In the psychoanalytic literature, it is generally conveyed by the metaphorical idea of psychological "poisoning" or "being poisoned" (Klein, 1981, p. 220), and is often unconsciously associated with faeces. In the organizational literature, Frost & Robinson argue that certain managers may take on the role of "toxin handler", shouldering pain on behalf of others and reducing its spread (Frost & Robinson, 1999; Frost, 2003). In the literature on leadership, Lipman-Blumen (2005) refers to "toxic leaders"; Krantz (2006) talks about the toxicity of the betrayal of leaders (2006, p. 235); while Offerman (2004) refers to toxic followers. In the area of decision-making, Maitlis & Ozcelik (2004) refer to "toxic decision processes". Despite these references, the application to customer-service situations has not yet been made.

The theoretical underpinnings of the toxicity image as used in this chapter are as follows. First, the service encounter is best understood if we postulate that a boundary region (Miller & Rice, 1967; Stacey, 2001) exists between front-line workers and customers. While the long-established concept of a boundary is a valuable one in organization studies (and will also be used in this chapter), it is supplemented here by the idea of a boundary region because this indicates more clearly the notion of a space shared by customers and employees alike, one that acquires its character by virtue of being so shared. This boundary region is governed by implicitly agreed norms specific to the employee–customer relationship. Further, while being influenced by geographic space and the design of work, the boundary region refers essentially to a phenomenological, experiential dimension: as Hirschhorn & Gilmore write, "boundaries ... aren't drawn on a company's organizational chart but in ... minds" (1992, p. 105), and this applies equally well to the notion of boundary regions.

Second, crucial to the healthy functioning of the organization is the degree of permeability of its boundary regions (Hernes, 2004; Miller & Rice, 1967; Shumate & Fulk, 2004). Inadequately permeable boundary regions may thwart effective work because they restrict the contact between customers and employees; they may also lead to a rigidity—or excessive "differentiation" (Schneider, 1991, p. 184)—that precludes adaptation and learning. Boundary regions that are too permeable, on the other hand, risk the effectiveness of the work in a different way. In such cases, there is excessive "integration" (Schneider, 1991, p. 184), with contact between the two parties being too intense or too invasive. Measures such as "buffering" (Lynn, 2005) and "thresholds"

(Hernes, 2004) may be used to manage the permeability of boundary regions, but getting the balance right is not always possible.

Third, excessive boundary permeability and lack of control over it may lead front-line workers to have the unconscious fantasy that they have inhaled or have been fed something poisonous, resulting in their being polluted by toxic substances. Such fantasies, which connote "unconscious mental content[s]" (Isaacs, 1952, p. 81), are so painful that they are often denied entry into the conscious mind. If and when these contents do become conscious, this may occur only in part and with difficulty: at a deeper level, these may be too threatening and may remain largely unconscious. This focus on corporeality and the unconscious is in line with the work of Anzieu (1984) and Diamond, Allcorn & Stein (2004). Further, observing related phenomena, the anthropologist Mary Douglas has argued that, when boundaries are permeated or become confused, the fear of pollution or contagion becomes heightened (1975, p. 56).

Fourth, when a front-line worker has an unconscious experience of being poisoned by an initial perforation, this may be felt to lead to further and sometimes multiple flows of toxicity. "[T]oxins", as Frost argues, "spread and seep" (2003, p. 5), damaging the work environment so that people can "barely function" (Frost & Robinson, 1999, p. 98); Barsade (2002) describes similar phenomena using the term "the ripple effect of emotional contagion". Returning to body-boundary imagery, one could say that, once a lesion has formed, a variety of toxic substances may flow. For example, employees at the receiving end of toxicity sometimes find themselves influencing other employees in a negative way, resulting in further damage to the provision of service. These kinds of toxicity may be experienced as traversing a variety of boundary regions, such as those between one person and another, one department and another, and one period of time and another. In such circumstances, employees may feel that the entire work environment has become toxic.

Fifth, as toxic substances cannot be digested or easily eliminated in a healthy manner, there is a possibility that revenge will be exacted. Revenge—"a defence against annihilation anxieties" (Sievers & Mersky, 2006, p. 241)—may thus be understood as the expelling of undigested toxic experience back into others. It is, however, important to point out that revenge is neither necessarily conscious nor necessarily deliberate: in particular, harassed and beleaguered employees may find themselves exacting revenge without fully intending to, and without being entirely aware of what they are doing: as Sievers & Mersky argue, "revenge often is wreaked unconsciously" (2006, p. 241). Revenge is discussed later on in this chapter.

The manifestations of toxicity

We now turn to the manifestations of toxicity and—consistent with the approach taken in this chapter—draw on ideas from psychoanalysis. Central in psychoanalysis is the notion that symbols—such as words, jokes, dreams, slips of the tongue, actions, or objects—may represent unconscious, hidden meanings (Laplanche & Pontalis, 1973, p. 442); these meanings are unconscious and hidden because they are too painful to enter consciousness. In an organizational context, Brown & Starkey (2000) apply this by showing how certain organizational symbols may come to represent inner ideas and complexes, while Schwartz (1985) focuses on the symbolic role of myths, and Gabriel (1995) on stories; Gabriel concludes that the words to be found in "gossip, nicknames, legends … and … stories …" are "symbolic elaborations" (1999, p. 199) that shed light on the unconscious experience of the organization's members. In a similar manner, therefore, employees' words and deeds are used here to support the contention of experiences that have unconscious meanings. In exploring the evidence for such interpretations, it needs to be acknowledged at the outset that there are, of course, other possible readings of the material.

Customers and toxicity

One way in which employees may experience toxicity is via customer actions and words. At the previously mentioned "Brady's Bar" (Spradley & Mann, 1975), waitresses were regularly confronted by customers who they found to be "obnoxious", a word etymologically related to "noxious". Indeed, the term "obnoxo" was a key part of the waitresses' lexicon and their informal system for classifying customers (Spradley & Mann, 1975, p. 61). As well as speaking of something noxious, such workers also referred to the related idea that they were "given shit"; on one occasion, for example, a waitress described how a group of men became "really obnoxious … [and were] … giving me shit" (Spradley & Mann, 1975, p. 124—emphasis in original). This is consistent with the psychoanalytic view which, as has been mentioned, suggests that "excreta are [symbolically] equated with poisonous substances" (Klein, 1981, p. 220), representing something unwanted, dirty, and polluted. The imagery of excreta is also used elsewhere: a credit salesman, for example, spoke of a customer "making me eat crap for four years, to make me collect my money" (Terkel, 2004, p. 93).

If employees feel themselves to be subject to toxicity when in face-to-face contact with customers, such a presence is not a necessary requirement for such experiences: other cases—in which customers are not physically present—exemplify even more starkly the toxic quality that words alone can have in the customer–employee interchange. In one telemarketing call centre, for example, a supervisor described how each of his evening-shift staff would "get sworn at and cussed out" (Bowe, Bowe & Streeter, 2000, p. 16) by abusive customers. He reported that very regularly—"about ten times a night"—each employee got exposed to something "venomous" (Bowe, Bowe & Streeter, 2000, p. 19), an allusion to the toxic quality of the experience. This toxicity frequently led to the employees crying, hiding in the corner, or leaving the job: "[m]ost quit by the third day" (Bowe, Bowe & Streeter, 2000, p. 19).

Toxicity may affect other parts of employees' work as well as their relationships with colleagues. In an extensive study of call centres, Korczynski found evidence that customers who expressed hostility over the telephone caused employees to feel distressed and dejected, which in turn adversely affected their relationships and their work. Employee comments that "[a]t the next call you're not going to say '[g]ood morning'" (Korczynski, 2003, p. 67) or that "[t]wo bad calls can kill a day" (Korczynski, 2003, p. 66) help us understand the enduring damage that "bad calls" can wreak. Further, as elsewhere, some of the employee language—such as the reference to customers as "obnoxious" (Korczynski, 2003, p. 66)—suggests an experience of being poisoned. These problems can spread beyond the worker and affect others: as one employee put it, "[s]ometimes the customer is rude ... [and] ... will say 'fuck off'. These comments are rare but they stick. They affect us all; they rebound round the whole team" (Korczynski, 2003, p. 66).

Such pressures can also affect relationships between employees and their bosses. One hat saleswoman, for example, related how the pressure of the job often caused her to lose her temper, which, in turn, affected her relationship with her boss. She commented: "I've been fired many times, I've quit many times, and I've fired her a couple of times" (Bowe, Bowe & Streeter, 2000, p. 166). In a similar vein, a saleswoman in a gift shop described how—in order to deal with a "high-maintenance customer"—she and her mother (her boss and the store owner) spent a "miserable" time working at night and "cussing each other" (Bowe, Bowe & Streeter, 2000, p. 128); this was in contrast with other times, when the two generally got on well.

Relationships between employees and workers in other organizations may also be affected. For example, a social worker who acted as an advocate for clients in court cases frequently found herself being yelled at and mistreated by her clients and their families. She commented: "You have to develop a thick skin ... . Still, of course, there's times when it really hurts. It's those few times when they get you between the cracks" (Bowe, Bowe & Streeter, 2000, p. 516). Such phrases indicate not only the palpable need for a boundary that cannot easily be permeated, but also the notion that such a boundary may sometimes fail. However, the social worker's life was made more complicated by employees from other organizations who treated her as if she were the same as her clients, whom they despised. In her view, "the D.A.s [District Attorneys], the cops, the judges, all the courtroom personnel ... think we work for the scum, the slime. We're closely equated with our clients" (Bowe, Bowe & Streeter, 2000, p. 511). As a result, she concluded, "We're shat on" (Bowe, Bowe & Streeter, 2000, p. 511).

There is also evidence that such toxicity may remain with employees well after the end of the working day, and that it may affect their home lives and their relationships with family and friends. One supermarket checkout clerk commented: "Sometimes ... . I'm a total wreck. My family says, 'We better not talk to her today. She's had a bad day'" (Terkel, 2004, p. 285). In a similar vein, a receptionist who spent much of her time on the phone dealing with the public observed that "things happen to you all day long, things you couldn't get rid of ... . There didn't seem to be any relief about going home ... Boy! Did I have a lot of garbage to put up with!" (Terkel, 2004, p. 31). This suggests that, like the employees mentioned above, this worker had an experience which unconsciously evoked in her the idea of being a recipient of something dirty or toxic that she had difficulty shedding.

Toxicity and revenge

We now turn to examine the issue of employee responses to toxicity. As we have seen, what is especially problematic is that employees cannot process or absorb toxic experiences and may consequently carry the effects of such experiences for significant periods of time. A number of responses may follow, such as employees engaging in subversive forms of humour (Taylor & Bain, 2003); having a run after work (Bowe, Bowe & Streeter, 2000, p. 510); going on "automatic pilot" (Van Maanen, 1991, p. 75); going out to "smoke pot in [the] Jeep" (Bowe, Bowe & Streeter, 2000, p. 20); or moving on to another client (Bowe, Bowe & Streeter, 2000, p. 161). While many of these may be understood to involve fleeing from the problem, there may come a point when flight is no longer possible. In such cases, front-line workers feel they can neither manage nor flee, and one remaining way to deal with this is to engage in revenge and attempt to expel the toxicity into someone else. Revenge, therefore, is sometimes the only remaining option.

The concept of revenge—the retaliation for an offence or injury—has long occupied an important place in human thought and experience: versions of the principle *lex talionis* (Latin for the "law of retaliation") appear as early as the code of Hammurabi and the laws of the Old Testament, and the theme of revenge is a central organizing motif in a wide range of stories from the Bible, Greek mythology, and Shakespearean tragedy. Many of these stories concern situations in which goods and services are created and exchanged: the Biblical Cain murdered Abel as an act of retribution towards a brother who made a sacrifice that was more pleasing to God than his own, while Shakespeare's Shylock literally demanded a "pound of flesh" as an act of revenge from a customer who had not repaid a debt.

While the literature on organizations tends to frame revenge in a negative way, Seabright & Schminke (2002) disagree with this and suggest that it may be creative and resourceful. This exception aside, the damaging aspects of revenge have been highlighted in a range of contemporary settings: Hopfl (2004) uses revenge to frame her understanding of consumer society; Stein (2005) links retaliation with envy and jealousy in explaining the demise of the Gucci family dynasty; while Sievers & Mersky (2006) see leadership revenge as playing a key role in the fortunes of companies such as Chrysler and Ford. Andersson & Pearson (1999) further suggest that, especially when it constitutes an over-reaction to the initial offence, revenge may facilitate the spiralling and escalation of workplace problems.

Psychoanalytic accounts argue that inclinations to exact revenge are likely to be stimulated by (partly or entirely) unconscious memories of earlier wounds, traumas, and losses. Terms such as "developmental injury" (Temple, 1998), "narcissistic injury" (Kohut, 1972), and early "trauma" (Gibb, 1998; Young & Gibb, 1998) give voice to the notion of emotional wounds experienced earlier in life which—often unconsciously—strengthen the desire for revenge. This would suggest that employees' tendencies to take revenge in toxic situations are likely to be particularly intense when such situations unconsciously evoke memories of earlier wounds and traumas. Further, these acts of revenge are not necessarily successful and, on occasion, may make matters considerably worse for those who engage in them.

Employees may sometimes respond to customer toxicity by explicitly desiring revenge, but not acting this out. Conscious or unconscious fantasies of revenge or retribution are familiar, for example, to flight attendants, many of whom suffer considerable abuse (Hochschild, 1983). As one airline employee put it—in response to an offending customer—she found herself wanting to engage in "something mean, like pouring Ex-Lax into his coffee" (Hochschild, 1983, p. 114). Indeed, Hochschild found that most conscious desires for revenge involve a strong oral component in which the offending customer is fed something unpleasant, poisonous, or problematic in some other way (Hochschild, 1983, p. 114). This therefore suggests that—in response to the transgression of their corporeal boundaries—employees may sometimes have a conscious or unconscious fantasy of retribution involving the transgression of the bodily boundaries of the customer.

In some examples, revenge fantasies are acted out, but there is a degree of ambiguity about the extent to which employees are in control and fully conscious of what they are doing. In one incident, a flight attendant tried her best to appease and tend to the needs of a passenger who complained about "absolutely everything" (Hochschild, 1983, p. 114). Already provoked, the flight attendant felt even more deeply angry when the passenger began yelling at her black colleague, calling her a "nigger bitch!" (Hochschild, 1983, p. 114). Shortly after this, the flight attendant tripped, spilling a Bloody Mary all over the offending passenger; in the interview with Hochschild, she recalled this incident with a grin, recounting how "that Bloody Mary hit that white pants suit!" (Hochschild, 1983, p. 114). It could be suggested that, following the psychoanalytic view of slips of the tongue, the act of tripping may be understood to be imbued with unconscious meaning. More specifically, this boundary transgression could be seen to have involved an unconscious attack—the spilt Bloody Mary symbolizing the spilling of blood—for the defilement of the black colleague by symbolically "cutting" the white skin—represented by the white pants suit—of the customer.

A similar ambiguity about employees' awareness of—and their capacity to control—their revenge fantasies may be found in the account of a waitress in a country bar, a workplace which, as she put it, "burnt me out" (Bowe, Bowe & Streeter, 2000, p. 236); as before, this term can be understood to allude to an unconscious fantasy of physical damage. One incident concerned a customer and his friends who kept on requiring the waitress to pour small amounts of salt on their necks so that they could do "body shots" (whereby someone else licks the salt off the person's neck and then drinks a shot of tequila). She continued that, having served the customer and his drunken friends "rounds of drinks and rounds of drinks and rounds of drinks" (Bowe, Bowe & Streeter, 2000, p. 235), and, in the absence of receiving a tip, "I started pouring the salt on his neck, and I just suddenly lose it. Right out of nowhere, I doused his head with salt" (Bowe, Bowe & Streeter, 2000, pp. 235–236). This can be seen as having the unconscious meaning of a toxic retaliation—the salt being likely to burn the customer's skin and eyes—in response to the waitress' feeling of being "burnt out" by the workplace and its customers.

In yet other cases, revenge fantasies may be acted out in an apparently more deliberate manner; at Disneyland, for example, while used only rarely, various repertoires of revenge activity were mentioned by ride operators (Van Maanen, 1991). These included the "seatbelt squeeze" that leaves the customer "gasping" for the duration of the trip; the "break-toss" so that "the driver flies on the hood of the car (or beyond)"; the "seatbelt slap" involving the customer receiving a snap of the hard plastic belt across the face or body; or the "Sorry-I-did-not-see-your-hand" tactic, a "savage move designed to crunch a particularly irksome customer's hand (foot, finger, arm, leg, etc.)" (Van Maanen, 1991, pp. 71–72). All of the above examples from different sectors and industries—whether involuntary or deliberate, conscious or unconscious—involve the principle of *lex talionis*.

The toxic environment

Problems of toxicity become particularly acute when they extend over space and time; in such cases, we may speak of the experience of a "toxic environment". One example emerged from my research with CapitalAirport, a state-run airport authority (Stein, 1995, 2000).

Employees taking payments at the airport car park exits, for example, faced customers who were frequently in distressed states. Like workers elsewhere, car park staff repeatedly referred to customers as "obnoxious", suggesting an experience of something polluting or poisonous being transferred to them; they also complained bitterly about the levels of pollution in the car park. One employee, especially angry that staff numbers were diminished by the requirement to use a "car starter machine" to assist those unable to start their vehicles, spoke of the new machine as "that bloody thing". When he offered me a cup of coffee (I interviewed him in the small work cabin situated in the car park), his colleague said that he would have to "scrape the carbon out of the cup" before he gave it to me. Although I accepted the offer, he never poured the cup. What this suggests is a pervasive feeling among these staff that they inhabited a contaminated world, permeated by a range of toxic substances that had dangerously transgressed their boundary regions. Like poisonous gases—where combinations of substances may vastly increase toxicity—these sources spiralled in a mutually reinforcing way. This combination of pressures, familiar to those working in a service environment (Foote Whyte, 1946), contributed to the experience of a toxic environment.

Further, the inclination to exact revenge or retribution may play an important role in the development of the toxic environment. One example concerns a flight attendant who, on occasion, had been hit, spat on, and had objects thrown at her (Bowe, Bowe & Streeter, 2000, p. 196). In one situation, after working eight days in a row, she was faced by a plane full of skiers, many of whom were upset that they had to put their bags in the hold. Already angry about the bag problem, one passenger became quite abusive when served with a cheeseburger rather than a turkey salad, an option that had run out. He shouted at the flight attendant: "What the fuck is this? ... You can take your fucking cheeseburger and shove it up your ass" (Bowe, Bowe & Streeter, 2000, p. 197), following which he threw the cheeseburger at her, hitting her face: the flight attendant, a vegetarian, found this "pretty gross" (Bowe, Bowe & Streeter, 2000, p. 196). The cheeseburger then landed in the lap of a woman passenger who sat up immediately, spilling her drink onto a third passenger, after which she began yelling at the flight attendant. The flight attendant, who could no longer cope, reports that she then "just lost it .... I was just hanging on a thread .... I started screaming" (Bowe, Bowe & Streeter, 2000, p. 197). With other passengers still waiting for food, and with colleagues in a state of confusion, the flight attendant refused to serve any more food until the guilty passenger apologized. However, when his apology was forthcoming, it was accompanied by the accusation that the flight attendant had been "disrespectful" and a "bitch" (Bowe, Bowe & Streeter, 2000, p. 198), leading to her upping the stakes and demanding a further, unequivocal apology over the PA system. The customer eventually did this, but the flight attendant lost a week's pay because of the incident. At least for a period of time, therefore, here too the work environment was experienced as toxic, with the desire for retaliation playing a key role in the spiralling of problems.

Discussion

Having explored various manifestations of toxicity, I now turn to relate these ideas to theory. I begin by examining how the toxicity theme undermines the idea of the autonomous subject. I then argue that the toxicity concept carries implications for our understanding of the processes and mechanisms that underpin problematic front-line worker interchanges. In particular, the concept implies an underlying process of regression, while the idea of revenge as a response to toxicity may be understood to involve the mechanism of "projective identification". The implications for certain of the systems and dynamic phenomena of service work are then examined. Finally, noting the focus on problems of boundary impermeability in certain areas of the literature, I argue that—by exploring the difficulties created by excessive boundary permeability—this chapter takes the debate into relatively new territory.

First, the toxicity theme implies an undercutting of the concept of employees as autonomous, conscious subjects who should have little difficulty controlling their feelings, and thereby influencing their fate; this concept is implicit, for example, in notions of them being "empowered" (Moss Kanter, 1983) or becoming "winners" (Peters & Waterman, 1982). Statements by managers that "[w]e own our own emotions" (quoted in: Korczynski, 2003, p. 68) and employees that "no-one makes you feel the way you do without your permission" (quoted in: Sturdy & Fineman, 2001, pp. 139–140) are therefore necessarily grounded in illusion: employees are vulnerable to the indeterminacy and difficulty of the work environment they operate in, as well as to the shaping of that environment by their feelings and by the unconscious. The undermining of the autonomy of the subject is especially poignant when we examine the relationship between front-line workers and customers: front-line workers are expected not to defend themselves, to accept abuse, and to appease those who try to provoke them.

Second, the toxicity image helps us understand the processes underlying problematic front-line experiences; this focus on process occupies an important part of theory development (Hammersley & Atkinson, 1983). Specifically, the toxicity idea articulates the notion that front-line workers may become involved in processes of regression to infantile mental states (Bion, 1961, p. 142) that involve having the fantasy of being attacked or poisoned by toxic substances. This connects with the ideas of the psychoanalyst Bick (1968), who has argued that the experience of the skin plays a central role in the formation of the infantile ego. In its most primitive form, she argues, the parts of the personality are "held together ... by the skin functioning as a boundary" (Bick, 1968, p. 55). Similar arguments have been formulated by Anzieu, who coined the term "skin ego", "a mental image of which the Ego of the child makes use ... on the basis of its experience of the surface of the body" (1989, p. 40). If the skin is central to the development of the infant's boundaries and sense of self, the threatening of adult ego functioning is likely to involve a regression to sensate, corporeal experiences of toxicity. Further, as implied by the notion of the "group ego-skin" (Anzieu, 1999), these processes may occur at group level, as well as at the level of the organization (Diamond, Allcorn & Stein, 2004).

Third, the toxicity image helps us understand not only the primitive processes involved in generating employees' feelings, but also the mechanisms implicit in their reactions; the specification of such mechanisms are also a key to good theory (Hammersley & Atkinson, 1983; Tsoukas, 1991). In particular, a key feature of toxicity—that it cannot be absorbed or processed—may lead front-line employees to react by attempting to expel it, forcing others, especially those from whom the toxicity has emanated, to absorb it. Psychologically, this sometimes translates as revenge, the forcing of others to deal with what you have to deal with yourself, or feel what you have been compelled to feel. In her formulation of the notion "projective identification", the psychoanalyst Klein (1980) provided us with a useful idea of a mechanism that underpins the phenomenon of revenge: projective identification involves the attempt to rid oneself of unpleasant feelings by forcing someone else to feel as you do. While the concept has been used in different ways

(Rosenfeld, 1987, p. 157), central to our purposes is the notion that projective identification involves an activity undertaken in relation to a recipient who will experience—and may well be transformed by—that activity (Klein, 1980); this transformation, in some cases, may lead to the recipient engaging in "enactments" (Bott Spillius & Feldman, 1989, p. 48). Thus, the suggestion is that employees may feel unable to contain certain experiences and therefore respond with specific enactments that involve vengefully projecting these back into customers. Revenge reactions could thus be seen as employees' conscious or unconscious attempts to unburden and detoxify themselves by returning—via projective identification—unbearable toxic experiences back into the customer.

Fourth, the toxicity image also goes further than certain of the other images in so far as it casts light on some of the systemic and dynamic phenomena associated with such subjects in their work in the service of customers. In particular, the image throws into stark relief the complex manner in which excessive permeability across one boundary may transfer and cause difficulties in other areas. Following Schneider (1991), we may posit the notion of a number of distinct levels or types of boundaries. Thus toxicity across an employee–customer boundary can produce problems across a range of other boundaries. It can, for example, have a knock-on effect and produce problems across the employee–team boundary, the employee–external employee boundary, the employee–boss boundary, and the work–home boundary. In extreme cases, in a manner similar to that shown elsewhere by Andersson & Pearson (1999), the systemic inter-relatedness of these boundary transgressions may lead to a downward spiralling of toxicity and the development of a toxic environment. In articulating these systemic and dynamic phenomena, the image therefore connects with, and potentially deepens, the systemic and psychoanalytic literatures that have pioneered the understanding of such matters.

Fifth, the toxicity image also contributes to the writings on boundaries within the related fields of psychoanalysis, organizational dynamics, systems psychodynamics, and socio-technical systems by taking them in a relatively unexplored direction. While these traditions did much important work on the articulation of the boundary and boundary region concepts, a great deal of this work—entirely appropriately—has focused on concerns about boundary rigidity and impermeability. In outlining the principles of socio-technical design, for example, Cherns argues that "boundaries should not be drawn so as to impede …" (Cherns, 1987, p. 156—emphasis in original). Similar arguments are formulated in his earlier paper (1976), but nowhere in these papers does Cherns examine the converse problem of boundaries that are excessively flexible or permeable. Further, more recent authors such as Diamond, Allcorn & Stein (2004) have focused on organizational boundaries as "silos" that isolate employee groups from each other in an especially problematic way. By way of contrast, therefore, this discussion seeks to make a contribution by examining the opposite problem of excessive permeability of boundaries and boundary regions.

Conclusions

My aims in this chapter have been to further our understanding of certain of the more problematic experiences of front-line workers as well as to contribute to the debates on the theories of organizational images. Having argued that some of the difficulties of employee–customer interchanges are not conveyed by the images currently in use, and drawing on a range of words and phrases used by front-line employees themselves, I thus introduced the new image of toxicity. This image encapsulates the notion of experiences that are felt to be poisonous and that cannot easily be dealt with. I have drawn on ideas from psychoanalysis and its application to organizational dynamics to explore the functioning of toxicity and understand its ramifications. I have also taken these themes further in the discussion by making a number of links with existing theories. This study makes a contribution to two areas of literature: first, it contributes to the literature on images and metaphors by articulating the hitherto overlooked dimension of toxicity; second, it adds to the literature on revenge by showing how it may occur as a consequence of toxicity in front-line service situations.

Finally, the theme of toxicity enables us to connect the employee–customer interface with a deep reservoir of primordial human experience which uses the tangible (body) to symbolize the intangible (emotions). Such uses of symbolization—which employ many "dead metaphors" (Tsoukas, 1991, p. 568) whose symbolic nature we are usually no longer aware of—may occur at so fundamental a level that they are barely noticed. For example, we commonly refer to emotions using the generic term "feelings", a word that implies tactile, physical experience. Similarly, we talk of being "touched" or "struck" by emotion, terms that, once again, suggest sensate experiences. Positive emotions may sometimes be represented in a physical way by words such as "warm" or "glowing", while more negatively, we may refer to "cold" or "hard" feelings. We also speak about "abrasive" personalities and "rubbing someone up the wrong way", both of which suggest something rough, uncomfortable, and distinctly corporeal. It is in the context of this symbolism that the toxicity idea may be less of a surprise than at initial inspection, because, I would argue, this corporeal notion is the natural extension of these familiar ways of thinking and speaking. It is hoped that these ideas further our understanding of these matters.

Note

I owe much to Anton Obholzer for stimulating my initial interest in toxicity, some years ago. I also own many thanks to Andrew Brown, Adrian Fronda, William Halton, Antje Netzer-Stein for their feedback on earlier drafts of this chapter. This research was supported by a personal bursary from the Tavistock Institute of Medical Psychology, for which I am very grateful. The responsibility for the views expressed in this piece is entirely my own.

Notes

1. This paper was first published in 2007 in *Organization Studies* (28/08: 1223–1241), and is reprinted here with permission from Sage.
2. Mark Stein received the Richard Normann Prize for an abridged version of this paper, and has in fact been the only ever recipient of the prize. Held in trust during the years 2005 to 2008 by Templeton College, University of Oxford, the Richard Normann Prize was intended to reward "outstanding insights into the service economy, value co-production, and business innovation and change".

References

Andersson, L. M. & Pearson, C. M. (1999). Tit for tat? The spiralling effect of incivility in the workplace. *Academy of Management Review*, 24(3): 452–471.
Anzieu, D. (1984). *The Group and the Unconscious*. London: Routledge.
Anzieu, D. (1989). *The Skin Ego*. New Haven: Yale University Press.

Anzieu, D. (1999). The group ego-skin. *Group Analysis, 32(3)*: 319–329.

Barsade, S. B. (2002). The ripple effect of contagion: emotional contagion and its influence on group behaviour. *Administrative Science Quarterly, 47*: 644–675.

Bick, E. (1968). The experience of the skin in early object relations. *International Journal of Psychoanalysis, 49*: 55–59.

Bion, W. R. (1961). *Experiences in Groups and Other Papers*. London: Tavistock.

Bott Spillius, E. & Feldman, M. (1989). "Introduction to part two". In: E. Bott Spillius and M. Feldman (Eds.), *Psychic Equilibrium and Psychic Change: Selected Papers of Betty Joseph* (pp. 47–50). London: Tavistock/Routledge.

Boulding, K. E. (1956). *The Image*. Michigan: Michigan University Press.

Bowe, J., Bowe, M. & Streeter, S. (Eds.) (2000). *Gig: Americans Talk about Their Jobs*. New York: Three Rivers.

Brown, A. D. & Starkey, K. (2000). Organizational identity and learning: a psychodynamic perspective. *Academy of Management Review, 25(1)*: 102–120.

Burrell, G. (1988). Modernism, post modernism and organizational analysis 2: the contribution of Michel Foucault. *Organization Studies, 9(2)*: 221–235.

Carlzon, J. (1987). *Moments of Truth*. Cambridge, MA: Ballinger.

Cherns, A. (1976). Principles of socio-technical design. *Human Relations, 29(8)*: 783–792.

Cherns, A. (1987). Principles of socio-technical design revisited. *Human Relations, 40(3)*: 153–162.

Clark, T. & Salaman, G. (1998). Creating the "right" impression: towards a dramaturgy of management consultancy. *Service Industries Journal, 18(1)*: 18–38.

Cornelissen, J. P. (2004). What are we playing at? Theatre, organizations and the use of metaphor. *Organization Studies, 25(5)*: 705–726.

Cornelissen, J. P. (2005). Beyond compare: metaphor in organization theory. *Academy of Management Review, 30(4)*: 751–764.

Cornelissen, J. P. (2006). Making sense of theory construction: metaphor and disciplined imagination. *Organization Studies, 27(11)*: 1579–1597.

Diamond, M., Allcorn, S. & Stein, H. (2004). The surface of organizational boundaries: a framework of analysis. *Human Relations, 57(1)*: 31–53.

Douglas, M. (1975). *Implicit Meanings: Essays in Anthropology*. London: Routledge.

Folgero, I. S. & Fjeldstad, I. H. (1995). On duty—off guard: cultural norms and sexual harassment in service organizations. *Organization Studies, 16(2)*: 299–313.

Foote Whyte, W. (1946). *Industry and Society*. New York: McGraw-Hill.
Foucault, M. (1970). *The Order of Things: An Archaeology of the Human Sciences*. London: Tavistock.
Foucault, M. (1977). *Discipline and Punish: The Birth of the Prison*. Harmondsworth: Penguin.
Frost, P. J. (2003). *Toxic Emotions at Work: How Compassionate Managers Handle Pain and Conflict*. Boston, MA: Harvard Business School Press.
Frost, P. J. & Robinson, S. (1999). The toxic handler: organizational hero and casualty. *Harvard Business Review, 77(4)*: 96–105.
Gabriel, Y. (1995). The unmanaged organization—stories, fantasies and subjectivity. *Organization Studies, 16(3)*: 477–501.
Gabriel, Y. (1999). *Organizations in Depth: The Psychoanalysis of Organizations*. London: Sage.
Gibb, E. (1998). Dreaming after a traumatic bereavement: mourning or its avoidance? In: C. Garland (Ed.), *Understanding Trauma: A Psychoanalytical Approach* (pp. 123–138). London: Duckworth.
Goffman, E. (1967). *Interaction Ritual*. Garden City, NY: Doubleday.
Goffman, E. (1971). *The Presentation of Self in Everyday Life*. Harmondsworth: Penguin.
Hall, E. J. (1993). Smiling, deferring, and flirting: doing gender by giving "good service". *Work and Occupations, 20(4)*: 452–471.
Hammersley, M. & Atkinson, P. (1983). *Ethnography: Principles in Practice*. London: Routledge.
Hernes, T. (2004). Studying composite boundaries: a framework of analysis. *Human Relations, 57(1)*: 9–29.
Hirschhorn, L. & Gilmore, T. (1992). The new boundaries of the "boundaryless" organization organization. *Harvard Business Review, May/June*: 104–115.
Hochschild, A. R. (1983). *The Managed Heart: Commercialization of Human Feeling*. Berkeley: University of California Press.
Hopfl, H. (2002). Playing the part: reflections on aspects of mere performance in the customer-client relationship. *Journal of Management Studies, 39(2)*: 255–267.
Hopfl, H. (2004). Demeter and the curse of consumption. In: Y. Gabriel (Ed.), *Myths, Stories and Organizations: Premodern Narratives for Our Times* (pp. 192–204). Oxford: Oxford University Press.
Isaacs, S. (1952). The nature and function of phantasy. In: M. Klein, P. Heimann, S. Isaacs & J. Riviere (Eds.), *Developments in Psychoanalysis* (pp. 67–121). London: Hogarth.
Jakobson, R. (1962). *Selected Writings*, vols 1–4. The Hague: Mouton.
Klein, M. (1980). *Envy and Gratitude and Other Works 1946–1963*. London: Hogarth and Institute of Psycho-Analysis.

Klein, M. (1981). *Love, Guilt and Reparation and Other Works 1921–1945*. London: Hogarth and Institute of Psycho-Analysis.

Kohut, H. (1972). Thoughts on narcissism and narcissistic rage. *The Psychoanalytic Study of the Child*, 27: 360–400.

Korczynski, M. (2003). Communities of coping: collective emotional labour in service work. *Organization*, 10(1): 55–79.

Krantz, J. (2006). Leadership, betrayal and adaptation. *Human Relations*, 59(2): 221–240.

Lackoff, G. & Johnson, M. (1980). *Metaphors We Live By*. Chicago: University of Chicago Press.

Laplanche, J. & Pontalis, J.-B. (1973). *The Language of Psycho-Analysis*. London: Hogarth Press and Institute of Psycho-Analysis.

Lipman-Blumen, J. (2005). *The Allure of Toxic Leaders*. New York: Oxford University Press.

Lynn, M. L. (2005). Organizational buffering: managing boundaries and cores. *Organization Studies*, 26(1): 37–61.

Maitlis, S. & Ozcelik, H. (2004). Toxic decision processes: a study of emotion and organizational decision making. *Organization Science*, 15(4): 375–393.

Mangham, I. L. (2005). The drama of organizational life. *Organization Studies*, 26(6): 941–958.

Mangham, I. L. & Overington, M. A. (1987). *Organizations as Theatre: A Social Psychology of Dramatic Appearances*. Chichester: Wiley.

Marshak, R. J. (2003). Metaphors and analogical reasoning in organizational theory: further extensions. *Academy of Management Review*, 28(1): 9–12.

Miller, E. & Rice, A. K. (1967). *Systems of Organisation*. London: Tavistock.

Mills, P. K., Chase, R. B. & Marguilies, N. (1983). Motivating the client/employee system as a service/production strategy. *Academy of Management Review*, 8(2): 301–310.

Morgan, G. (1980). Paradigms, metaphors, and puzzle solving in organization theory. *Administrative Science Quarterly*, 25: 605–621.

Morgan, G. (1983). More on metaphor: why we cannot control tropes in administrative sciences. *Administrative Science Quarterly*, 28: 601–607.

Morgan, G. (1986). *Images of Organization*. Beverly Hills: Sage.

Morgan, G. (1997). *Images of Organization* (new edition). Thousand Oaks: Sage.

Moss Kanter, R. (1983). *The Change Masters: Corporate Entrepreneurs at Work*. London: Unwin.

Normann, R. (1984). *Service Management: Strategy and Leadership in Service Businesses*. Chichester: Wiley.

Offermann, L. R. (2004). When followers become toxic. *Harvard Business Review*, 82(1): 54–60.

Ogbonna, E. & Harris, L. C. (2004). Work intensification and emotional labour among UK university lecturers: an exploratory study. *Organization Studies, 25(7)*: 1185–1203.
Ortony, A. (1975). Why metaphors are necessary and not just nice. *Educational Theory, 25*: 45–53.
Pentland, B. T. (1999). Building process theory with narrative: from description to explanation. *Academy of Management Review, 24(4)*: 711–724.
Peters, T. & Waterman, R. H. (1982). *In Search of Excellence: Lessons from America's Best Run Companies.* London: Harper & Row.
Rosenfeld, H. (1987). *Impasse and Interpretation.* London: Tavistock.
Rosenthal, P., Peccei, R. & Hill, S. (2001). Academic discourses of the customer: "sovereign beings", "management accomplices" or "people like us". In: A. Sturdy, I. Grugulis & H. Willmott (Eds.), *Customer Service: Empowerment and Entrapment* (pp. 18–37). Houndmills, Basingstoke: Palgrave.
Schneider, S. C. (1991). Managing boundaries in organizations. In: M. Kets de Vries and associates (Eds.), *Organizations on the Couch: Clinical Perspectives on Organizational Behaviour and Change.* (pp. 169–190). San Francisco: Jossey-Bass.
Schreyogg, G. & Hopfl, H. (2004). Theatre and organization: Editorial introduction. *Organization Studies, 25(5)*: 691–704.
Schwartz, H. S. (1985). The usefulness of myth and the myth of usefulness: a dilemma for the applied organizational scientist. *Journal of Management, 11*: 31–42.
Seabright, M. A. & Schminke, M. (2002). Immoral imagination and revenge in organizations. *Journal of Business Ethics, 38(1)*: 19–31.
Shumate, M. & Fulk, J. (2004). Boundaries and role conflict when work and family are collocated: a communication network and symbolic interaction approach. *Human Relations, 57(1)*: 55–74.
Sievers, B. & Redding Mersky, R. (2006). The economy of vengeance: some considerations on the aetiology and meaning of the business of revenge. *Human Relations, 59(2)*: 241–259.
Spradley, J. P. & Mann, B. J. (1975). *The Cocktail Waitress: Woman's Work in a Man's World.* London: Wiley.
Stacey, R. (2001). Complexity at the edge of the basic-assumption group. In: L. Gould, L. F. Stapley & M. Stein (Eds.), *The Systems Psychodynamics of Organizations* (pp. 91–114). London: Karnac Books.
Stein, M. (1995). Unpublished doctoral thesis, Brunel University.
Stein, M. (2000). "Winners" training and its troubles. *Personnel Review, 29(4)*: 445–459.
Stein, M. (2005). The Othello conundrum: the inner contagion of leadership. *Organization Studies, 26(9)*: 1405–1419.

Sturdy, A. & Fineman, S. (2001). Struggles for the control of affect—resistance as politics and emotion. In: A. Sturdy, I. Grugulis & H. Willmott (Eds.), *Customer Service: Empowerment and Entrapment* (pp. 135–156). Houndmills, Basingstoke: Palgrave.

Taylor, P. & Bain, P. (2003). "Subterranean worksick blues": humour as subversion in two call centres. *Organization Studies, 24(9)*: 1487–1509.

Temple, N. (1998). Developmental injury: its effects on the inner world. In: C. Garland (Ed.), *Understanding Trauma: A Psychoanalytical Approach* (pp. 155–166). London: Duckworth.

Terkel, S. (2004). *Working: People Talk about What They Do All Day and How They Feel about What They Do*. New York: New Press.

Toffler, A. (1980). *The Third Wave*. New York: Morrow.

Tsoukas, H. (1991). The missing link: a transformational view of metaphors in organizational science. *Academy of Management Review, 16(3)*: 566–585.

Tsoukas, H. (1993). Analogical reasoning and knowledge generation in organization theory. *Organization Studies, 14(3)*: 323–346.

Van de Ven, A. H. & Poole, M. S. (1995). Explaining development and change in organizations. *Academy of Management Review, 20(3)*: 510–540.

Van Maanen, J. (1991). The smile factory: work at Disneyland. In: P. J. Frost, L. F. Moore, M. S. Louis, C. C. Lundberg & J. Martin (Eds.), *Reframing Organizational Culture* (pp. 58–76). Newbury Park: Sage.

Vera, D. & Crossan, M. (2004). Theatrical improvisations: lessons for organizations. *Organization Studies, 25(5)*: 727–749.

Weick, K. (1989). Theory construction as disciplined imagination. *Academy of Management Review, 14(4)*: 516–531.

White, H. (1979). Michel Foucault. In: J. Sturrock (Ed.), *Structuralism and Since: From Levi-Strauss to Derrida* (pp. 81–115). Oxford: Oxford University Press.

Young, L. & Gibb, E. (1998). Trauma and grievance. In: C. Garland (Ed.), *Understanding Trauma: A Psychoanalytical Approach* (pp. 81–95). London: Duckworth.

CHAPTER THREE

Different organizations—different burnouts
Burnout as interplay between personality pattern and organizational structure[1]

Mathias Lohmer

Introduction

Burnout is a major threat to physical and psychological health. As a result of growing expectations, workload, and the blurring of boundaries between work and free time in organizational life, burnout as a form of depression is becoming a serious problem. We can differentiate several risk factors that can lead to burnout. There are risk factors due to the individual lifestyle and the personality of a person, which we call personal risk factors. On the other hand, there are also risk factors in the work environment of a person, which we call organizational risk factors.

Besides general risk factors in most modern work environments with a rapid rate of change and great demands of flexibility, we can differentiate particular organizational risk factors depending on different types of organizations. When they interact with different types of personality styles, they produce "different types of burnout". Appreciating this interaction will help us to identify the individuals who are at risk from organizational burnout.

My hypothesis is that those individuals who fit especially well in a certain type of organization—like compulsive personalities in bureaucratic types of organizations—are also particularly at risk of suffering burnout in these types of organizations, because they tend to overlook the hazards involved due to an unconscious collusion of personal and organizational structures.

In the following, I will first present a case of burnout, then define forms and phases of burnout and differentiate different types of risk factors for burnout and their interaction with each other. I will conclude with some considerations about prevention and treatment of burnout.

A case of burnout[2]

Miss D., a thirty-three-year-old woman made an appointment in my office where I see coaching clients as well as psychotherapy patients. She was not clear what kind of help she would need and reported that she had been suffering from depressive exhaustion, fear of failure, and existential anxiety. In addition, she complained about physical fatigue, difficulty in sleeping through the night, headaches, whining sounds in the ears, and problems with "sorting out her life". For years, she had been severely addicted to cocaine. At the point of coming to see me, there remained some alcohol and nicotine abuse.

Miss D. presented as an assertive, tough-looking woman, not too feminine in her conservative business dress, but at the same time a bit "unreal", as if she was hiding a very vulnerable aspect of herself.

She told me that she worked as a consultant who specialized in the financial stabilization of middle-sized enterprises. She usually worked alone and reported that she was chronically overtaxed by demanding projects, professional trips, and a lack of free time. She carried on a "long-distance" relationship with an older man who worked as a banker in another city. Apparently his plan was to move back to the city where she lives within a year or two. They wanted to have children but have been unable to conceive, therefore she was in hormone treatment. The client entertained vague ideas about "dropping out" of her profession and doing something entirely different "maybe a shop, a bar, something with flowers?"

She found it hard to concentrate, and tended to become aggressive when drinking. In her relationship, she gave an impression that, in many ways, she had adjusted to fit into her partner's rather conservative circle of family and friends. She had a great ability to satisfy people's expectations and avoid offending anyone. She tended to be successful at winning others over. The flip side of this "ability" was, however, that she hardly had any authentic, unburdened contacts. Thus, during the interview, she gave the impression of being cogent, measured, and in general "too mature" for her age.

As a child, she was an "elitist outsider". A "daddy's girl" with a certain largess, she learned early to take on responsibility, avoid creating problems, and to be successful and independent. These abilities also played a major role in her professional success as a consultant. In an unconscious inner conflict between her autonomy and her own neediness, she was locked into an active mode of caring for others. Therefore, her own wish to be cared for remained unfulfilled, and she could not activate sufficient energies to take better care of herself. The client attempted to compensate this deficit of self-care and "being cared for" by her addictive behaviour—including work addiction. Her love relationship also failed to provide much real satisfaction; her partner was himself burdened by his professional work and, in addition, was affected by a severe chronic illness. This boded for her a future in a helping role. Due to the client's current habits in cultivating relationships, the realm of friendly contacts scarcely presented options for emotional nourishment or support. The client was locked into a mode of object-manipulation, granting her a great deal of control over her objects, but offered no real and significant experience of authentic relationships. She was thus in danger of developing a "false self".

Overall, the client can be characterized as a depressive personality with compulsive and narcissistic traits. Due to rising demands in her professional life, the compensation mechanisms were no longer sufficient, and this resulted in a state of burnout with the severe symptoms described earlier.

Due to the neurotic nature of the conflicts which seemed to be imbedded in her personality structure, I suggested psychotherapy (with coaching elements) rather than coaching *per se*.

Later on, I will discuss what psychotherapy versus coaching would have meant whilst working with this client.

Definition, phases, and effects of burnout

Definition

The term "burnout", originally coined in English, is now used internationally. The concept was introduced by Herbert Freudenberger in 1974. It denotes the effects of chronic fatigue due to overworking, manifested physically as well as emotionally. There is a consensus about three core dimensions of the burnout experience: exhaustion, depersonalization, and inefficacy. Exhaustion (physical, emotional, and cognitive) is the most widely reported, the most thoroughly analysed, and one necessary criterion for burnout (Maslach, Schaufeli & Leiter, 2001). Depersonalization describes the attempt to distance oneself from other people, especially one's customers/clients, by developing an indifferent or cynical attitude (Maslach, Schaufeli & Leiter, 2001). Inefficacy means reduced personal accomplishment and constitutes the third burnout core dimension.

Five phases of burnout syndrome

In the individually centred approaches of burnout (Freudenberger, 1974), the burnout syndrome is seen as a result of the frustration of job expectations. It develops in different phases, as a four-stepped process of disillusionment.

At the beginning of the employment, idealistic enthusiasm is the dominating emotion, which is characterized by unrealistic expectations and exceeding engagement. The idealistic enthusiasm is then followed by a phase named stagnation. In this phase, dissatisfaction with general organizational conditions emerges, while exceeding engagement is retained. In the third phase, frustration, the idealistic job expectations are frustrated. As a consequence of this, in phase 4 apathy, frustration, cynicism, and emotional retirement are predominant, the affected person also avoids contacts to her or his clients. Phase 4 leads to the full syndrome of burnout in phase 5.

Effects of burnout syndrome

If burnout has occurred, a series of effects are typical. Loss of motivation is a very common indicator: at work, people with loss of motivation drag themselves to work and have trouble getting started once they arrive. Disorganization and the inability to handle complex tasks also occur as a result of the burnout syndrome. On the emotional and cognitive level, disillusionment (resignation) with loss of courage and existential despair are typical effects of the burnout syndrome. Common physical symptoms that can occur are a weakened immune system or heart arrhythmia. Furthermore, burnout-specific effects on the psychological and physical level are, for example, depression and aggressiveness, anxiety, and often panic or addiction disorders. People who suffer from burnout often withdraw from their friends and their further social network. Finally, from the economic perspective, an important and frequent result of burnout is the status of occupational disability, ranging from temporary to permanent.

Risk factors for burnout

There are different risk factors that can lead to burnout. There are risk factors due to the individual lifestyle and personality of a worker, which we call personal risk factors. On the other hand, there are also risk factors in the work environment, which we call organizational risk factors. In the following section, I will describe both types of risk factors for burnout, making distinction between general and particular risk factors. However, let us consider the personality risk factors first.

Personal risk factors

One general risk factor for individuals is the overemphasis on work. When work becomes the most important part of life, the work–life balance is disturbed and work addiction can arise. Burnout can be a consequence of work addiction.

Beside this general personal risk factor, there are several particular risk factors for the emergence of burnout. Especially susceptible are persons who exhibit (one or more of) the following attributes and personality styles in the extreme form:

1. Inner performance script due to their role in the family of origin, where recognition was only granted on the basis of achievement. Later on, a high ego ideal is developed and peak achievement is regarded as the norm.
2. Depressive personality structure, frequently found in the helping professions (health or social care, education). In the family of origin, self-esteem and recognition were based on helping others. This makes it difficult to set limits to one's own work-based contribution to the service/organization.

3. Compulsive personality structure with a need for control, coupled with perfectionism and difficulty in delegating tasks to others.
4. Narcissistic personality structure with massive self-esteem conflict. Recognition by others is never sufficient and must be re-mobilized constantly. Executive personnel are particularly susceptible, since their work—as opposed to family life or recreation—involves constant recognition of visible success.

Organizational risk factors

In addition to personal risk factors, there are also organizational risk factors that can advance the development of a burnout syndrome. As in the case of personal risk factors, we can also distinguish between general and particular risk factors.

General risk factors in organizations which are always present are, for example, stress originating from inevitable changes in the work situation (such as a new role, new boss, new organizational structure) or situations in which goals of the organization contradict one's own values. One can see this dilemma, for example, in the common cynicism among advertising professionals during midlife crisis.

Due to recent developments in the professional world, there are also several particular organizational risk factors, for example an increasingly rapid rate of change, a dramatically reduced predictability (global markets, short-term planning, for example when quarterly outcomes supplant longer-term profit estimates), and greater flexibility demands (regional mobility, shifting tasks, or rapid acquisition of new knowledge, such as IT handling) in organizational life.

Whereas these factors stem from an increasing feeling of helplessness due to sociopolitical changes, we can also identify psychodynamic factors which can seduce (especially) executives into excessive overworking. In this sense, managerial work can take on an "erotic cast" (Kasper, Scheer & Schmidt, 2002), because it provides constant fulfilment—while the family is shunted into a "reification trap", spouse interaction being reduced to the coordination of family life.

For these executives, work offers a well-structured situation with clear expectations and rewards (Hochschild, 2002), whereas the home environment presents diverse, unpredictable, and relatively unstructured demands. It is tempting to enjoy the affirmative experience of serving as a "good parent" for employees around the clock, while avoiding frustrating conflicts at home—for example, interacting with or controlling defiant teenagers. Business trips, with their "down time" free of responsibility when staying in hotels during the evening, can thus become a source of respite from the strains and demands of family life.

Such factors make it more difficult to achieve the balance between professional life and other areas of life—the famous "work–life balance"!

Furthermore, the postmodern professional world presents new challenges to employees. Workers are expected to see themselves as "work enterprisers" (Pongratz & Voß, 2003) or as "entrepreneurs within an enterprise", identifying as fully as possible with the aims of the company and personally committed in the way a partial owner would be. We also see an increasing of informal structures with flat hierarchies and only few directives: employees are not presented with a clear structural framework but are expected to use self-organization, which in turn necessitates greater mental investment, so that employees are more and more absorbed by their work (Baecker, 1995).

Finally, we can observe a growing "boundlessness of work" (Schreyögg, 2005) caused in part by the development of new technologies, which in turn give rise to the corresponding organizational structures (Valcour & Hunter, 2005). Modern technology in manufacturing results in work schedules that assume readiness around the clock—so that private life is increasingly "colonized" by work. Modern computer technology supports new forms of work at home, with mobile phones, Blackberries, and iPhones providing and creating expectations of constant availability on work issues.

Besides these general and particular risk factors in most modern work environments, we can differentiate particular organizational risk factors depending on different types of organizations. When they interact with different types of personality styles, they produce "different types of burnout".

In the following section, I will present the findings of my research about the interactions between different types of organizations and different personality styles. I derived these data and my conceptual conclusions by extensively treating and coaching executives from different types of organizations, by observing and consulting to different types of organizations, and by conducting interview surveys with human resources departments of different types of organizations (see Lohmer 2004, 2008a, 2008b).

Risk factors in different types of organizations and their interplay with different types of personalities

Particularly risk-laden, in my view, are three types of organizations, which are fundamental to differentiate and which I would like to categorize in the following way:

- Bureaucratic-formalized type of organization
- Unrestricted-informal type of organization
- Emotionally demanding type of organization

Bureaucratic-formalized type of organization

Large firms, administrative agencies, and civil authorities correspond to this type. Here, the hazards lie in the restriction of individual initiatives and the existence of too many limitations. There are too few options for integrating one's personal expertise, abilities, and needs into the professional role. Rigid directives reduce leeway for actions and decisions, and lead to a sensation of powerlessness. Employees hardly participate in decisions or strategic discussions, are given little responsibility and many routine tasks rather than diverse challenges, often resulting in their being under-challenged (and thus distressed). This leads to a constant feeling of frustration and can produce forms of burnout that tend to be chronic and "silent" in character: depressive disorders or psychosomatic reactions such as pain syndromes and somatic disturbances. Individuals with compulsive traits "fit well" into such organizations, but also tend to overlook the hazards involved, since there is an unconscious collusion of personal and organizational structures.

Unrestricted-informal type of organization

Typical here are young and upcoming enterprises in areas such as IT or biotechnology. The temptation is to invest all of one's energy in work, which then becomes the main source of meaning in life. There are few formal directives to deter employees from high commitment and passionate feelings about their own effectiveness. This tendency can escalate into work addiction, since personal limits are no longer perceived, and boundaries between work and private life begin to fade. This work addiction forms the basis for chronic overtaxation (distress), and finally results in sudden and acute burnout. It can take the form of fatigue syndrome or a narcissistic crisis. In the background of this breakdown there may have been chronic abuse of addictive substances, often alcohol or cocaine. Individuals with narcissistic personality traits are attracted to work for and show high "fit" into this type of organization, but they are also at particularly high danger of burnout.

Emotionally demanding type of organization

This often applies to institutions in health, social care, and education. Teachers, physicians, nurses, psychotherapists, and others working with those who are ill, needy, or in training are at risk of sliding into a chronic imbalance: their emotional commitment "bounces back" at them, thwarted by the structural lack of narcissistic recognition for their efforts on the part of the clientele. This leads to an emotional overload due to an unfulfillable, asymmetrical demand for relational exchange. In this process, personal resources are spent and not regenerated—"the battery runs down". Work in such organizations can become especially critical if the management neglects the factors of reward, recognition, and containment. This can develop into chronic burnout with a high risk of addiction and massive depression, and potentially even suicidal tendencies. Particularly, persons with a depressive personality structure or narcissistic traits (the "helper syndrome"—Schmidbauer, 2002) are attracted to work and also "fit" well into these organizations, and they are at particular risk of burnout since their personal and the institutional defence mechanisms are congruent and ego-syntonic!

Prevention and treatment of burnout

As there are risk factors on the personal and the organizational levels, the burnout syndrome can be prevented or treated on the personal and the organizational levels.

Prevention and treatment on the personal level

The motto by Mundle (2007): "Don't give up your profession or your job, give up your destructive patterns of thought and behaviour!" shows an important approach for the treatment of burnout.

Generally, the treatment of burnout (psychotherapy or coaching) is divided in three phases. In the first phase, the following aspects are relevant:

- Acute relief and recovery
- Fundamental reorientation of self-care
- Relearning to satisfy basic physical needs

In this phase, it may be advisable that the patient leaves his or her living environment for a few weeks and be treated in an in-patient psychotherapy with its multi-modal therapy options. In this phase, some remedial measures might be necessary, for example the abstinence from addictive substances, sufficient sleep, healthy nutrition on a regular basis, systematic exercise and phases of relaxation, work breaks, and work time that is free for reflection, re-establishment of recreational and social activities, and intimate dialogue with the spouse.

In the second phase, aspects as the psychodynamic alteration of inner patterns through coaching or psychotherapy, an analysis of personal stress patterns, the perception of suppressed affects and needs, and an analysis of fundamental unconscious conflict patterns and personality styles are important.

In the third phase, the aim is to develop a more healthy life concept and a new work–life balance (this phase overlaps with the second phase). Burnout should be understood as a vital signal from the body and the psyche—"the positive side of something negative". This opportunity should be used for a re-definition of life goals and professional aims, the work–life balance. Furthermore, the cultivation of awareness and mindfulness as well as a deepening intuition and the ability to follow one's "inner voice" are important learning goals in the treatment in this phase.

The central question in this phase is: "what really nourishes me?". What contributes to enriching my life, gives my life a sense and meaning, as opposed to just passing the time, such as by zapping through television programmes (Sprenger, 2007).

Further important aspects are the planning of the future shape of one's work situation with regard to new limitations, priorities, and goals, as well as the reframing of everyday life, rearranging emphases, for example playing with one's children or going to the theatre as important activities (Sprenger, 2007).

Differential indication for coaching or psychotherapy

Depending on the individual form of burnout and the fundamental unconscious conflict patterns or personality styles at its root, it is essential to be able to differentiate and chose the most appropriate intervention. Should coaching or psychotherapy be indicated? The more ego-syntonic the attitudes and behavioural patterns leading to burnout, the more pronounced neurotic posture or personality disorder, the stronger the indication for psychotherapy would be. Also to be factored in: the ego strength of the client, along with his or her ability to accept help and ability to translate insight into behavioural change.

Where psychotherapy is indicated, it can be short-term or long-term therapy. It has proven particularly favourable to combine timely in-patient psychotherapy with subsequent out-patient treatment. In-patient treatment at intervals may also be recommended. In cases associated with addictive disorders, participation in self-help group meetings will also be necessary.

Getting back to my client Miss D., we can now see that she did need psychotherapy with regard to the prevailing conflict between autonomy and neediness, her severe addictive tendencies, and because of her strong features of creating "false self". She clearly needed some space to develop her personality and balance her needs differently.

Some of her problems, however, were suitable for a coaching context: working too much alone, not having enough breaks between projects, having a too-narrow professional specialization, lacking clear vision for one's own future, a missing work–life balance which produces vague ideas of "dropping out". These would be topics that one would address in a coaching process. In the case of Miss D., psychotherapy could also have addressed these problems by focusing not only on the transference processes of the patient, but also by challenging the very realities of the work situation and by advocating ideas that could improve work–life balance.

Burnout prevention measures at the organizational level

General changes in the professional world as described earlier—acceleration, forced flexibility, and the intrusion of work issues into private life—cannot be undone, but they can be reflected upon regularly and reconfigured into a new balance on the personal and organizational levels. For the three different types of organizations proposed here as potential triggers for burnout, the following consequences may be drawn in the context of burnout prevention:

Prevention in the formalized-bureaucratic type of organization

Important aspects here are the expansion of employees' options to take the initiative or make decisions and more delegation of decision-making and accepting responsibility for work processes. In addition, measures in the area of organizational development that help to alter work processes, styles of communication, and elements of organizational culture (such as management coaching, team-development techniques, future-search workshops for departments or entire organizations) are important preventive strategies.

In favourable cases, this can encourage the experience of a state of "flow", as described by Csikszentmihalyi (2003), of satisfaction within an organization previously perceived as "sterile". This implies complete immersion in an activity that is enriching and that promotes a feeling of identity and connectedness with other colleagues and the organization: "The task at hand, in its complexity, absorbs us so completely that we identify fully with it. There is no distinction between thought and action, between oneself and the environment" (Csikszentmihalyi, 2003, p. 59). But be aware of the dark side of that "flow": work addiction!

Viktor Frankel described it thus: "Happiness should emerge as the unintended consequence of working toward a goal that is larger than the person himself" (Frankel, 1963, as cited in Csikszentmihalyi, 2003, p. 81). Such moments of satisfaction then strengthen organizational identity, the wish to belong and to participate in the meaning of the institution.

Prevention in the unrestricted-informal type of organization

Here, we have the opposite to the type of institution described above, therefore, measures to be taken must promote structure and boundaries rather than relaxing it. It is important to establish clear limits and functions. Tasks, competencies, and responsibilities need to be defined and distributed, roles to be clarified, and above all, in this type of organization, high-level personnel must learn to regard themselves not only as professionally expert, but also as responsible for management and leadership in the sense of guiding employees and steering work processes. When they can identify with this leadership task, they are able to promote a containing function for the organization through structure and mental space.

Prevention in emotionally demanding organizations in health/social care and education

The culture of helping and teaching has its own code, which needs to be observed. Organizational measures must reinforce the important distinction between desirable commitment and a "helper syndrome" that can lead to burnout. It is particularly important that the management formulate expectations clearly but also communicate the message that limits are helpful and necessary. Organizations active in the psychosocial field need to pursue containment efforts on a constant basis in order to maintain a balance of tension among individuals, their roles, and the organization. Continuous participation in Balint groups or team supervision circles can lead towards learning and maintaining an appropriate approach to professional burdens. Productive time out , such as sabbaticals or rotation schemes, can help in sustaining vital professional energy, curiosity, commitment, and creativity, and in reducing the risk of burnout.

Interim conclusions

There is often a very thin line between commitment and overtaxation, between enjoyment of formative tasks and work addiction, between the ambition to perform well in managerial or helping roles and the loss of one's work–life balance. Moreover, personal needs and organizational realities can vary greatly.

Concepts such as "role analysis" do help in working with clients at risk, since they allow a systematic reflection on the interactions between the demands of the organization, the needs and emotional life of the person, and the options and constraints of the specific role as the intersections between organization and person.

So one could state: "get to know your personality patterns and the type of organization you are working in, and you can discover what type of burnout is waiting for you round the corner!"

Acknowledgements

My grateful acknowledgement goes to Prof. Dr. Götz Mundle and Dr. Bernd Sprenger for their stimulating exchange about the field of burnout.

Notes

1. This paper has been presented at the ISPSO Symposium in Philadelphia in 2008.
2. This is a composite case.

References

Baecker, D. (1995). Durch diesen schönen Fehler mit sich selbst bekannt gemacht. Das Experiment der Organisation. In: B. Heitger, C. Schmitz & P. W. Gester (Eds.), *Managerie, 3. Jahrbuch. Systemisches Denken und Handeln im Management*. Heidelberg: Auer.
Csikszentmihalyi, M. (2003). *Good Business: Leadership, Flow, and the Making of Meaning*. New York: Viking.
Freudenberger, H. (1974). Staff burnout. *Journal of Social Issues, 30*: 159–165.
Hochschild, A. (2002). *Keine Zeit*. Opladen: Leske + Budrich.
Kasper, H., Scheer, P. J. & Schmidt, A. (2002). *Managen und Lieben. Führungskräfte im Spannungsfeld zwischen Beruf und Privatleben*. Wien: Redline Wirtschaft bei Ueberreuther.
Lohmer, M. (Hrsg.) (2004). *Psychodynamische Organisationsberatung. Krisen und Potentiale in Veränderungsprozessen* (2nd ed.). Stuttgart: Klett-Cotta.
Lohmer, M. (2008a). Competition and coherence: creating a new balance between economic change and organizational identity in mental health care organizations. *Organisational and Social Dynamics, 8(1)*: 1–17
Lohmer, M. (2008b). The loss of meaning and motivation: "burnout" as interplay between personality style and organizational structure. Unpublished manuscript.
Maslach, C., Schaufeli, W. B. & Leiter, M. P. (2001). Job burnout. *Annual Review of Psychology, 52*: 397–422.
Mundle, G. (2007). Burn Out—von der Spitzenleistung zur Erschöpfung. Die Unfähigkeit, die eigene Balance zu finden. Unpublished manuscript.
Pongratz, H. J. & Voß, G. (2003). *Arbeitskraftunternehmer. Erwerbsorientierungen in entgrenzten Arbeitsformen*. Hans Böckler Stiftung. Berlin: Sigma.

Schmidbauer, W. (2002). *Wolfgang Schmidbauer: Helfersyndrom und Burnoutgefahr*. München/Jena: Elsevier GmbH, Urban & Fischer.
Schreyögg, A. (2005). Coaching and work-life balance. *Organisationsberatung, Supervision, Coaching, 4*: 309–319.
Sprenger, B. (2007). Burnout und Sucht bei Führungskräften. Unpublished manuscript.
Valcour, P. M. & Hunter, L. W. (2005). Technology, organizations, and work-life-integration. In: E. E. Kossek & S. J. Lambert (Eds.), *Work and Life Integration: Organizational, Cultural, and Individual Perspectives* (pp. 61–84). Mahway, NJ: Lawrence Erlbaum Associates.

PART II

PSYCHOANALYTIC REFLECTIONS ON THE FANTASTIC OBJECTS OF DESIRE

CHAPTER FOUR

Money as a phantastic object

Claudia Nagel

Introduction

As a former banker, and by now also a trained Jungian psychoanalyst, I have found that there is a "natural" attraction to money and its meaning for the individual and society. Furthermore, I think that this attraction can also be seen and understood from a psychoanalytic standpoint. In this chapter, I shall describe the results of my ongoing reflections and will share a number of insights about the archetypal nature of money. This analysis is based primarily on the history of the origin of money and ascriptions found in mythology and fairy tales. The recent financial market crisis of 2008 has led me to take another look at the phenomenon of money. I have found it far too simplistic to blame the investment bankers and their greed solely for this rather complex psychological development within the society. One of the outcomes of the financial crisis has been that the bankers served as scapegoats for a broader societal phenomenon which could be identified as a perverse attitude or a perverse state of mind in which they were not the only actors. The logical conclusion was that money was (and is) a fetish of this perverse attitude in society. Instead of using the term "fetish", it could also be termed a "phantastic object". There are some differences between these two terms which will be discussed at a later stage. However, the questions remain: what makes money so special to us, and why does it tend to polarize people's views?; why is it that we either renounce money or want more of it?; what is so fascinating about it?

In this chapter, I would like to lead you through the idea of "money as a phantastic object" firstly by examining its archetypal roots. This will then be followed by a discussion of money as a symbol of the self as well as the importance of money in relationships and the symbolic function of money.

The term "phantastic object" already evokes a huge amount of phantasy itself and when connected to the word "money" tends to make people wonder. This is probably due to the phantasies we all have about money and the attraction which can be found in the word "phantastic". It contains the world of the imaginary, the work of the unreal, of unconscious wishes, dreams, and ideas. It implies that it does not belong to "the real world". The real world consists of matter, whereas phantasy is part of the mental world and also the world of the soul. "Mental" could also mean spiritual, and the attraction of money may have to do with the split between spirit and matter, as will be shown later. Phantastic also contains the notion of magic, both white and black magic, which may also say something about the original roots of money. What also comes to mind in relation to the term "phantastic object" are concepts such as self-object or transitional object. These will be considered through my exploration of the meaning of money. Perhaps there is a difference between money as a phantastic object, as a fantastic object, and as a fantasy object. These ideas will be examined in detail later on in the chapter.

The technical term "phantastic object" was introduced into the psychoanalytic discussion of financial market phenomenon by Tuckett & Taffler in 2003. The authors used this term to describe the cause of stock market bubbles (e.g., the dot.com bubble of 1995–2000) where market instability arouse out of ambiguity and uncertainty. Stock market bubbles are usually described in highly emotional terms, and as Tuckett & Taffler point out, they follow a pattern of predictable sequential emotional stages. They start with patchy excitement about an innovation leading to growing, then to manic or euphoric, excitement, turning to panic, and finally resulting in blame. In the excitement phase, a dominant portion of the market participants think that something "phantastic" is happening while they are also somehow incapable of assessing existant information in a realistic way. Do these stages not strongly remind us of the financial market crisis in 2008?

Tuckett & Taffler derive the term "phantastic object" from two psychoanalytic concepts. They use the term "object" in the sense of a mental representation of something but not as the thing itself. The term "phantastic" is based on phantasy and refers to an imaginary scene in which the inventor of the phantasy is imagining his wishes (unconscious or conscious) fulfilled. Thus a "phantastic object" is a mental representation of something (or someone) which in an imagined scene fulfils the protagonist's deepest desires to have exactly what she wants exactly when she wants it. We might say that the phantastic object allows individuals to feel omnipotence like Aladdin (who owned a lamp which could call a genie); or like the fictional bond trader, Sherman McCoy (who felt himself a Master of the Universe (Tuckett & Taffler, 2008, p. 395f; Wolfe, 1987). In my view, it is not only the stock or the investment vehicle which plays the role as the phantastic object, but money itself can also be seen as a fantastic object. This will be demonstrated over the course of this chapter.

The archetypal dialectics of money

The basic psychological structure of money is highly ambivalent and difficult to grasp. It contains godlike-creative as well as diabolic-destructive aspects which stand in dialectic opposition to each other. They can transform us and allow us to develop more individuality as well as destroying our soul when it leads us to obsessively wanting to amass wealth. Money in its double sense is a shimmery, shiny, and tricky thing. Due to its origin and symbolic power, we can understand money as a symbol of the Self. This explains its overwhelming meaningfulness.

Looking at the archetypal base of money might help us to get a deeper understanding of its slippery and shiny power of attraction. An archetype represents the *a priori* (Kant) of all human action and thought, an "innate and thereby pre- and unconscious individual structure of the psyche" (Jung 1938, § 151). These preconscious structures, which cannot be described, are a form of unconscious predispositions to act in certain human ways and manners. Archetypes have no concrete contents and must therefore be understood as patterns or "primary images". Content is added to archetypes by means of an individual experience. Every archetype is said to have two poles, a positive and a negative one. Although its meaning for the individual derives from specific experiences, an archetype always has a supra-individual, common, and collective core, which is primarily reflected in symbols and images. The supra-individual collective experiences which determine the content of an archetype are communicated and thus "transported" to these experiences within the collective through fairy tales, myths, stories, and pictures, as well as in other forms of artistic products. They represent archetypal themes of general importance for human existence. In order to understand an archetype, it is therefore helpful to look at the "stories" associated with it; this enables us to approach the archetypal core meaning.

Where does money come from, and how did it develop? The modern English word "money" is derived from the Middle English *"monie"*, which is, in turn, derived from the French *"monie"*. The common root is the Latin word *"moneta"*. *"Moneta"* developed into the German *"munizia"* and later into *"Münze"* (coin), into the French *"monnaie"* and the English "money" (Kluge, 2000). Moneta is a goddess; her Greek name is Mnemosyne, who is regarded as the mother of the muses. She was also the goddess of memory. *"Moneta"* is derived from the older word *"moneo"* and signifies "to remind" and also to advise, to admonish, and to warn. What appears to be interconnected in the word "money" are recollection, storage, and creative force—because of the connection to the muses—as well as an element of warning (Hillman, 1983). All of these elements play a role in today's perception of money.

To get a modern understanding of the word, we need to also look at what money means for an economist. There it has three different functions:

- money stores value,
- money is a medium of exchange, and
- money is a unit of account.

Although these functions sound very technical, they will also help us approach the archetypal nature of money. The first function means that money has a containing function. The holding or elementary character of money (I am applying a concept of Neumann (1956) which he used to examine the archetype of the Great Mother) relates to its role as a means of storage and preservation of value and the meanings associated with these functions. It is concerned with storing, "containing", recollection—as we have already been advised by the goddess Moneta. The idea of containing also plays an important role from a psychological point of view, because the origin of self-esteem and identity lies in the containment the mother provides for the child. Money might later become not only a symbol for this containment but also to replace it.

In the second function as a medium of exchange, we find the first roots for money in the hoarding of precious and desirable objects such as seashells, furs, and amulets which represent one component of the historical development of money. This meaning has been ascribed to an assumed primary human desire for decoration and status, which was developed by women, to be taken up later by men in the form of rank or status decorations and, as such, "was integrated into the development of money" (Schmölders, 1966). Gerloff expresses this in quite a typical point of view for a man of his time in 1952: "Women invented jewellery, men turned it into money". Initially, jewellery was made of seashells and teeth, but soon metals such as gold, iron, copper, and zinc came into use. However, it can be assumed that jewellery was not only used as decoration, but also carried magical and mythical meanings. The person wearing the jewellery thereby symbolically introjected strength and divine power. Jewellery thus served to ward off evil spirits and to establish a bond with good spirits, gods, and magic powers. It was particularly the latter which created the value and the special character of the object.

The divine and magic power also plays a significant role in the origin of money in Europe.

The divine power of money—sacrificing the bull

In early human civilization, blood sacrifices had to be offered to the Great Mother to fertilize her land and thereby to ensure a good harvest. The sacrifices offered to the Great Mother and other deities in a plea for a good harvest or support were, in principle, the first acts of bartering. Money developed from this exchange of one "commodity" for another, the sacrifice being "a tax payable to the gods" (Laum, 1924). In early Greek and Roman times, sacrificial beasts were slaughtered on the house altar or at public festivals. While a part of the sacrificial beast was burned in its entirety, the large remainder was destined for common consumption. In this central religious ritual, humankind connected with the god through the medium of the sacrificed animal and thereby acquired or introjected its divine powers.

In occidental or European cultures, it is the bull in particular that has a special role as a sacrificial beast. It frequently represents the highest deity. Thus "Il", the highest Syrian deity, also bears the name of the bull, and in the Old Kingdom of Egypt, Apis is revered as a symbol of fertility. Through death, it merges with Osiris and is depicted as the god of death in the form of a plate, representing the sun. The Greeks also associate Zeus with the bull (Lurker, 1984). The derivation of money from the bull sacrifice relates the special sacrificial role of the bull to its use as a unit of account and as a means of exchange. In Homeric times, arms, slaves, and objects of art were traded for bulls, while wealth was measured in herds of cattle.

In the Greek bull sacrifice, just as in Indian, Roman, and Celtic cultures, the meat of the beast was roasted on a skewer. Both the roasted pieces of meat and the skewer itself were named "obelos". (The original meaning of the term "obolus", which is still used today for a small monetary donation, is "skewer" (Kluge, 2002) and can be traced back to this origin (Laum, 1924).) The most widely known small coin in ancient Greece is also called an "obelus". Antique temple inventories frequently record a large number of skewers/obeloi, and it has been argued that due to the connection between the large number of sacrifices and the compensation which the priest would receive in the form of a sacrificial animal, temples were indeed the first, pre-economic sites of exchanges. In temples, skewers, which were considered items of value in themselves, as well as votive plates and animal idols, were traded. The latter were purchased and sacrificed instead of the original sacrificial beast (Laum, 1924).

The original sacral character of money is also reflected in the first coin stamps, which frequently depict an image of the bull. A seal or an amulet is said to possess the magical powers of the totem animal. The seal, and later the coin stamp with an image of the animal, thus connects the sacrificial beast with the token sacrifice in the form of the coin. Still today, the symbol of the bull signifies economic prosperity: it stands for the hausse, that is, for positive developments on the stock market—and thus represents growth and profits.

The bull sacrifice as the origin of today's money provides some important symbolic clues for the archetypical meaning of money: each sacrifice is made in memory of a person's ancestors, and to appease both ancestors and the individual's parents. Classical psychoanalytical theory therefore interprets the desire for money as a longing for parental love. Desmonde (1977) even goes beyond this in his analysis and perceives the bull sacrifice as a desire to unite with the Great Mother. The desire for unification stands for all-encompassing, intimate motherly protection and complete emotional security. This idea of security and protection is transferred to and, in turn, is expected of money. In more than one sense of the word, it conveys material, primordial motherly security. This is interesting, in today's world of finance, where even the most technical terms (credit, trust, security, bonds, savings, etc.) somehow refer to the psychological notion of protection and security.

Money also represents some kind of wholeness. At the centre is a vigorous, creative, and brave animus figure (the bull). This, by means of the sacrifice, connects with the anima, the divine principle of fertility and earth, forming a union from which new life comes forth. The connection of male creative power with Mother Earth as a symbol of female procreation further serves as an indicator of the desire for self-fertilization, which is also symbolized in the bull sacrifice. Money represents the male, creative part of the self, which must connect to the anima aspect inherent in the sacrifice. The inherent creative power of money results solely from the union of the two spiritual powers, this then leads to the transforming power money is said to possess. On the one hand, gold and money signify divine powers and nearness to the gods; money conveys the feelings of security and safety. On the other hand, it has to be returned to the gods as a sacrificial offering, in order to achieve the true formation of a unified self. The elementary character may be said to store and contain the sacral image of the self.

It is certainly this "magic" or phantastic effect which encapsulates a large part of the attraction money holds for many of us even today. As a symbol of the self, money embodies this creative spiritual power, in which the female, nourishing and the male, spiritual aspect are united. Yet the development does not result from holding and hoarding, but from devotion and sacrifice. However, the creation myth is not about possession and wealth; the true creative power of the symbol is realized only through voluntary sacrifice.

The desire for security, which we have also observed in the bull sacrifice, and the wish for creative power, lead us to long for the preservation of the acquired money, to prolong its effect through accumulation. Yet in hoarding, which in its extreme form becomes miserliness and greed for more, the positive effect of money is reversed, as described and immortalized by the myth of Midas. This is the turning point of the containment character, where the magic-creative power is transformed as a result of false use into its very opposite. Wherever the "good" gods are found, the devil is not far away.

The evil quality—does money smell?

Money is frequently described as dirty—the saying *"pecunia non olet"*, i.e., money doesn't smell, actually means the exact opposite. A look at Goethe's *Faust* will help us to understand this.

The anal character (Freud) or obsessive-compulsive individual is characterized by qualities such as orderliness, thriftiness, and stubbornness, which may lead to excessive miserliness and can be traced back to a disturbed personal hygiene development in early childhood (Freud, 1999). Since faeces are what infants first produce themselves—their primary possession—the child learns through the parents' approach to "potty training" indirectly about the use of power, that is, the economical withholding of faeces versus generous giving. An individual's attitude towards money, according to Freud, results from their coping with experiences in the anal phase. He also discovered the equation money = faeces in tales of devils and witches, where gifts of money are transformed into faeces. The anal or faecal characteristic is therefore inherent in money (Harsch, 1995).

The most famous treatment of the devil topic with unequivocal references to the money-faeces equation, however, can be found long before Freud lived, in Goethe's *Faust*. Faust presents a box containing pieces of gold jewellery to Gretchen to gain her favours. It was Mephistopheles who provided the box by a magic trick. When Gretchen concedes with the famous words:

> Toward gold throng all
> to gold cling all
> yes, all!

her mother realizes the truth of seduction behind the gold/the money.

Mephistopheles relates this to Faust as follows:

> The mother gets to see the thing:
> That woman has a fine sense of smell
> Always sniffing in the prayer book
> From every item can she tell
> Whether it's heaven or it's hell
> And with the jewels she clearly guessed
> That it was not the least bit blessed.
>
> (Goethe, *Faust I, Abend und Spaziergang*)

The smell of faeces betrays the transformation into gold, and it is thereby identified as a gift from the devil (Harsch, 1995). In Part II of *Faust*, which already contains a critique of future economic development, Goethe also alludes to the anal character of gold: "I shall treat gold just as wet clay, for this metal can be transformed into whatever you may" (*Faust II, 1. Akt, Weitläufiger Saal mit Nebengemächern*).

Faust represents the devil which—as Satan—was the enemy of God (Satan signifies opponent/enemy), he used to put men's good qualities to the test. Only later, in Christian religion, the devil, as God's and also man's opponent, embodies sin, an external obsessive power from which humans must free themselves (Kasper, 2000). The inescapable fate of hell and the great significance of the devil as its lord is a Christian, modern concept, which is not found in pre-Christian religions (Campbell, 1968/1996). This is interesting because it gives us a hint that the mind–body split which developed in early Christianity can explain partly the still predominant dirty side of money. But before we come back to this thought, we need to look at the consequences of the anal aspect of money.

As lord of the underworld, the devil is also understood as lord of the unconscious. The power and energy of the unconscious can possess, control, and steer us without our being aware of it. Obsession, also obsession with money, results from the strength of this power and of the "diabolic" (black magic) side, which initially appears to be uncontrollable. Only by consciously dealing with this energy can we free ourselves from control and obsession.

In his depth psychology analysis of *Faust*, Jung interprets Mephistopheles as a split-off shadow complex of Faust, characterized by repressed sexuality, power, but also by vitality (Jung, 1920). The anal, diabolic, or dirty side of money thus represents a part of the shadow, in which dark character traits, inferior and negative aspects, are found. These possess the individual because the shadow, as long as it is unconscious, holds a certain autonomy at the emotional level (Jung, 1950). To some degree, this also applies to money: "The rich do not possess their money, they are possessed by it" (Blaton, 1977). If money and gold are also understood as symbols of the shadow, it becomes apparent that the previously described characteristics of greed and miserliness are projected on the rejection of money as something dirty. This is, however, not a characteristic of money. Instead, it is man who projects his "dirtiness" onto money as a symbol of his own shadow.

Yet the confrontation with the shadow also offers the potential for liberation and development, which can be supported by creative destructive powers. For Faust, the confrontation with Mephistopheles, who represents the principle of evil and destructiveness, also has a liberating effect upon him. As a dried-up intellectual and scientist who is about to put an end to his life, he experiences for the first time sensuality, emotions, and lust. We should therefore aim to become aware of our shadow, in order to integrate it and to experience this integration as liberation. The shadow projection on money can revert into liberating, creative redemption if it becomes possible to break free from the fixation on and the hoarding of money.

The divine and the demonic constitute the two sides of the same coin.

The hope for divine transformation ...

The divine quality of money and the possibility to introject divine power also implies the wish for positive transformation. Money is wanted because of its secretly hoped for and expected main purpose, that is, to make people happy. Owning money is perceived as happiness, and everyone harbours the secret hope to achieve happiness through money (despite the common knowledge that money does not make one happy). Moreover, happiness is frequently a prerequisite for the acquisition of wealth. Interestingly, in ancient times, wealth and health were seen as interrelated, as were poverty and illness (Meier, 1949).

As the projection surface for receiving and reflecting many wishes, money can assume (almost) any form, and humans hope that it will enable them to change themselves as well. The transformative character thus also serves a dual function.

Let us think of Grimm's fairy tale "Star Coin". Seen from the viewpoint of depth psychology, money can have the described magical or phantastic character, which is manifest in the stars falling from heaven. The fairy tale can also be interpreted as a story of the transformative power of money—represented by the gold coins—which is not about external, but internal, wealth. This inner lifelong wealth is achieved only after having given away the bread, a necessity for life. To attain a self-determined goal, the individual must be prepared to give away life and himself. The sacrifice (here also) is the first step in a transformative process. This has to be supported by liberation from all externalities, the clothes must be given away, the image of the external identity, the persona, must be liberated. And finally, a dark forest has to be traversed. The individual must set out on a journey into the dark unconscious and there endure the night—fear, loneliness, and depression. Only then can the path to the inner wealth, which "falls from heaven", be found. The sky is therefore also a symbol of an inner heaven, which enables individuals to recognize their own internal wealth. The money is then also a symbol of the wealth received as a reward for having fulfilled a difficult task, or for giving up or renouncing something held dear. It is a symbol for the result of an inner transformative process and of the inner wealth, which can be attained by the individual who engages in this difficult process. This inner wealth is then transformed into external wealth.

... and the risk of selling love for wealth

Why is it common knowledge that money does not make one happy? Probably because one instinctively knows that wanting (to make) money keeps you away from what really matters in life: love, relationships, and friendships. The fairy tale "The Cold Heart" (the most important one in Wilhelm Hauff's collection *The Caravan* (Hauff, 1826/2002)), best tells the story of blind obsession and the sale of the protagonist's heart to achieve economic and social success. It could be a story of today's top executives and businessmen.

Peter Munk, the young protagonist, is a charcoal burner who lives among glass makers in the Black Forest. In the forest also lives a good spirit, the glass kobold by the name of "Schatzhauser", as well as "Holländer-Michel", a huge, broad-shouldered evil spirit, in the guise of a rafter. Peter Munk, who strives to be something better than a poor charcoal burner, asks the glass kobold for help. But his wishes are so foolish that the riches are as rapidly lost as they are gained. Disappointed and wanting all, he then decides to sell his heart to Holländer-Michel, receives a stone in exchange, becomes incredibly rich, extremely parsimonious and fraudulent, and kills his wife in an outburst of rage. Her death eventually affects him deeply and he wins back his true heart with the help of a ruse. After feeling real and deep remorse, which leaves him longing for his own death, the glass kobold brings his wife back to life, returns her to him, and they live happily ever after.

In this fairy tale, the transformative power of money, which turns Peter Munk into a heartless human being, becomes evident. Out of dissatisfaction with his own situation, Peter Munk longs for money and wealth, which he believes would turn him into a respected "Someone". It is thus only by means of "external" values that Peter Munk gains worth as a human being—or so he believes.

He sells his heart, psychologically speaking his soul, his anima, and in exchange he receives a cold heart of stone, wealth, and social status. His turning towards and obsession with money prevents the "rich man" from having deep feelings and establishing friendships (without giving something in exchange, i.e., without buying them), or from his heart speaking to him. The friendly young man Peter Munk was prior to being seduced by money is turned into a cold, stingy, greedy man and compulsive gambler. This fairy tale illustrates the negative changing character of money.

What is problematic is that this negative aspect of money initially appears to be a positive transformation. Wealth and social status provisionally help to fill the void which constitutes a lack of self-confidence. The fulfilment of wishes made possible through material wealth is perceived as pleasant and the feeling of want is gone. This leads to the alleviation of psychological stress and pressure on the individual to change.

Peter Munk is looking for social recognition which, however, due to his wealth, is not granted to himself as a person, and can thus never be true recognition of his own value. Money is a token for a sense of self-esteem and self-love, and in the present context represents the self, respectively, the lack of self-development and the longing for a self (cf. Kernberg's 1979, S. 302) definition of narcissistic personalities). The fairy tale represents a warning in so far as the desire for money for narcissistic reasons leads to the satisfaction of instincts, but eventually also to internal hardening and thus to the exact opposite of what is desired, that is, love and recognition.

Although help comes from the outside in the form of an innocent virgin, whom Peter Munk marries—an anima aspect—the obsession with money is so strong that nothing changes initially. It is only when all spiritual life, his wife, dies and he himself feels guilty of this death that he begins to think a little. The feeling of guilt causes him to turn back. Besides emotional strengths, this fairy tale is also about moral qualities, as evidenced by the glass kobold as the archetypal old wise man. At the time when he had a heart made of stone, Peter Munk was not helpful, kind, and good-natured, but hard-hearted, destructive, and exploiting the poor. In the second part of the fairy tale, Peter Munk trades in gold and wheat—both of which are products of the soil, representing fertility and life. However, due to his exploitative and treacherous practices, people lose their land and their basis for life. Here, a destructive and evil force, contemptuous of life, is represented by Holländer-Michel as the embodiment of the archetype of evil and of the devil. The frequent appearance of Holländer-Michel in the fairy tale is representative of the self-enhancing destructive force of the negative transformative character of money. Once it has started to take effect, it appears difficult to free oneself from it, in addition to which it continues to return. It is further enhanced by society's consent and support of such behaviour. The result, on the one hand, is emotional coldness, boredom, and emptiness combined with the wish for more money and more wealth, embodied by parsimony and greed, which, in turn, lead to greater coldness, and so forth: a vicious circle in the true sense of the word.

The analysis of the tale "The Cold Heart", which seems to exist in very similar versions in different cultures, shows that money has the power to compensate for the lack of self-esteem for the price to destroy other feelings such as friendship, love, and compassion. This very theme with identical moral is also explored in a Russian fairy tale called "The Gold Fish".

Money embodies the mind–body duality

Money may be seen to contain both the good spiritual aspect and the evil, diabolic material aspect. The differentiation between the spiritual and matter has existed in this form only since the emergence of

Christianity (Hillman, 1983). Prior to that, the material and spiritual forms of money were still interrelated, as shown by the stories regarding the containing character.

The first dualistic concepts may be found before Christianity, developed by the Zoroastrians. The introduction into Christianity started probably with Augustinus (AD 354–430). Different from the Greek thinking, he put soul and body into a hierarchical relationship in which only the soul could comprehend divine truth, whereas the body was defeated. Based on the somatophobic ideas of the gnosis and Manichaeism, and the concurrent repression of sexuality and reproduction, the true human being had to deny the body and consist only of the inwardly and godwardly turned soul. The material, fleshly world of the body was seen as being demonic and having been created by the evil demiurge. Later, this attitude continued in the Christian persecution of the sorceresses which had very close ties with the persecution of the Jews (Hexensabbat).

In the notion of Hexensabbat, the witch is connected with the Sabbath—this is the Jewish holiday, a day of rest, when work is not allowed and contact with money is forbidden. Since the Middle Ages, Jews were often excluded from exercising a craft because they would have to belong to a guild, but the only profession they were admitted to was money-lending. Christians were not allowed to lend money against interest. Somehow the negative, evil side of money, which was expressed through the persecution of the Jews and their business of lending money, still seems to be noticeable in the archetypal-evil side of money.

Based on what was demonstrated, one could say that in pre-Christian times material and spiritual aspects were still connected within money. This supports the idea of money as a symbol of the self. Only later the split between mind and body was established. This differentiation between the good spiritual/soul and the mind/body/evil has had a profound effect on spiritual life in the Western world. The result of the differentiation made in Christianity is—to speak with the words of Hillman—one in which the world is bereft of the soul and the soul is bereft of the world.

> The soul is left on a spiritual path of denial and the world is left in the sins of luxuria, avarice and greed. Then the soul is always threatened by the money and the world needs the spiritual mission of redemption from the evil caused by the Weltbild that cuts Caesar

from God. That money is the place where God and Caesar divide shows that money is a "third thing" like the soul itself, and that in money are both, the inherent tendency to split into spirit and matter and the possibility to hold the together. ... As long as our belief system inherently depreciates money, it will always threaten the soul with value distortions.

(Hillman, 1983, p. 56f).

Money as a mirror

Taking together what is now known about the archetypal aspects of money, the coming together of divine and evil, of material and spiritual elements, we could argue that money can be regarded as a symbol of the (Jungian) Self. Among the indicators viewed against the discussed mythological background is certainly also the round-shaped form of coins. The round stands for wholeness or completeness and symbolizes the totality, the Self. Lockhart (1983) understands money even as a talisman of the Self, which can support the individual on his or her path to individuation. As an example for this, he cites the gold doubloon which is nailed to the mast of the *Pequot* by Captain Ahab in Melville's *Moby Dick*.

Money by outer form and by inner quality reminds us also very much of the mirror in the tale of Narcissus—this can help us to gain a deeper understanding of the suffering in narcissism. The more action-oriented aspects were already described in the fairy tale of "The Cold Heart".

The basic forms of money were metal coins—shining and shimmering and looking somewhat like a mirror. In a double sense, the (golden) coin is the mirror in which Narcissus regards himself. In Ovid's tale, Narcissus had to be punished by the gods because he did not treat the other beings well who fell in love with him because of his beauty. As a penalty, the gods decided that he had to fall in love with the first being he would see next. He then looked into a pond of water and saw his mirror image in the water and fell in love with his own image. Every time he wanted to touch the image, the other, it was destroyed. He finally died from his desire and unfulfilled love. This tale gives a very good picture of the need of mirroring which stems from a lack of motherly mirroring and containment. The narcissist appears as turning only around himself and using the other continuously as self-objects. But behind that is a deep suffering and longing for being mirrored, being seen and being loved for being himself.

Interpreting the tale, one could say his external beauty represents external wealth. The mirror reflects his own image, an image he receives from the external world, with which he falls in love and which he loves. Since he wishes for his love to be returned, he dies—as a result of his longing for the impossible. Narcissus looks for love in a mirror. Love is outside the mirror and therefore corresponds to recognition received from the external world, but it is also his mirror image, he himself, and thus within him. Yet both are united in one person and, thus, impossible.

The mirroring quality of money explains very well how money replaces the ego—it can be understood as a "borrowed ego". Making money stands for building up power and the possibility to get what you want, to fulfil all wishes, to make other people obey and do what you want—just to get a feeling of significance and finally of being seen. This is part of the phantastic quality of money.

One can see the power of money in organizations and the role money plays to make hierarchical differences visible, and here I do not wish to allude just to top management bonus excesses! Money demonstrates the value of the recognition of the organization. Money can transform this recognition into an even greater power outside of the organization, since money can be changed into anything that promises prestige, status, and influence. In my experience with/in top management, the number of narcissistic managers is growing. Behind the narcissistic appearance there may lie feelings of emptiness and inadequacy with symptoms of depression, as well as compulsive structures or other anxieties. (See also Chapter Three in this book, on burnout, by Mathias Lohmer.)

As a "borrowed ego", money may then have the ability, so to speak, to reflect both this "borrowed ego" and the "desired ego", as already shown in the discussion of the Narcissus myth. Coins seem to permit the reflection of the ego as well as the pond did with Narcissus. The basic problem of the narcissistic need for a borrowed ego is a lack of self-worthiness and the possibility to value one-self. This seems to form an interesting link with money being defined as a store of value and as a unit for account.

Money as transitional object—the phantastic quality of money

In the realm of phantasy and imagination, which we can also call the potential space, money plays a specific psychological role. The potential space is the intermediary realm of experiences into which inner and outer reality flow. It as a linking function between the subjective and the objective experience.

All life long, it remains an important task to relate inner and outer reality. Play and creativity, philosophy and religion, can be understood better as results of this intermediary space. The transitional object is its first appearance and the basis; the roots for creation of symbols are laid in this early phase of life. First, the possibility to symbolize, and later the development of the symbolic attitude, is key in the individuation process.

The terms "potential space" and "transitional object" introduced by Winnicott refer to important accomplishments in child development. Briefly, of interest here is the phenomenon that infants as young as four months already occupy themselves with fabrics, blankets, teddy bears, and suchlike. These transitional objects are established in a psychic potential space between the Me and Not-Me. A transitional object functions as a bridge, connecting the area of experience with subjective objects, and experiences with objectively perceivable objects (Tenbrink, 2002). The transitional object exerts a soothing and anxiety-relieving effect in the potential space. It symbolizes the mother and the non-mother at the same time.

Winnicott views the potential space as "the third area, … an area of experience". It is different from the inner reality and the outer reality, and it is of a symbolic nature. Later in life, the potential space continues to have a role as mediator between inner and outer reality, it is the space of phantasy, of games, creativity, music, and art. After what we have seen so far, money has obviously the quality of a transitional object. Money has the ability to interconnect intrapsychic phantasies, wishes, and conceptions to a translation into external socially relevant objects and possibilities.

This interconnecting capacity has a very important effect which also explains part of the attraction: money can help to create (social) identity, but also a phantastic object.

This seems to be a very obvious statement, but it has a more profound reason than one might think at first sight. Identity creation is a process of continuous reflection—by observing the outer world and relationships, a wanted self-representation is adapted and shaped. Identity is the outcome of a dialogue between inner and outer world resulting in a constantly changing and adapting psychic constructing. Identity is also a balance between "outer expectations and social role play on the one hand and the inner reality with its fantasies and wishes on the other" (Bohleber, 1992). Money clearly plays a role in translating inner and shaping outer world.

The potential space is the space of the symbolic. Green (1975) points out that mirror allegories used in psychoanalysis to form pairs consisting of image and object always also require the third element, the mirror. This third object represents the symbolic. "The operator representing the symbolic re-establishes, on the level of psychic processes, the oneness of a subject, which is nevertheless described as separate. The origin of the question as to the division of the subject lies in the relationship to the other" (Green, 1970, p. 90). This means that identity formation also requires symbolic interaction structures and social categories of meaning (Bohleber, 1992). From that perspective, money is a symbol and mirror at the same time. But that is part of the problem and the risk which the use of money creates. If one cannot make a distinction between the symbol and the mirror, between phantasy and reality, money takes over and the obsessive and possessive aspects dominate.

Money is a central symbol, which can be described as both the expression of mirroring and as the mirror itself. It can be conjectured that in the presence of a healthy self-worth development, the symbolic function of money as a mirror is given an importance which does not lead to a distortion of the mirror image. A sensible attitude in the handling of money might be the result of an undistorted feeling of self-worth. As a mirror and projection surface, money is understood symbolically only, because the actual feeling of self-worth is independent of the symbolic mirroring function.

If money is used as mirror only and is not used in a purely symbolic sense, but rather as identification with the mirror function, a disturbance in the feeling of self-worth may be present.

Money has a symbolizing function, that is to say it symbolizes a multitude of (self-) worth-related aspects. Out of this symbolizing function arises the possibility of the projection of these symbolic aspects onto money. Subsequently, money no longer symbolizes, but it is virtually equated and identified with these projections. A projection always contains an unconscious aspect. From this factual aspect of money and from its symbolic character emerges that which is transferred in the projection. These projections are the core of the money complex, because they can be traced back to archetypal conceptions.

Because of the fundamental archetype of money to "assess oneself/ as self-worth" and the associated attachment and relationship aspect, money can be ascribed a mirroring function. It obtains this function from its archetypal core meaning, which contains the development of self-worth on the basis of relationship experiences.

Depending upon whether the individual confronts his or her money complex, more or less consciously, the sooner money can serve to develop the own Self (development function), or to compensate for the not, or only partially, existing Self, or, respectively, for pain and mortification (hurt feelings) inflicted on the Self.

Money as a fetish

We have now discussed some very basic aspects of money which derive from its sacral origin and archetypal nature. In this perspective, we were able to get an understanding of the symbolic qualities or the nature of money, especially as a symbol of the Self.

The use and the abuse of the symbolic quality of money as a phantastic object are closely connected, and by looking at what happened in the financial market crisis of 2008, another inherent phantastic quality became apparent to me. Not only that the financial market instruments could be understood as phantastic objects, as Tuckett & Taffler argue, but also money itself has that quality. This idea came up through the understanding of one potential cause for the crisis being a perverse state of mind on a societal level.

One could argue that in the development of the financial crisis, the classical mechanisms of denial and splitting were at work on different levels. Also the use of others as objects played a role as the illusion of grandiosity combined with the fear of incompetence and helplessness (Nagel, 2009).

In general, the role of the fetish has different aspects in the perversion. While it serves the pleasurable satisfaction of the sexual drive, on the one hand, it may also be understood as an extended self-object. Comparable to the use of the other as object, the fetish serves to stabilize and complete the self. It replaces that which is missing, the missing piece, the missing other.

In the financial market crisis, the fetish character of money becomes particularly apparent in CDS (credit default swaps) speculation. CDS are highly abstract speculative investment vehicles which were designed to insure against the loss of value of an underlying bond. But over the course of time, they became completely detached from this underlying purpose and became an instrument of speculation only. The fetish character finds expression in the "casino mentality" with a zest for betting in manifestly deregulated markets. This lust for gambling combined with instrumentalization and illusions of grandeur has taken on enormous proportions, so that an instrument originally intended to serve as an insurance against loss had reached a ten-fold value of the bond against whose loss it was insuring.

A broker explained this development: "But around 2003/2004 I was getting increasingly nervous, because I could see how the CDS market changed from a very legitimate instrument into something more *hot-blooded* and *interesting*, although it also held much greater dangers" (Blumberg, 2009b, p. 41, author's italics).

It is precisely the term "hot-blooded" which describes the lust in speculating with CDS. In my view, CDS and the CDS market stand for the speculative-playful-lust attitude towards money. The detachment of the original underlying is part of the fetish character. However, not only were CDS used as a fetish, but other investments and money itself have assumed more and more of a fetish character, caused by the ongoing detachment and estrangement. The almost sensual zest for speculation, betting, and gambling is immediately apparent in conversations with traders. But it also affects many private investors who speculate on the stock market. In the extended view of perversion, dealing with money and money products may be experienced as a sensation filled with lust. On the level of the system, this pleasure has contributed to compensate for a lack of eros and the dehumanization of relationships.

Aladdin's magic lamp, which Tucket & Taffler were talking about in their paper (2008), at the beginning functions like money itself. The magic lamp has to be rubbed for a genie to appear and fulfil the owner's every wish. This is what money will do when it is spent to (hopefully!) fulfil the wish for beauty, prestige, power and influence, control, desire, and also lust.

The projection function of money (Nagel, 2008) results from the possibility that it can be changed and exchanged. And thus enables the projection of unconscious wishes, needs, hopes, and cravings on money. When the possibilities for projection on the basis of the archetypal qualities of money, which are represented by eros and power, come together with individual experiences and conceptions, the money complex develops (Nagel, 2008).

The money complex becomes effective, because, as a self-object, money is able to reflect the "borrowed ego" symbolically and thereby permits the identification with it. This mirroring—which corresponds to the mirroring of the child through the mother—also corresponds symbolically to the mirroring Narcissus experiences when he falls in love with his own mirror image in the pond. The bonding relationships which were hoped to come into being through the described mirroring are replaced by money. Money is then used for projective identification purposes. With its help, anguish and hurt can be temporarily compensated. The bonding relationship money was to replace has, however, become impossible through the compensatory use of money, leading to a cycle of a lack of emotional relationships, compensation, and a new lack of emotional relationships (Nagel, 2008). The vicious circle of money characterizes the mechanism of perversion as a whole.

The alienation of money

The aspect we have not considered thus far is the more recent emergence of different variations of money. While money initially evolved from exchange objects and oboli, to develop from there first into coins and later into paper notes, which were long backed by gold (the gold standard), the character of money has changed completely today. The money (production) process is currently—especially as a result of globalization and computerization—completely detached from the merchandise markets, there is frequently no longer any connection at all. "Money has become a pure abstraction detached from anything of real value" (Korten, 2001, p. 179). Korten cites an assessment by Kurtzman (1993), the former editor of *The New York Times* and current editor of the *Harvard Business Review*, who claims that for every dollar from the productive world, approximately twenty to fifty dollars circulate in the world of finance. These figures are probably obsolete, because in recent years additional, and increasingly less understandable, products have been developed on a derivative basis on the money markets. The detachment and abstraction of money from the respective commodity production and the computerized trade in ever changing forms of investment and risk may also be described as the "alienation" of money.

I would therefore conjecture that the alienation process of money further contributes to the emergence of a great number of fantasies and projections. Because money is, so to speak, no longer attached to anything, it can even more readily become anything and everything.

Money—a phantastic or fantastic object?

The alienation of money and the delinking from every real value alleviates the use of money as a phantastic object. Is money also a fantastic object, and what would be the difference? Based on the *Oxford English Dictionary*, Charles Rycroft argues that the difference is basically based on the difference between American and British English, where British psychoanalysts rather use the term "phantasy". Then it is defined as "imagination, visionary notion", whereas "fantasy" stands for "caprice, whim, fanciful invention" (Adams, 2004, p. 2). Another explanation seems to be that "The English translators of Freud adopted a special spelling of the word, 'phantasy', with the ph in order to differentiate the psycho-analytical significance of the term i.e., predominantly or entirely unconscious phantasies, from the popular word, 'fantasy', meaning conscious day-dreams, fictions, and so on" (S. Isaac, 1952, pp. 80–81, cited after Adams, 2004, p. 2).

Adam explains further that he uses the word "fantasy" as a synonym for "imagination", whether conscious or unconscious. "All the functions that are active in psyche converge in fantasy" (Jung, 1934, par. 292 [translated from the original German by the author]). In contrast to the (former) Freudian idea of phantasies being unconscious wish-fulfilment, imaginations are expressions of the unconscious which need to be understood but not necessarily changed or cured. In Jung's view, psyche consists essentially of images, and every psychic process is an image or imagining (Jung, 1939 , par. 889). "Psyche is composed of images and that reality is constructed in and through those images ... I would say that reality is not only constructed but, as Jacques Derrida might say, deconstructed by the imagination" (Adams, 2004, p. 6).

Fantastic objects are than any kind of imaginal concepts of something, and the idea of analysis is to increase consciousness by interpreting or experiencing the meaning of those fantasies. As Jung says, fantasy is "a natural expression of life which we can at most seek to understand, but cannot correct" (Jung, 1963 par. 1249 [translated from the original German by the author]).

Using the term "fantastic object" instead of "phantastic object" can allow us to approach the symbolic meaning of money for each individual from a broader perspective, which might give us more insights into the nature of the individual psyche and the ideas of the inner world of this person. The use of this term might imply less pathology and a more natural way of dealing with the fantastic possibilities of money.

Summary

The fascination, the shimmery, shiny character of money, can be explained by its archetypal nature of being a symbol of the self with a sacral, containing, and evil destructive side. This dialectic is also represented in the basic contradiction of money standing for love and eros whilst using/abusing power. Money is all about relationship. It has its roots in the nature of secure bonding and mirroring experiences and is strongly linked to individual development, both from a phylogenetic perspective and most likely also perhaps from an ontogenetic perspective.

As we have seen, money and social relationships, particularly attachments, seem to be of similar importance with regard to their contribution to developing self-worth and identity. The focus in social and attachment relationships is always on the Eros aspect in relationships, and love in a broader sense. An equation might therefore be appropriate here:

$$Money = Love/Eros$$

Whenever love comes into play, its reversal—power—is also involved. But as Jung and also others already said: "Where love is, power cannot reign ... Because money promises to be, but actually does not compensate for unrequited love, it also stands for power."

The equation should therefore be:

$$Love = Money = Power$$

Is it not possible to attribute all self-worth disturbances to this dichotomy: love or power?

In addition, we can also summarize the psychological functions of money.

Money has a symbolizing function, that is to say it symbolizes a multitude of (self-) worth-related aspects. Out of this symbolizing function arises the possibility of the projection of these symbolic aspects onto money. Subsequently, money no longer symbolizes, but it is virtually equated and identified with these projections. A projection always contains an unconscious aspect. From this, factual money and its symbolic character emerges which become transferred to the projection. These projections are the core of the money complex, because they can be traced back to archetypal conceptions.

Because of the fundamental archetype of money "assess oneself/ as self-worth" and the associated attachment and relationship aspect, money can be ascribed a mirroring function. It obtains this function from its archetypal core meaning, which contains the development of self-worth on the basis of relationship experiences.

Depending upon whether the individual is able to confront his or her money complex, money can consciously serve to develop one's own Self or unconsciously compensate for the only partially existing Self, for the pain, mortification, and hurt feelings inflicted upon the Self.

In the contemporary world, the latter has become its predominant role, based on the growing detachment and denial of the spiritual aspect of money which already existed in antiquity.

References

Blaton, S. (1977). Die Masken des Geldes. In: E. Bornemann (Ed.), *Psychoanalyse des Geldes* (pp. 319–335). Frankfurt am Main: Suhrkamp.

Blumberg, A., Davidson, A. & Glass, I. (2009a). Die Finanzkrise: Teil 1. Der globale Geldtopf in: NZZ [*Neue Züricher Zeitung*] Folio (pp. 23–35), January.

Blumberg, A., Davidson, A. & Glass, I. (2009b). Die Finanzkrise: Teil 2. Das Wall-Street Massaker. In: NZZ [*Neue Züricher Zeitung*] Folio (pp. 37–45), January.

Bohleber, W. (2002). Identität. In: B. Waldvogel & W. Mertens (Eds.), *Handbuch psychoanalytischer Grundbegriffe* (pp. 333–339). Stuttgart: Kohlhammer.

Campbell, J. (1959). *Mythologie der Urvölker. Die Masken Gottes.* Band 1. München: DTV, 1996.

Campbell, J. (1968). *Schöpferische Mythologie. Die Masken Gottes.* Band 4. München: DTV, 1996.

Desmonde, W. H. (1977). Der Ursprung des Geldes im Tieropfer. In: E. Bornemann (Ed.), *Psychoanalyse des Geldes* (pp. 134–151). Frankfurt: Suhrkamp.

Freud, S. (1906–1909). Charakter und Analerotik. In: S. Freud (Ed.), *Gesammelte Werke*, Band VII. (pp. 203–209). Frankfurt: Fischer, 1999.
Harsch, W. (1995). *Die psychoanalytische Geldtheorie*. Frankfurt am Main: Fischer.
Hauff, W. (1826). *Die Karawane. Märchen*. Berlin: Aufbau, 2002.
Hillman, J. (1983). A contribution to soul and money. In: J. Beebe (Ed.), *Money, Food, Drink and Fashion and Analytical Training: Depth Dimensions of Physical Existence*. Fellbach-Oeffingen: Bonz.
Jung, C. G. (1920). Psychologische Typen. GW Band 6. Düsseldorf: Walter, 1995.
Jung, C. G. (1934). Die Beziehung zwischen dem Ich und dem Unbewussten. G: Band 7 Zwei Schriften über Analytische Psychologie. Düsseldorf: Walter, 1995.
Jung, C. G. (1938). Die Psychologischen Aspekte des Mutterarchetypus. GW Band 9.1. Die Archetypen und das kollektive Unbewusste. Düsseldorf: Walter, 1995.
Jung, C. G. (1939). Vorwort zu Daisetz Teitaro Suzuki: Die grosse Befreiung. GW Band 11 Zur Psychologie westlicher und östlicher Religion. Düsseldorf: Walter, 1995.
Jung, C. G. (1950) Aion. GW Band 9.2. Aion. Beiträge zur Symbolik des Selbst. Düsseldorf: Walter, 1995.
Jung, C. G. (1963). Vorwort zu Wickes „Von der inneren Welt des Menschen". GW Band 18.2. Das symbolische Leben. Düsseldorf: Walter, 1995.
Kasper, W. (2000). *Lexikon für Theologie und Kirche*, Band 9. Freiburg: Herder.
Kernberg, O. (1979). *Borderlinestörungen und pathologischer Narzissmus*. Frankfurt am Main: Suhrkamp.
Kluge, F. (2002). *Etymologisches Wörterbuch der Deutschen Sprache*. Berlin, New York: de Gruyter.
Korten, D. C. (2001). *When Corporations Rule the World*. San Francisco: Kumarian.
Laum, B. (1924). *Heiliges Geld. Eine historische Untersuchung über den sakralen Ursprung des Geldes*. Tübingen: Mohr.
Lockhart, R. A. (1983). Coins and psychological change. In: J. Beebe (Ed.), *Money, Food, Drink and Fashion and Analytical Training: Depth Dimensions of Physical Existence* (pp. 17–31). Fellbach-Oeffingen: Bonz.
Meier, C. A. (1949). *Antike Inkubation und moderne Psychotherapie*. Zürich: Rascher.
Nagel, C. (2008). *Geld—Teufelswerk oder Stein der Weisen? Die archetypische Bedeutung des Geldes für Identität, Beruf und Individuation*. Unpublished thesis, The International School for Analytical Psychology, Zürich.

Nagel, C. (2009). Die Psychodynamik der Finanzmarktkrise. *Freie Assoziation*, 3: 61–84.

Neumann, E. (1956). *Die große Mutter. Eine Phänomenologie der weiblichen Gestaltungen des Unbewussten.* Olten: Walter, 1985.

Tenbrink, D. (2002). Übergangsobjekt, Übergangsraum. In: W. Mertens (Ed.), *Handbuch pschoanalytischer Grundbegriffe* (pp. 750–754). Stuttgart: Kohlhammer.

Tuckett, D. & Taffler, R. (2008). Phantastic objects and the financial market's sense of reality: a psychoanalytic contribution to the understanding of stock market instability. *International Journal of Psychoanalysis, 89*: 389–412.

CHAPTER FIVE

With memory and desire: the function of the insurance industry in the world that we create

Matthieu Daum and Silvia Gollini

Introduction: a glimpse of today's (perfect?) world

"It is 6 am as I wake up this morning in my apartment (for which I managed to get a great all-comprehensive insurance); a hard day ahead of me, as I prepare to travel to Rome for work. I quickly sign the confirmation that I've subscribed an insurance policy for my children at school, and jump into my car to travel to the airport. As I drive along the motorway, I congratulate myself for having subscribed the all-comprehensive insurance with the same broker as for the apartment, bringing me further discount and fewer bills to attend to.

At the airport, I grab a coffee for one of my favourite chains, and notice the cups have changed design—a big sign saying "caution—hot beverage" is now printed all across the back of it. I venture a cheap morning joke with the bar-tender: "have you had complaints that you served cold coffees before?", but then learn that the chains insurance company, following several cases of successful litigation by scolded customers, have requested the new sign be printed on the new cups.

My plane is late; to my relief, my policy's "terms and conditions" for loss of earnings seems comprehensive enough to cover the possible damage with my clients. In any case, the credit card used to pay for this trip has its own travel insurance built into it; with a bit of luck, I might even win both claims!

My return trip is trouble-free, until I'm told my luggage is lost … but don't worry sir, it's covered on the insurance! I head for the car park. The childminder rings me to let me know that the washing machine has just broken down, a cunning two weeks after the end of the manufacturer's warranty! Luckily, we had preferred to buy the shop's extension of the warranty …. She asks me if she can leave the kids in the house for five minutes whilst she pops to the shop in the pouring rain to get the essentials for tonight's dinner. I feel uneasy … you never know what could happen, do you? In the end, I tell her that I'll pop into the local supermarket that opens till late and will do the shopping myself …"

An industry with a long history

As we see for the above vignette, the possibility of insuring most of what we do permeates our everyday life. Today, in exchange of a small payment, we can (in theory) cover ourselves against damages that we, and our family, could (in theory) inflict on others (in our apartments, playing at school, etc. …) for which we could be liable to pay important sums of money. Similarly, those who provide us with a commercial service have subscribed to an insurance that will protect them if they fail to meet the standard they claim to guarantee. In addition, if customers want a higher level of "protection", they can take out, at their own expense, further insurance that is available …

For the purpose of this chapter, it is this collection of all the commercial services, aimed at protecting against future misadventures, which we will refer to as the insurance industry.

This industry has not been born out of thin air; it has evolved, through various forms, into what it is today, in perfect symbiosis with the evolutions in social, political, and economical contexts of the various times it has traversed.

Below is a very short overview of this evolution, gathered through the work of Trennery (2009).

One could argue that the first trace of "insurance-type behaviour" can be noticed in initial religious behaviours such as rituals and sacrifices. As a way to conjure up favourable weather, or protect one's community against unfortunate events, the local sorcerer would perform some rituals or sacrifices of animals in order to claim the benevolence of gods and spirits. Whilst these rituals hold much more to them (connecting to the

Earth, spirituality, respect, and humility, and so on), one can, however, see the basis of the process: "if I do this, that will not happen—or I will be protected against that". Results, however, were not guaranteed, and rituals were still performed in profound recognition that, whilst one could offer gifts to gods/spirits, one could never control them.

The first record of a specific, commercial service of insurance comes from Babylonian times, in which the code of Hammurabi contains some traces of what could be seen as an insurance shipping policy: a payment from the traders in the form of a loan to guarantee the safe arrival of their goods against bad weather, ruptures, thefts, and so on; after that, there is something similar during the times of the Phoenicians and the Greeks. Then during the Roman age, we find something like a burial insurance: people pay collectively the funeral expenses to the family members. The first traces of guarantee against a loss by fire with shipping insurance are during the medieval age. The guilds pay ransoms to pirates and assure their members against loss by fire of the shipping charge.

The first formalization took place in 1347 in Genoa, where a group of people had underwritten (and this term is still in use) a contract for sharing an amount of risk that they were willing to assume about shipping. Starting from this moment, underwriters begin to play a big role in the insurance industry: they are the ones who calculate risk and decide what the premiums will be. Their calculation is based on statistics: in 1693, the astronomer Edmond Halley developed the first mortality table, but with a mistake—this table used the same rate for all ages, an error that was corrected in 1756, and that made it possible to scale the premium rate to age.

In 1688, following a practice of insuring cargos, the first insurance company was created, at the Lloyd's Coffee House of London, and grew into one of the most important insurance companies, Lloyd's of London. Starting from this moment, in the US and UK mainly, many insurance companies were born, the risks began to be classified, and people accepted as normal the idea that they had to pay for being protected from losses and others' risks.

As a consequence of the great fire of 1835 in New York, and the big payments that insurance companies had to make, the idea of reinsurance began to be diffused, together with the obligation, for insurance companies, to have reserves to protect them from big events.

During the twentieth century, business and private life became more and more complex, and so did the scope of insuring moves from a strictly business sphere to a few areas of private life. By the 1950s, with the start of the economic boom, the insurance industry grew and developed as more and more people owned cars, houses, bank accounts, and financial policies.

Towards the last quarter of the twentieth century, along with the spread of credit cards and later of Internet shopping, the insurance industry grew again along two axes: 1) the range of things that can be insured, leading to different forms of insurance being created, such as life insurance, health insurance and pensions, crop insurance, deposit insurance at the bank, travel insurance, dogs insurance, kids insurance; 2) the numbers of people being insured, along a trend of democratization of insurance, as more and more people gain access to the goods and services that can be insured—and then choose to insure them.

Our world according to our insurance industry

For a physicist, the world is a collection of atoms, electrons, and various laws and forces that govern their movements. For a musician, it is a collection of sounds, of silences, of intensity, and rhythm. For a psychotherapist, it is rather the result of a range of acted-out expressed and repressed feelings—themselves imprints of childhood traumas. For an insurer, however, the world is a collection of risks. The prism through which he sees the world is that of incidents, disasters, misadventures; and his role is to mitigate the impacts of those on his clients. In that way, one is always insured "against" something. It is a service in case something bad, unpleasant happens—but not as a way of increasing the opportunities for something good, creative, generative to happen.

In other words, the insurer promises us a world with less unhappiness—but not one with more happiness (it would, indeed, be unlawful to promise to do so). However, whether by the magic of marketing or our own investment in believing in it, we can often associate insurance with inducing happiness. Would we perhaps be more inclined to settle for fewer ills than for true joy, and then delude ourselves into taking the former for the latter?

Insurance and anxiety

Our insurance industry (for it is us who have collectively created it) is therefore dealing with the realm of our anxieties. Initially, one is tempted to say that it carries, at a collective level, individual anxieties that we may have about events we might encounter in the future. As if it were separate from us, this industry presents us a world of unpleasant future possibilities, and offers us protection from them—offering us, thereby, a relief against the anxiety that the future might bring.

On closer look, however, the picture appears a bit different. The psychodynamics at work here seem to involve a triad: us today, us in the future, and the insurer as a mediator/mitigator of the two. In that triangle that our relationship with the insurance industry by nature involves, the future is always a persecutory one. Something bad arising from this persecutory future is coming our way. Some split-off parts of us, that we've projected into the future, are coming back to haunt us. In that scenario, we are powerless victims, and the future, filled with projected disowned parts of us, is powerful and threatening. The insurance therefore becomes a defence against this persecutory future.

As with most defence functions, the relief is short-lived, and soon a vicious cycle settles in. Indeed, presenting us with an unpleasant future ends up reinforcing our anxieties about this future; by a set of positive feedback loops, the defence system expands to cover ever larger parts of the world in which we interact.

All those risks we (don't) take everyday

This industry has not sprung out of nowhere, landing on Earth on the back of some asteroid. To the contrary, it reflects our own relationship with risk-taking; it comes in and occupies the space left vacant when we let our own capacity to live with, and manage, risks recede.

This surrendering to risk-aversion starts in the matrix of all social systems: the family.

At the beginning of last century, most families in Western Europe still lived in rural areas; children, when not working on the farm, were left to interact with their surrounding environment, learning first hand the meaning of falling, hurting oneself, getting bitten, catching diseases. Parents were spending most of their waking time working, and therefore had very little time to watch their children. Risk management was therefore a mix of distributed responsibility amongst the adults and the older children, and implicit delegation to the younger ones to manage themselves as best as they could.

The ever increasing urban population of Western Europe, throughout at least the first three-quarters of the twentieth century, spent, from a young age, some of its time too interacting with the external environment, a mix of gardens, parks, and streets. When out, a certain type of social network provided some containment (local shop-keepers, other parents, older friends …). From as early as five or six years old, children were left going to school, parks, shops, without adults, often in little groups, and sometimes on their own. If they went on holidays, these city-children often encountered a much less clearly boundaried environment in which they discovered new threats and learned to deal with them.

In those days, incidents did occur, trivial as well as serious, sometimes even lethal. Most children went through a series of "childhood illnesses" (chicken pox, measles, whooping cough, and so on) as there were no widespread vaccines for them. They got into cars without seat belts, sometimes on adults' laps on the front seat (some young babies even lying on the dashboard!). Physical and sometimes sexual assaults, rape, and murder did also happen[1] throughout that century, as they did in the centuries before.

In other words, throughout most of the twentieth century, illness, misfortune, accidents, deaths of relatives—all these were expected to happen in one's close, or at least extended, family (Kubler-Ross, 2005). Parents and grandparents had died during one of the two world wars, the ones still alive having lived through shortage of food, bombing, and ruins.

Today, most children are vaccinated against more and more childhood diseases. Cars are built as fortresses in which children up till the age of ten have their own private armoured seat. Driving has become the primary mode of taking children to school; not only fewer parents walk their children to school, but even fewer parents let their children walk there by themselves, or go by public transport, in any case, without a supervising adult. The issue of safety and security, a recurrent aspect in most election campaigns in Europe, is subtly being distilled through many advertising campaigns.

Hence cars are now insured not only for third-party, fire and theft, but also for accident and recovery. With virtually all household appliances, beyond the manufacturer's warranty, an extended guarantee is being offered by default. Sales staff are being trained to both praise the quality of the product they are trying to sell, and at the same time to present an extended warranty as unavoidable, without undermining the attractiveness of the product—a complex juggling exercise ...

Travelling too has grown under the protective film of insurance. Having graduated from being "organized" to being "packaged", it is now a product in its own right, for which quality must be assured. The discovery of new countries must not overshadow the request for tranquillity and peace of mind. Another juggling exercise must take place here: providing the opportunities for customers to be "disturbed" out of their habitual life through foreign experiences, whilst at the same time controlling the level of that disturbance.

In summary, the ending of the twentieth century has marked a real transition, in Western Europe at least, of society's attitude to life, and the management of risks inherent to being human[2]. Announced by the successes of all industries throughout the "Roaring Thirties", which brought about peace, stability, predictability, and the idea of ever-increasing material Progress, we have seen a move from the onus being on humans to learn to deal with what life brought their way, to a growing expectation that life itself should be sufficiently tamed so that whatever it may want to bring our way can be controlled, managed, and, ultimately, not fully nor directly experienced.

The inner origin of the desire for insurance

Insuring means reducing the various routes that the future might take; it expresses our desire to control the range of scenarios that we may be faced with. It is therefore, by nature, antithetic to the experience of Not-Knowing. In the words of Alistair Bain (1999), insuring is a "defence against the present moment".

Whilst the illusion may be that taking out insurance enables us to be more tranquil about the present, the very act of taking out insurance kills the present moment, because it reduces it to a set of finite possibilities. Whereas, to paraphrase French philosopher Emmanuel Levinas (1980), the present moment is where/when the infinite can be experienced—and with it the wide range of possibilities that may surprise us, cause us to rejoice, bring us pain; in other words, all sorts of experiences that will disturb our intrapsychic *status quo*, but for which the desire to control can only be a phantasy, thereby illusory.

In following Levinas, the inner desire for insurance could therefore be seen, at a spiritual level, as a refusal to accept "that which is bigger than us humans". As an expression of our desire, as humans, to no longer be submitted to, or at best work with, but actually control, the complex, interconnected web of life. In that way, it marks a real rupture with the initial rituals and sacrifices performed by sorcerers, which were, fundamentally, enacted in profound respect for "that which is bigger than us".

In psychodynamic terms, the desire for insurance can also be seen as a phantasy for control; that of an omnipotent ego over the reality that surrounds it. In defending us against the present moment, it actually shields us from the reality principle, and its inevitable reaffirmation of the limits of our potency. It is that reaffirmation, experienced as castration, that we try to avoid.

For Lacan (1999), castration creates lack; and lack opens up the space for desire, in other words for the movement of the Life forces. In following Lacan, we could therefore hypothesize that insurance defends us from experiencing castration, and therefore from experiencing ourselves fully alive.

By erasing the present, by locking ourselves in a binary past–future relationship to time, we develop a relationship to life, to our external reality, that is the precise opposite of Bion's disposition as a psychoanalyst. Where his invitation, in encountering a patient or a group, was to meet them "without memory or desire", we, in fact, relate to the unfolding of our life journey with partial memory and plenty of desire. Partial memory, because we tend to filter out what can go well to focus only on what could go wrong; and plenty of desire[3], because we frame the unfolding of our future in an attempt to control its outcome.

Interestingly, one of the key shifts we can notice through the development of insurance is the move away from the collective, the whole, to a focus on the individual, the part. And, in that process, from learning to predicting.

Indeed, until nearly the end of the twentieth century, as one could expect nothing but the unexpected, the emphasis was placed on developing capacities to deal with and managing risk, and developing resilience in the face of adversity. The extended community operated as a safety net, on which one could call in times of personal hardship. As part of a whole, the individual developed learning through the sometimes harsh experiences he traversed. By learning here, we mean, in the sense of Maturana & Varela's (1980) understanding of cognition, that the internal structure of that individual was modulated through the impact on it from the external reality. Of course, that modulation could also generate defences, or even denial, but in any case, the internal was directly impacted by the external.

Since the latter part of the twentieth century, co-existing with the fragmentation of the traditional social networks in the West, a shift has occurred to attempt to provide individuals with direct protection. From being an individual member of a larger whole, whose life journey relied upon capacity-building and initiative in the face of adversity, one has become a fragmented, stand-alone part, whose artificially fed protection and sense of security have brought about a diminishment in one's capacity to deal with adversity. An external individual "blanket-cover" has replaced an internal strength-building for individual members of resilient communities. In that way, it seems as though the development of insurance in all areas of our lives is fulfilling an age-old phantasy of returning to a womb, in which one would be protected from the external reality through a reassuring matrix of policy covers. In that phantasy, learning recedes, as one is protected from direct interaction with external reality; instead, predictability sets in, just as with the predictability of the type and rate of nutrients flowing through the umbilical cord.

Creating our own unwanted future

Two issues seem important to clarify at this stage. Our hypothesis is that the insurance industry has developed, through a set of mutual feedback loops, from this inner reluctance to live in the present moment, from this human inner desire to control—and not work with—our external reality. The growth of the industry is for us a reflection of this shared inner state—and has in no way induced it. The sets of mutual positive feedbacks are what make a growth in one generate a growth in the other.

We are aware of writing this chapter as Western citizens, at a time in our history when the very tranquillity and predictability that surround us create the conditions in which we can take time to write about an inner desire to not face the realities of life. Put it another way, our historical understanding suggests that, of course, when one was surrounded by epidemics, wars, and economic hardship, a life-giving response was to try to find ways of reducing the overwhelming, sometimes arbitrary, impact of such events. However, perhaps it is worth exploring whether the response that we have collectively contributed to creating actually meets those needs we had in the first place—or whether something has evolved that no longer provides us with what we had imagined.

The basic principle is that we invest a fairly small amount of money in insurance, so that we can be protected in case of loss, damage, or incident in the future. The amount of money is small in comparison to what we would lose should the dreaded event happen; and we pay now so that the future does not deal us an unpleasant hand. This, as we have discussed earlier, provides us with a defence against a phantasized persecutory future.

However, for the insurance industry to work, and to make business sense, the income from policies needs to be invested in the markets so that it can generate profits. Until recently, very few investors used SRI[4] criteria, and therefore money has been generally invested in markets primarily for performance alone criteria[5]. As a result, the money that we pay for our insurance policies can be used to fund pharmaceutical companies that discover life-saving drugs, or that manufacture drugs such as Mediator. It can be used to fund a new electric-car programme for one of the big manufacturers, or it is more likely used to fund the manufacturing of millions of petrol-fuelled cars to be sold to those countries not yet saturated with those individual carbon-producing machines. The money invested might serve the creation of new companies and jobs, or it will more likely serve the decisions for downsizing and delocalization, bringing unemployment to some of the very people who, through subscribing to a policy, have provided the means for this decision to happen. It may even be used to bet against the Euro, or some other currency, contributing to blowing a wind of panic throughout Europe, leading to drastic cuts in public expenditure.

In other words, as we believe to be paying for a protection against a persecutory future, our money may actually create the conditions for the future to be (not just in phantasy, but in reality) less hospitable: because of increased pollution, job losses, wars, global warming, etc. ... The transactions that we believed to be operating, under controlled conditions, only in a triad (me now, me in the future, and the protecting insurer), actually turn out to be propelled into a highly complex system of investment and return on investment, the outcome of which is certainly not controlled (indeed, not controllable), and could easily, in the long run, generate for us more negative effects than the ones we paid to be insured against.

When that highly complex system actually dysfunctions, as, for example, in the case of the subprime crisis, then the outcome is sure to be disastrous. The millions of billions of dollars lost by banks and financial institutions[6] has prompted a set of systemic responses that have not only generated drastic cuts in public expenditure (i.e., the money used by governments to run public services tailored to us, the public) but has also brought the economy to a halt, tinkering on recession, hence increasing job cuts and reducing job and development opportunities. Connected to this, many national and international governmental initiatives to bring about significant responses to the challenges of global warming have been put, as it were, on the back burner.

So, yes, I may have an additional private health insurance, but have I stopped and thought about whether my transactions have actually contributed to making the world less healthy? I may be happy to have subscribed to an insurance on the monthly payments for my new car, but what if I won't have the money to pay for the petrol needed to run it?

The examples above point to the fact that whilst we invest in a defence against a phantasized persecutory future, our investment transactions may actually contribute to creating a real persecutory future. In that case, however, the defence mechanism can still hold its defensive function, in so far as the consequences brought about by our transactions are displaced in time, and sufficiently diffused to make it difficult to perceive the circular causalities involved.

That defence mechanism, however, can suddenly break down when we make a claim. For we realize, at this moment when life erupts back into our present to claim its right to surprise us, that being covered doesn't mean being fully taken care of. It is not because something breaks down that it will be reimbursed or replaced. The insurer may try to limit the repaying amount; they may have set a rather high excess on the policy, the reality of which you only discover in times of incidents. There may be a range of excluding clauses that they will try to use in order to refuse liability[7]. What had initially appeared to be a solid defence is now being toppled over by some small prints …

The risk, in other words, is that if an unfortunate event does actually happen and one has to make a claim, the insurer suddenly becomes the persecutor. The policy, that had hitherto served as a defence, actually becomes the one against which there is nothing left to serve as a defence. The persecution, which we had hoped to escape from, is nonetheless happening …

Insurance, leadership, and management

As we have seen, insurance is intricately linked to predictability; to framing in advance the range of outcomes with which one may be faced. It creates a structure supposed to defend us against unpleasant surprises. As organizational consultants, two questions emerge for us at this stage:

- How might the nature of the work itself, that of providing insurance, impact on the leadership and management culture of an insurance organization?
- How, more broadly, might the expanding societal culture of insurance pervade into organizational attitudes to leadership and management?

In answer to the first question, our ten-year experience in working with high potentials and on leadership issues, with people in this kind of industry, in consulting multinational insurance companies, has been very particular. Below are a few of our reflections.

The nitty-gritty of the business has been (is still) very difficult to understand for external people, and sometimes also for people who have joined the industry within the last couple of years. There is something like a lack of information from people speaking about their business. The business is very complicated by nature, but there is also the fact that people seem to have a lot of difficulties in connecting their results with the whole enterprise and explaining what that whole is. This often results in an experience of being in a cloud, or in some kind of big cottonwool ball.

This behaviour is a big obstacle for the exercise of leadership because, in a complex environment, in which in any case some information is not known and not available for action, it contributes to increasing the level of risk in decision-taking … perhaps without possibility to be insured.

Hence, a compensatory behaviour that we have often noticed can be seen in the decision-making process, and how authority and delegation are being exercised. Indeed, decisions may be moved laterally, or upwards, or both, before being taken, thus diffusing the level of personal accountability. Decisions can sometimes be felt to emerge out of this set of circular communications, witnessed by the boss (at times, the

CEO), yet it would be hard to pinpoint who took the final decision and can be said to be accountable for it.

Another defensive behaviour that we observe is the richness of technical details that are provided in order to explain each phase in delivering the service that often makes people of the same organization feel at a loss in understanding each other. Sometimes it seems, again, to be done to hide the real process. However, a more disturbing hypothesis, perhaps, would be to think that this "verbal diarrhoea" is useful for containing the anxiety due to the perception of emptiness within the process: as if there is nothing real to discover behind what is being talked about.

The broader issue of leadership and management in organization shares, in our experience, quite a lot of similarities with the more specific issue of organizational culture within the insurance industry.

The issue seems to play itself out in the creative tension between leadership (holding a vision to move towards) and management (organizing resources within the current sets of constraints). Leadership operates in the field of the yet-to-be-experienced, of the unpredictable. It is a constant reworking of the response an organization can provide to a quickly evolving context, and as such, it does not know whether the response will work—it has not been tried out in this particular situation.

Management operates in the field of the tangible; of targets. It has tools, processes, methodologies. It starts from the reality as it exists, and works out how to process it into a predictable future.

At both extremes, management can be said to be taking its cues from the cards that reality has already dealt, whereas leadership is about shuffling and dealing a new hand to play with.

Our experience of consulting to people in leadership and management roles is that that tension is often difficult to hold. Personal accountability is at stake, in particular when a decision needs to be taken. Standing up to say "this is what needs to be done, and I can be held accountable to that decision" is far more risky than saying "our studies suggest that X could be better than Y", or "this is what our performance indicators are saying, therefore ...".

Indeed, organizations have been developing entire internal structures and processes to institutionalize these behaviours, through risk assessment processes and health and safety procedures. With these, the locus of control, judgement, and action gradually moves from individuals to these procedures, which can end up governing for us[8].

When human decisions can't be avoided, they can end up being passed around like hot potatoes, so that the accountability gets diffused throughout the system, or relayed all the way up to the CEO, as another way to "cover one's back".

As actors within the organizations tacitly take out protection covers against what misfortunes the Not-Known might bring, the whole organization develops a sort of homeostasis that stifles innovation and learning. Leadership, for the results of which there can be no insurance, then becomes increasingly difficult to exercise.

The role of the insurance industry in transforming this situation

As alluded to above, whilst the insurance industry may stem from a life-giving attempt to render one's experience of life less chaotic and arbitrary, the way it has developed may not necessarily have been the best way of meeting the intrinsic needs of the insured. In particular, our hypothesis is that the insurance industry, in the way that it currently operates, may actually be reinforcing the problem it is supposed to solve in two ways. Firstly, through a complex set of positive feedbacks, it tends to reinforce our fears of a persecutory future, extending them to an ever increasing range of areas in our life. Secondly, the money collected through the policies is not rigorously invested so as to ensure risk reduction from the external environment. In other words, insurance companies tend to operate in order to protect and compensate, but not to reduce future risks.

In psychodynamic terms, we could say that the industry operates as a receptacle of our persecutory anxieties; that receptacle is supposed to act as a defence against those anxieties, but can be seen to leak at times when confronted by the test of reality (i.e., claims).

One way to transform this situation, therefore, would be to move away from being a receptacle, to being a container of those persecutory anxieties, metabolizing them and feeding them back to their clients in a new form—one that enables learning and growth.

Some have already shown leadership in starting to do that. One of the companies we worked with, for example, realized that it was more costly for them to try to avoid paying out claims (in particular through staff time involved in defending the case for non-payment, and sometimes through court cases). They therefore transformed their policy from "fighting" claims as a stance, to accepting claims as a stance. Customer satisfaction has increased, overheads have been reduced, business and profits are on the increase. In this example, real leadership has enabled innovation, moving from managing the existing to shifting paradigm; in doing that, however, they've ensured that the defence remains solid enough not to let out any persecutory bits.

Another company, for which an important market share was the business-to-business sale of insurance policy against staff sickness and long-term absence, realized that one way to reduce claims was to ensure that the workplace became healthier and more conducive to good working climate. It has therefore decided to fund stress-relief programmes for its client companies, coaching, and HR consulting, and sometimes crisis intervention. Whilst holding companies' anxieties about loss of performance through staff absence, it literally fed back initiatives aimed at reducing the likelihood of absence.

More broadly, the insurance industry, with its huge financial leverage power, has an important role to play in shaping the future. As such, it could decide to use that power to bring forth a more hospitable world, one with less obesity, heart disease, poisoning through pollution, and damage from catastrophic natural events (floods, hurricanes, oil spills, and so on). The issue is not about being philanthropic here; the issue is, first and foremost, a business one. As private health insurance is on the increase, so is the rate of claims and the cost of those claims. Triple bypass operations, organ transplants, all these highly technological interventions cost a lot to the industry, when they are actually the downstream consequences of problems that it may be much more cost-effective to address much more upstream (through health-awareness programmes, but also through investment in companies that produce or distribute healthy food rather than just profitable foods).

As claims linked to freak climate-related incidents are also on the increase, it will also be important for the industry, if it is to anticipate rising costs, to take an active role—through investment, for example—in the fight against climate change. (See Chapter Twelve on climate change in this volume.)

In conclusion, a future where risk and harm have reduced will remain an object of phantasy, if we retain the insurance industry in the role of defensive receptacle against our fears of what the future may bring. In contrast, we can transition towards a more mature world, in which this industry will still have a role, albeit evolved towards an actor that not only protects against, but also actively works at reducing, potential future risks and harm.

Notes

1. Many studies show that the incidence of such assaults has not significantly increased in recent years; rather, their media coverage, coupled with the exponential increase of information technologies throughout the different medias, has greatly increased, giving us the impression that the number of assaults has increased.
2. "Life is a sexually transmitted condition, of which you always end up dying." This phrase is attributed, amongst others, to R. D. Laing, and to Woody Allen.
3. Bion's use of the concept of "desire" is, of course, very different to Lacan's; for the former, it is synonymous to a wish, i.e., an actual thing we want to see happen or realize in the future; for the latter, it is not about a thing as such, but a libidinal force, or energy, without necessarily being object-related.
4. SRI: Socially Responsible Investment, i.e., an approach to investment that ranks companies according to environmental, governance, and ethical criteria, and selects investment portfolios according to those analyses.
5. Performance is a general term, within which there can be various focuses: high return, long-term stability, capital guarantee, regular income, etc.
6. Some of the money they held being, of course, collected through private pension schemes, a system, highly developed in the US, for example, that favours individual insurance. This system is in stark contrast with the "solidarity" systems of some countries in the "Old" Europe, where the money collected from workers today directly serves to pay the pensions of those who have retired.
7 In these clauses, we can of course include: floods, wars, extreme weather, strikes, and other acts of gods. Interestingly, this is where the ambiguity of the insurance paradigm is expressed, as it attempts to differentiate "that which is bigger than us humans" from that over which we have control—in a spirit of increasing the former and declaring it non-insurable, and reducing the latter. So we see again how this paradigm is both responding to us at our phantasy level, and operating on fragmentation and splitting the whole into parts.
8. Sometimes creating serious accidents, like those heavy stock-market losses triggered by computer-controlled risk-assessment and selling procedures, that can set up positive feedback of massive sales of shares leading to panic in the markets, which in turn increases massive sales.

References

Bain, A. (1999). On being frozen in Time. In: R. French & R. Vince (Eds.), *Group Relations, Management, and Organization*. Oxford: Oxford University Press.

Bion, W. (1970). *Attention and Interpretation*. London: Tavistock Publications.

Kubler-Ross, E. (2005). *On Grief and Grieving: Finding the Meaning of Grief Through the Five Stages of Loss*. London: Simon & Schuster.

Lacan, J. (1999). *Écrits*. Paris: Éditions du Seuil. [Lacan, J. (2007). *Ecrits*: the first complete edition in English. New York: W. W. Norton.]

Levinas, E. (1980). *Le Temps et l'Autre*. Montpelier: Fata Morgana. [Levinas, E. (1987). *Time and the Other*. Pittsburg: Duquesne University Press.]

Maturana, H. & Varela, F. (1980). *Autopoiesis and Cognition: The Realization of the Living*. Dordrecht: D. Reidel.

Trennery, C. F. (2009). *The Origin and Early History of Insurance*. New Jersey: The Lawbook Exchange.

CHAPTER SIX

Psychodynamic reflections on the fashion system

Anna König

Introduction

Clothing and one's constructed appearance form a tangible boundary between the self and the external world. It is, therefore, remarkable that psychodynamic theory appears to have little to say about fashion and the manner in which it is used by individuals to reconcile internal and external identities. Amongst the numerous scholarly works to have been written on fashion in the past twenty years, there is a paucity of theoretical work on fashion from a primarily psychodynamic perspective. Even texts that purport to provide a broad range of academic perspectives on the history, culture, and business of fashion fail to offer psychodynamic frameworks of any description. This prompts the question: is it fashion theorists who have ignored psychodynamic interpretations, or psychodynamic theorists who have dismissed fashion?

Despite the proliferation of academic writings on fashion over the past twenty years, yet there appears to be an implicit assumption that fashion benefits from sociological rather than psychological investigation, and much is made of the "social" components of fashion and dress. The clothed individual is often posited as "playing" to a social audience, and therefore it is the social aspect of dress that is emphasized. The academic field that currently dominates the study of fashion is cultural and historical studies, a polymorphous discipline that borrows theoretical models from sociology, anthropology, and gender theory, amongst others. However, it makes scant use of psychodynamic theory. Indeed, the only time that psychodynamic theory is mentioned in fashion texts is in reference to J. C. Flugel, but by and large, fashion theorists appear to have rejected most aspects of psychoanalytic theory as a tool for understanding fashion. That said, some academics allude to psychodynamic ideas without explicitly acknowledging them as such. Perhaps this arises out of the historic mistrust that cultural theorists have of psychoanalysis as a discipline, preferring instead to locate argument within more "visible" and less ambiguously coded theoretical disciplines.

I would suggest that, in part at least, fashion theorists mistrust the inherently linguistic qualities of psychodynamic theory. Before anything can be understood within the psychoanalytic framework, it must first be translated into language, and invariably fashion—a material and visual phenomenon—defies straightforward translation. Although academics such as Roland Barthes have attempted to apply semiotics to the interpretation of fashion, the ambiguities that arise from such an approach have led most theorists to look elsewhere for explanations. Indeed, Barthes himself recognized that fashion images defy clear interpretation, hence the use of text to "anchor" the preferred meaning of the image within fashion publications and advertisements (Barthes, 1977).

Conversely, psychologists and psychoanalysts themselves have offered up very little on the subject of fashion. One has to ask why those who investigate the world from a psychodynamic viewpoint generally ignore fashion and its impact on individuals. Is it because fashion continues—despite forty years of cultural studies—to be seen as culturally frivolous and therefore not of interest to academics? Whilst sociologists and social anthropologists have overcome this institutional prejudice, psychologists have faltered, and the individual has become lost in a crowd of sociological explanations. It seems likely that gender lies at the root of this blind-spot, for psychoanalytic theory has always struggled to make sense of "woman", and fashion continues to be presented as a predominantly feminine cultural domain. Could it be that psychoanalysis has simply not yet got a grasp on woman, and therefore cannot hope to make sense of fashion? Furthermore, the aim of psychoanalytic enquiry is often to explore a problem in order to find a resolution, and though fashion is complex and ambiguous, one cannot honestly categorize it as a problem.

This chapter might, therefore, be seen as an attempt to address a theoretical void and consider what fashion can tell us about the unconscious. In doing so, I consider several facets of the fashion system, including trends in clothing, fashion imagery, fashion writing, and the use of fashion by individuals. I make no apology for the fact that I draw on psychodynamic theory from a range of schools. Whilst the seminal works of Freud and Jung facilitate some insights, it is perhaps more pertinent to draw on the work of Lacan and the work of feminist psychoanalytic theorists, for fashion is a cultural phenomenon that continues to be very clearly associated with "the feminine".

Fashion archetypes and the collective unconscious

Fashion is perhaps the single most visible indicator of cultural *Zeitgeist* at any given time. If we consider fashion in the twentieth century, there is a tendency to distil trends into ten-year divisions, and we talk of the fashions of the 1960s, 1970s, and so on. Arbitrary as these demarcations appear to be, within each period central themes emerge, unique to the social and cultural context at that point in history. These emergent motifs can subsequently be interrogated, making use of the tools of psychodynamic theory in order to ascertain some general insights into the ways in which unconscious impulses are expressed through fashion.

A useful methodological approach comes from Caroline Evans and her study of fashion design and imagery in the 1990s (2003). Here, she rejects the idea fashion designs should be read as the creative product of individual designers, suggesting instead that they speak of a collective *Zeitgeist*. This is an important theoretical shift, for fashion history, following the discourse of long-established art historical approaches, tends to privilege the individual creator. However, such an approach rarely produces anything other than hagiographic accounts hailing the "genius" of the subject without truly interrogating the designs. Evans's work, however, evokes the notion of Jung's collective unconscious, which is, perhaps, a more fruitful line of enquiry when looking at broad fashion trends.

Whilst it is duly noted that Jung's writings on the collective unconscious are often dismissed by theorists on the grounds of being too closely allied to mysticism, I nonetheless believe it to be helpful when looking at a group (as opposed to an individual) phenomenon, such as a fashion trend. Jung writes:

> In addition to our immediate consciousness … there exists a second psychic system of a collective, universal, and impersonal nature which is identical in all individuals.
>
> (2003, p. 43)

Moreover, the notion of archetypes is particularly pertinent to a discussion of fashion, as clothing and appearance can be used to "speak" these archetypes aloud. In fashion, there is the possibility of playing out identities that are embedded within the collective memory of a society or culture: one has to acknowledge that this manifestation may be more than simply an individual preference.

Retrospectively, this methodological framework can be applied to fashion trends of the twentieth century. Starting with the 1940s, we might conclude that the military, tailored fashions of that era reflected the fact that there was little room for individuality in a psychological sense. What becomes important in times of war is social cohesion rather than self-expression: the psyche enters survival mode and there is little appetite for pushing boundaries or experimentation. Moreover, as material resources were limited by rationing and the implementation of the Utility scheme, there was limited scope for playful expression through appearance. The detailing on Utility clothing (false pockets, slivers of contrasting fabrics) might be regarded as tiny neurotic motifs. The fussy little details of fashion provided the evidence that there was still a yearning for individuality, an attempt to resist the threat of psychic annihilation, even within the social and political devastation of the Second World War.

It might be argued that the economic and political stability of the 1950s was reflected in the fashions of that era. Though austerity came to be replaced by economic growth and a consumer boom in Western Europe and North America, social conformity was still incredibly important, and this was made manifest through dress. Although self-expression was deemed important—that was, after all, ostensibly what the war had been fought for—this was a paradoxical form of self-expression.

The explosion of mass-market consumer goods in the 1950s (including ready-to-wear fashion) was not characterized by a stylistic free-for-all. Rather, it reflected an illusion of personal freedom and choice within a carefully controlled system, an illusion that came to be reinforced through comparisons with the lack of choice in Eastern European and Soviet bloc countries.

By the 1960s, youth was challenging authority, and sex bubbled up through the collective unconscious in ways that had never before been possible. The contraceptive pill liberated women from the inevitable consequences of sex, and clothing peeled back from the body in fashions that revealed as much as they covered. In many ways, the 1960s represented an infantile regression to playful exhilaration, necessary, perhaps, after the punishing austerity of preceding decades. The baby-boomer generation failed abjectly to identify with their parents, choosing instead to tread new paths to adulthood.

Negotiation of gender identity was, perhaps, the prominent fashion motif of the 1970s, as both men and women tested out shifting social expectations through androgynous clothing and styling. However, this was not a straightforward shift towards an egalitarian utopia in which gender ceased to matter: in many respects, the changes that seemed within reach in the 1970s failed to materialize (Faludi, 1992). That said, at the time there was a sense of a shift in the rigid social demarcations between male and female. In Jungian terms, this might be regarded as a time when men and women most visibly recognized anima and animus respectively.

Rather different concerns dominated the 1980s: power, status, individualism, and hedonism. It might best be described an era of phallocentrism, a time in which the desires of the individual trumped the needs of the group. Thatcherism and Reaganomics provided the economic and political agenda, and this was reflected in fashions that spoke of personal wealth, power, and status for women as well as men. And yet the 1980s was also the decade in which men's fashion started to diversify, the era of the "new man" with his display of attributes previously perceived as "feminine" (Jobling, 1999). Thus it becomes evident that more than one set of issues may be made manifest at any given time period.

Stylistically, the 1990s was characterized by minimalism, and, to a degree, nihilism. The swaggering optimism of the 1980s ended in economic collapse, and with it came an aesthetic change. The fashionable figure was thinner and more childlike than ever before, but not in a joyful sense redolent of the 1960s. Instead, there was a kind of denial of self, present both in the clothing and the fashion imagery of that time (Arnold, 2001). Anxieties about the body were repeatedly played out in distressed, deconstructed clothing, whilst the androgyny of the 1990s became a retreat from rather than an exploration of sexuality.

So what might be said of the collective unconscious in recent years? Whilst the early years of the "noughties" started out with a consumer orgy of luxury and glossy hedonism—perhaps in relief as the world didn't come to an end as the millennium passed—it limped to a close in an aesthetic blur of identity confusion. The fashion system is—at the time of writing—a fractured, complex, and multidimensional matrix of plurality and mixed messages. Granted, the fashion media are still present (as discussed in a later section of this chapter), attempting to guide consumer taste, but there are now multiple "looks", and there are—apparently—dozens of fashion choices on offer.

Whilst a sociological or economic analysis would attribute this to the diversification of fashion production and the impact of the free-market economy, a psychodynamic take on the situation might be that culturally we have entered a phase of identity confusion. The over-inflated bubble of consumer activity burst spectacularly in 2008, and perhaps subsequently there has been an attempt to make sense of what has happened. Whereas in times of economic plenty, pleasure can easily be purchased, when funds run out, individuals are left to contemplate how else fulfilment might be obtained. For some, of course, it is just a matter of buying cheaper versions of desired fashion items, but for others, economic constraint may prompt the revaluation of a life lived through material objects, a self constructed through the purchase of mass-produced consumer goods.

Theories of postmodernism can also be utilized in order to explain the plurality of styles that is prevalent in contemporary fashion. Notably, Elizabeth Wilson suggests that fashion might become a substitute for a coherent sense of identity:

> Dress could play a part, for example, either to glue the false identity together on the surface, or to lend a theatrical and play-acting aspect to the hallucinatory experience of the contemporary world; we become actors, inventing our costumes for each successive

appearance, disguising the recalcitrant body we can never entirely transform.

(Wilson, 1992, p. 8)

Such an explanation contains within it the assumption that the individual's sense of self is fragmented and that existence itself is something of a hallucinatory experience, and from a psychodynamic perspective this is interesting: resolution of fractures within the psyche is, after all, the grand project of psychoanalysis. Moreover, as an increasingly globalized world provides myriad variations on style and dress; the sartorial toolkit that an individual might use to fashion their identity becomes ever more complex and multifaceted. Previous constraints on identity exploration have been lifted, or at least altered, in a postcolonial globalized world.

According to Jung, "there are as many archetypes as there are typical situations in life" (2003, p. 48), and clothing provides an obvious means of exploring such identities. The fashion industry encourages us to believe that we can tell a story about ourselves through the clothes we wear, but in the main it thwarts this possibilities by providing only pre-scripted stories. Mainstream fashion permits only a narrow range of "looks" that gives individuals little scope to genuinely tell their own personal stories: only the most daring individuals will venture outside of the socially acceptable fashion archetypes.

Even the expressive childhood game of dressing-up has been eroded by consumerism into a series of rigid identities. Instead of a collection of disparate items of clothing (the everyday and the special; items for both men and women; large and small; incongruous) from which a child can formulate their own playtime identities, dressing-up clothes are factory-made and sized to fit, usually evoking well-known commercial characters (for example, Disney's Cinderella). So even at an early stage, the expression of universal archetypes is curbed. If dressing-up is a form of play that permits experimentation with different identities, the diversity of those identities has been stunted by corporate consumerism.

Fashion archetypes: women, men, and children

Elizabeth Wilson writes that: "Fashion acts as a vehicle for fantasy .... All art draws on unconscious fantasy; the performance that is fashion is one road from the inner to the outer world" (2003, p. 246). However, at a time when there has never been more choice in fashion, why do so many consumers choose to look so alike by following very narrowly prescribed trends? If, as Wilson says, fashion provides an opportunity for fantasy, why does that fantasy manifest itself in such a uniform manner? Moreover, for many, negotiating the fashion system is something more of a challenge than an opportunity, whilst for others still, fashion is barely acknowledged.

For women, fashion presents all manner of contradictions, and this has been reflected in feminist critiques of the fashion system from the mid-nineteenth century to the present day. These discussions have ranged from functionalist critiques of specific fashion items, such as the corset, to ideological discussions concerned with the cultural importance—and construction—of a woman's physical appearance (de Beauvoir, 1997). Although the latter years of the twentieth century saw a brief flirtation with the somewhat simplistic post-feminist notion that fashion is empowering and therefore no longer problematic to women, some theorists would argue that no clear resolution has been reached (Walters, 2010).

In the nineteenth century, denied most other forms of creative expression, the dressed body became the site of all creativity for women (Pollock, 1981). Whilst in theory the twentieth century saw the elimination of those barriers that excluded women from artistic expression, I would argue that societal recognition of women's creativity continues to be problematic, dogged by spectres of long-established cultural biases that favour men. Denied other forms of expression, women have become adept at using the materials that are both at hand and socially acceptable: thus the body becomes a canvas. But this can be an unsatisfying process: the body has limits, as does clothing, and creative options are, in reality, restricted. Moreover, the labour of maintaining what has been described as a socially acceptable "performing self" (Featherstone, 1991, p. 186) can be every bit as futile, repetitive, and soul-destroying as the domestic chores which have traditionally fallen to women.

Even today, for many women, fashion is used to present a self that is so overtly "feminine"—according to social conventions—as to become a caricature of womanhood. The writings of Joan Riviere offer a useful perspective on this phenomenon. In her 1929 essay, "Womanliness as a masquerade", Riviere recounts the story of a successful, intelligent woman who would, after speaking in public, dissolve into coquettish and flirtatious behaviour that was quite incongruous with her otherwise professional demeanour in a "compulsive reversal of her intellectual performance" (1991, p. 94). Riviere's explanation for this is that so great was her fear of being found to be in possession of "male" attributes (intellect, professionalism), the woman was compelled to undo this in a public display of femininity. She writes:

> Womanliness therefore could be assumed and worn as a mask, both to hide the possession of masculinity and to avert the reprisals expected if she was found to possess it.
>
> (1991, p. 94)

Perhaps even now the fear of being caught in possession of "male" attributes is a spectre that continues to haunt professional women: it's not enough to be professional, one must be professional and feminine, in a manner that is essentially as prescribed and limited as that which was prevalent in the first half of the twentieth century.

For men, the fashion system holds different challenges. For most of the twentieth century, choice of clothing was dictated by social class and profession, but societal shifts and changing labour patterns have disrupted these certainties. Thus, although most discussions of fashion inevitably hone in on women's dress, it should be noted that, in many ways, men are now subject to the same pressures as women with regard to appearance. Much of the challenge of fashion—for men—has been to untangle masculinity from sexuality and to escape the constraints that expectations around social status place on clothing.

Continuing the process that came to prominence in the 1960s, fashion is still an arena in which intergenerational conflict is played out. However, there is no longer a simple split between boundary-pushing teenagers and their shocked parents. Rather, there is a blurring of boundaries between parents and children: clothing worn by a twenty-year-old is often no different to that worn by a forty-five-year-old: in the fashion system, everything is up for grabs. This can, perhaps, be seen as a manifestation of the contemporary phenomenon that many adults wish to be friends with, rather than parents to, their children. Yet simultaneously, there is direct intergenerational competition, at its worst, manifested in television programmes such as *Hotter than my Daughter* where mothers and daughters are pitted against one another in terms of their appearance, each scrutinized by a panel composed of members of the public. This might liberate older women, including mothers, from the social scrapheap to which they have historically been consigned once beyond the age of forty, but do their daughters pay the price? Perhaps by holding onto their sexual power, they inhibit the development of their daughters (or indeed simply younger generations). The bleakest assessment of this scenario is that no-one wants to "grow up" and no-one wants to relinquish sexual power: young women remain forever childlike, and older women feel they have no power other than their sexual power. By placing such an emphasis on youth and sexual desirability, one might argue that culturally we have inhibited our own personal growth, that psychologically we have stunted our development.

At this point, I wish to move away from general observations about the fashion system. Whilst it is useful to have an awareness of broad themes that influence fashion, the application of psychodynamic theory comes into its own when considering the individual.

Paper dolls

The image has become highly prized in contemporary culture, and nowhere is this more evident that within the fashion industry. In a spectacular coup that obviates the material basis of fashion, image has become more important than either the clothes or even the body. For many years, I have taught fashion design students, but few are interested in making clothes. Rather, the aspiration in fashion has become that of creating a design that is eye-catching enough to demand commercial attention, but not so obscure as to alienate a fashion-buying audience. Within this paradigm, there is little space for consideration of the physical and material aspects of fashion: the look is all.

"Fast fashion" has come to dominate the contemporary retail market, a production system that provides the consumer with a rapid turnover of exceptionally cheap clothing (Braham, 1997). However, the appeal—and therefore the key to the success—of fast fashion is that it delivers a look. There is often little concern for the quality or fabric of such clothing—what counts is that it emulates some of the basis stylistic features of luxury designer clothing. This is indicative of two prevalent themes in contemporary culture. Firstly, there is a widespread desire (particularly amongst the young) to base their appearance, and therefore a significant part of their constructed identity, on celebrities.

But secondly, there is a certain degree of disconnect between the image portrayed (or desired image) and the actual physical identity of the individual.

Old-fashioned paper dolls serve as a good analogy for this disconnect between image and body. The individual—and subsequently their identity—must be as flat and two-dimensional as possible if the proscribed clothes are to fit. By this, I am not referring to the desire for fashionable thinness (although this may be related). Rather, the identity of the individual must be "flattened out" if the image-clothes are to fit. Somewhat inevitably, this results in conflict as the individual fears obliteration by the image. Not only has the individual turned themselves into an image, they turn themselves into an image of someone else.

The psychological implications of such an action undoubtedly warrant further investigation: on the one hand, there is a quest for identity through appearance, but on the other, the tools with which this might be done are often self-defeating. As Boultwood & Jerrard write: "fashion seeks to mould the body into its own image. The individual, rather than using fashion, is used by it, and fashion ultimately fails" (2000, p. 306). Reconciling an actual body with a fantasy image (such as those present in fashion magazines) therefore becomes a fraught task. Whilst much as been written about the embodied nature of fashion (e.g., Entwistle, 2000), rather less theoretical work has addressed the relationship between fashion imagery and those who view it. Given the prominence of fashion imagery in contemporary culture, an examination of the subject is long overdue.

Psychodynamic theory and the fashion image

Above all, psychodynamic theory is concerned with the linguistic expression and investigation of the unconscious, therefore it is perhaps unsurprising that images and their meaning rarely feature. Images, and the individual's interaction with them, may be private and non-verbal, but this does not mean that unconscious processes are not taking place.

The reinvestigation of classic psychoanalytic case studies such as Freud's "Dora" presents useful insights into the mechanisms of the image-observer relationship. In the era prior to mass-circulation media images, portrayals of "ideal" women were predominantly manifested in paintings of the Madonna. Against this background, Bracha Ettinger (2006) re-evaluates Dora's absorption with a religious painting, and identifies in that moment a state of "fascinance". In contrast to Lacan's formulation of "fascinum", in which movement stops, life is frozen, and the subject becomes momentarily "mortified" (Lacan, 1964, p. 115), Ettinger's fascinance is a moment that has transformational properties, allowing a working-through of mother–daughter relations:

> In a matrixial encounter, the private subjectivity of the individual is momentarily unbounded. The psyche momentarily melts, and its psychic threads are interwoven with threads emanating from objects, images, and other subjects.
>
> (Ettinger, 2006, p. 62)

She goes on to suggest that not only is this image-interaction noteworthy, it may even be critical in the development of the female psyche: "Can a girl become a woman if she cannot receive admiring recognition of her femininity from another woman-Mother?" (2006, p. 67).

Given that in contemporary culture, fashion images have far greater exposure than any religious iconography, Ettinger's fascinance might usefully be applied to the process of reading fashion imagery. Certainly, it would help to explain the enduring appeal of some types of fashion image. As Diana Fuss (1994) argues, the "maternal face" is a dominant archetype in beauty product advertisements, characterized by a close-up, and "natural" look to the face, with an expression that is gently appealing—certainly not in any way threatening or hostile. This, Fuss argues, facilitates the rediscovery of the mother's face, a "cultural simulation" (1994, p. 220) of what has been lost.

Yet for other types of fashion imagery, there is little that could be discerned as comforting, or providing a sense of mutual adoration. Throughout the twentieth century, fashion photography has been dominated by images that dissemble and fragment the body, in what could be regarded as a symbolic act of violence against women. David Bate (2004) notes the prevalence of sado-masochistic imagery in the photographic works of the surrealists, artists whose work came to have a major impact on fashion imagery. It is also worth noting that the majority of fashion photographers working in the industry today are men, and thus, the agenda for representation is set by a male eye, and indeed, a male psyche. The words of Luce Irigaray become pertinent here: "Again and again we [women] become the captives of these fantasies, this ambivalence, this madness which is not ours" (Irigaray, 1991,

p. 42). Yet the very nature of fashion photography as a media product that is disposable and frivolous means that its cultural power is often overlooked: "extraordinary liberties are taken precisely because it is 'only' fashion" (Evans & Thornton, 1989, p. 82).

An unavoidably dominant feature of the contemporary fashion industry is that of hyper-sexualized imagery, now so ubiquitous as to be rendered unremarkable. Whilst once, sexualized images were utilized in advertising for their shock value, sex has become the *lingua franca* of the fashion industry. Bodies are repeatedly exposed, and, inevitably, fashion imagery is more concerned with bodies rather than clothing. Moreover, the banality of fashion imagery is such that one has to question its ability to reflect anything other than a bland and highly prescriptive version of "desire" in contemporary culture. Whilst one might certainly argue that fashion and fashion photography—like all the creative arts—have the potential to provide interesting and insightful commentary on contemporary culture, few designers or photographers actually utilize this opportunity. Market forces and economic considerations are such that opportunities for risk-taking in the industry are limited, for both designers and the photographers who present their work to consumers.

For Roland Barthes, meanwhile, the photograph always serves as a reminder of death. Indeed, he describes photographers as "agents of death" (1984, p. 92) and talks of the violence of a photograph, violent not because of the subject it depicts, but because it is a full, unalterable image, showing what has been and can never be again. From such a perspective, the fashion image might therefore be a symbol of melancholia, reiterating again and again the inevitability of the ageing process, and ultimately, death. Might, therefore, the fashion image be one of the few sites in contemporary culture where we attempt to reconcile ourselves to the finite nature of life? If so, Lacan's fascinum would seem to have a degree of potency. The celebrated fashion photographer Guy Bourdin compulsively produced beautiful but deathly images of women—captivating, but on some levels appalling. Interestingly, his photographs continue to influence fashion photographers today, suggesting that his aesthetic cannot be dismissed as a 1970s trend: it is a reiteration of beauty and death that continues to resonate. Likewise, the nihilistic imagery prevalent in fashion photography of the 1990s spoke of hopelessness and dereliction, a direct counteraction to the superficial energy and optimism of the 1980s.

It would be remiss to consider contemporary fashion imagery without at least touching upon the increasing prevalence of the self as a fashion image. Whereas in the past, images were restricted to those of professional models, photographed by professionals working in the industry, technological developments in recent years have facilitated the practice of self-representation. Since the 1970s, theorists such as Christopher Lasch (1976) have argued that the twentieth century has given rise to a new narcissistic personality type, obsessed with eternal youth. However, technological phenomenon such as the Internet have allowed this trait to develop further.

Although space prohibits anything other than a brief discussion of social networking websites, it is a highly pertinent to an overall discussion of fashion in contemporary culture. In particular, the popularity of sites such as Facebook indicates a widespread, and global, engagement with the concept of posting information about oneself in a public domain. As the updates are provided by the users themselves, the potential for self-exposure is limitless, and for many users, this will be in the form of photographs. One way of defining narcissism is that "one has only to be, to be loved" (Whitford, 2003, p. 31), and the compulsive posting of images of oneself that Facebook facilitates might well be seen as a manifestation of a desperate need just to be acknowledged. Although in theory, Facebook is a forum for the revelations of exciting or interesting ideas and images, in practice the content most users post is decidedly banal: in other words, little more than a reiteration of "I am here". It seems that it is no longer sufficient to secure the attention of those whom you personally know, it is necessary to alert the whole world to one's existence.

The most obvious explanation for this arises from the study of celebrity culture. As a media-consuming society, we have become so familiar with knowing the minutiae of the lives of people we have never met, this has set a standard for how we subsequently present ourselves to the world. As Kelli Fuery writes:

> New media's role in all of this has been to provide a mechanism whereby the individual can self-celebritize; by forming celebrity versions of themselves on the net, in blogs, in digital versions.
>
> (2009, p. 140)

For example, a fashion-conscious individual would be very careful about which images they posted of themselves, for fear of being seen wearing the same outfit twice. Moreover, Fuery argues that it is not celebrity *per se* that is fetishized in contemporary society. Rather, it is the notion of celebrity status that is revered. Whereas once celebrities were idealized, digital media has allowed ordinary individuals to do this to themselves, and perhaps most curiously, for themselves. For a further exploration of these themes, the reader is referred to chapters by Richard Morgan-Jones on celebrities and Philip Boxer on the Internet in this volume.

It becomes evident that fashion images—whether those generated by the media industry, or those generated by ordinary people—reveal much about the needs and desires of individuals in contemporary society. However, in the next section, I will show that the language used by the fashion industry similarly mediates the individual's relationship with and understanding of fashion.

Fashion writing: the superego and the id

In Roland Barthes' seminal analysis of fashion writing *The Fashion System* (1990), he identified specific features that make fashion writing unlike other forms of journalism. Of relevance here is his finding that the use of the imperative was a linguistic device used with both frequency and urgency in fashion magazines. Likewise, in my own analysis of fashion writing in UK *Vogue*, I found that fashion editors make use of the imperative to instruct readers on what must be bought and how it must be worn (König, 2006). They are in the know, that is, they have knowledge. Specifically, they have knowledge of the "right" way of being a woman; they have a degree of access to the world of celebrities, making them powerful semi-fictional characters in the drama of self-presentation.

Elsewhere, I have argued that the generalizations and hyperbole that dominate fashion writing create a curiously shrill domain in which much is broadcast, at great volume, but with a somewhat hollow authority (König, 2006). Fashion writing demands rights (to occupy space, to be heard, to be taken seriously in cultural life), but apparently has no responsibilities (to reflect reality, to take ethical work practices or environmental issues seriously). Thus, fashion writing might be conceived of as both superego and id: it asserts authority whilst simultaneously taking no responsibility for its actions or impact on the world.

However, in recent years, the collective authority of fashion editors has been challenged by expert amateurs operating on the Internet.

In many ways, this can be regarded as a healthy and long-overdue challenge to the stifling authority of the traditional fashion hierarchy. Amateur enthusiasts are less restricted by the need to secure advertising revenue, so in theory at least, there is potential for more honest discussion and celebration of fashion. An interesting offshoot of fashion blogs are those sites that seek the advice of other readers on specific outfits. So, an individual will upload a photograph of the proposed outfit and seek feedback from fellow blog-readers on whether or not it "works". This highlights the ongoing need for approval (but most of the posters on such websites are in their teens or twenties), but rather than seeking that approval from an authority figure, they turn to their peer group for feedback.

Conclusions

Space prevents a more detailed analysis than has been offered here, and it is acknowledged that some of the issues touched upon warrant far closer interrogation. However, the intention has been to identify the multifarious ways in which psychodynamic thought can be utilized in order to make sense of fashion, prompting, perhaps, rather different questions to those that have already been asked by fashion theorists.

In theory, fashion presents the individual with the opportunity to explore and present a unique story, yet in practice often ends in disappointment as attempts at individuality are often thwarted by conflicted internal voices, manifested through the authority ascribed to the fashion industry. The fashion system infantilizes, but without providing adequate tools with which the individual can subsequently develop and grow. "Fashion is a pleasure", we are told, yet often it becomes a repository for self-doubt, where the individual compulsively presents her best face to the world and asks for approval.

But why has fashion become such a dominant vehicle for this fractious display of identity uncertainty? A cursory survey of the landscape of popular culture tells us that we are inundated with information on self-help, self-knowledge, and self-expression, and yet we still don't know who we want to be, let alone who we actually are. We know we should be able to articulate our needs and desires, but we can't, so they manifest in rituals of identity exploration in the hope that one of the looks will "fit". But until the "work" of the inner self is resolved, contentment with the outer, visible self is highly unlikely. So the quest for external resolution is an ongoing process, just as inner work is for those who engage in the psychotherapeutic process. Perhaps this external work can indeed provide insights into the identity of the individual, but unless the individual makes use of their own dressing-up box (as opposed to one which has been pre-edited), it is unlikely to end in satisfaction.

Alternatively, it may be that the magic of fashion is its defiance of clear resolution. Forever, it articulates the ambiguities of human identity and, as an historically female form, resists the logic of phallocentric psychoanalytic theory. Juliet Mitchell writes: "If language is phallocentric, what is a woman patient doing when she is speaking? What is a woman analyst doing when she is listening and speaking back?" (1984, p. 288). Perhaps, in using fashion, women (and men) are dodging the bullets of psychoanalytic theory altogether, preferring instead to take refuge—and indeed, delight—in the mute power of ambiguity.

References

Arnold, R. (2001). *Fashion, Desire and Anxiety*. London: I. B. Tauris.
Barthes, R. (1977). *Image Music Text*. London: Fontana.
Barthes, R. (1984). *Camera Lucida*. London: Flamingo.
Barthes, R. (1990). *The Fashion System*. London: University of California Press.
Bate, D. (2004). *Photography and Surrealism*. London: I. B. Tauris.
Boultwood, A. & Jerrard, R. (2000). Ambivalence, and its relation to fashion and the body. *Fashion Theory, 4(3)*: 301–322.
Braham, P. (1997). Fashion: unpacking a cultural production. In: P. du Gay (Ed.), *Production of Culture/Cultures of Production*. London: Sage.
De Beauvoir, S. (1997). *The Second Sex*. London: Vintage.
Entwistle, J. (2000). *The Fashioned Body*. Cambridge: Polity.
Ettinger, B. (2006). Fascinance and the girl-to-m/Other matrixial feminine difference. In: G. Pollock (Ed.), *Psychoanalysis and the Image*. Oxford: Blackwell.
Evans, C. (2003). *Fashion at the Edge: Spectacle, Modernity and Deathliness*. London: Yale University Press.
Evans, C. & Thornton, M. (1989). *Women and Fashion*. London: Quartet.
Faludi, S. (1992). *Backlash: The Undeclared War Against Women*. London: Chatto.
Featherstone, M. (1991). The body in consumer culture. In: M. Featherstone, M. Hepworth & B. S. Turner (Eds.), *The Body: Social Process and Cultural Theory*. London: Sage.

Flugel, J. C. (1930). *The Psychology of Clothes*. London: Hogarth.
Fuery, K. (2009). *New Media: Culture and Image*. Basingstoke: Palgrave Macmillan.
Fuss, D. (1994). Fashion and the homospectatorial look. In: S. Benstock & S. Ferriss (Eds.), *On Fashion*. New Jersey: Rutgers.
Grove-White, A. (2001). No rules, only choices?: repositioning the self within the fashion system in relation to expertise and meaning: a case study of colour and image consultancy. *Journal of Material Culture, 6(2)*: 193–211.
Irigaray, L. (1991). The bodily encounter with the mother. In: M. Whitford (Ed.), *The Irigaray Reader*. Oxford: Blackwell.
Jobling, P. (1999). *Fashion Spreads: Word and Image in Fashion Photography since 1980*. Oxford: Berg.
Jung, C. G. (2008). *The Archetypes and the Collective Unconscious*. London: Routledge.
König, A. (2004). Sex and the City: a fashion editor's dream? In: K. Akass & J. McCabe (Eds.), *Reading Sex and the City*. London: I. B. Tauris.
König, A. (2006). Glossy words: an analysis of fashion writing in British Vogue. *Fashion Theory, 10(1/2)*: 205–224.
Lacan, J. (1964). *The Four Fundamental Concepts of Psycho-Analysis*. New York: Norton.
Lasch, C. (1976). *The Culture of Narcissism: American Life in an Age of Diminishing Expectations*. New York: Norton.
Mendes, V. & de la Haye, A. (1999). *Twentieth Century Fashion*. London: Thames and Hudson.
Mitchell, J. (1984). *Women: The Longest Revolution*. London: Virago.
Parker, R. & Pollock, G. (1981). *Old Mistresses: Women, Art and Ideology*. London: Pandora.
Riviere, J. (1991). *The Inner World and Joan Riviere: Collected Papers 1920–1958*. London: Karnac Books.
Walters, N. (2010). *Living Dolls*. London: Virago.
Welters, L. & Lillethun, A. (Eds.) (2007). *The Fashion Reader*. Oxford: Berg.
Whitford, M. (2003). Irigaray and the culture of narcissism. *Theory, Culture and Society, 20(3)*: 27–41.
Wilson, E. (1992). Fashion and the postmodern body. In: J. Ash & E. Wilson (Eds.), *Chic Thrills: A Fashion Reader*. London: Pandora.
Wilson, E. (2003). *Adorned in Dreams: Fashion and Modernity*. London: Virago.

PART III

PSYCHOANALYTIC REFLECTIONS ON THE WORLD OF INTERCONNECTIVITY

CHAPTER SEVEN

The Twitter Revolution: how the internet has changed us

Philip Boxer

> Psychoanalysis always likes to be able to eliminate all factors that are environmental, except in so far as the environment can be thought of in terms of projective mechanisms. But in examining usage there is no escape: the analyst must take into account the nature of the object, not as a projection, but as a thing in itself.
>
> —Winnicott, 1969, pp. 711–716

Preface

This chapter explores what psychoanalytic thinking can add to our current understanding of the ubiquitous "Twitter" phenomenon, and considers how it might be changing our object relations and our societal relatedness. The chapter examines several interconnected aspects of the information revolution, including the Internet's impact on individuals, markets, and society. It ends by considering how the "Twitter Revolution" might be changing the relationship between the individual and the realm of the political.

Introduction

The Twitter Revolution reflects a change in our online experience. This chapter considers the impact of this online experience on our relationship to an increasingly dynamic environment, and how this impact may be changing us, whether as individual, enterprise, or psychotherapist. I am an engineer who came late to psychoanalysis. I have spent most of my life working in enterprises that face structural challenges to their competitive identity. As consultant, I worked on these questions of strategy arising from these structural challenges, which always involved questioning the basis of the relationship between the enterprise and the way it understood its environment.

The quote above from Winnicott identifies the difficulty those with an analytic background have when consulting to enterprises competing in these dynamic environments. This difficulty arises because of the need to work with the relationship between objects both as part of the environment and also as psychic phenomena (Winnicott, 1969). In effect, psychotherapists are comfortable with working across the psychic boundary between conscious ("surface") and unconscious phenomena ("below the surface"). But their way of thinking has difficulty working across the boundary created by the way their clients define the environment itself. This difficulty is not unique to psychotherapists. Enterprises also have difficulty including the dynamic impact of changes in the way their environment is organized.

The chapter starts by considering the impact of the Twitter Revolution in terms of our current online experience. It then draws parallels with Gutenberg's Printing Revolution spanning the fifteenth and sixteenth centuries, to consider how the current Twitter Revolution might be affecting us. It explores how a return to Freud can help us understand what is happening, particularly with respect to the three forms of identification he described in group behaviour (Freud, 1921c). These distinguished between a direct emotional tie to another (for example, falling in love), the taking up of a way of being (for example, emulating an admired approach to life), and the taking up of some aspect of another's relationship to themselves (for example, by following a fashion). In these terms, the online experience is seen as changing the balance between these three aspects of who we take ourselves to be. The chapter concludes by drawing out some of the implications of this change for the nature of work and for politics.

The Twitter Revolution: something more than an information revolution

The Twitter Revolution is not just another way of accessing information that could ultimately be found in books. It is a revolution in the way we interact with each other. Reading a book is something individuals do alone. But despite appearances, and unlike reading a book, the online experience is an interactive experience in which it is not possible to be wholly private. Twittering takes this interactivity to an extreme. A Twitter is a 140-character text message broadcast by an individual to the world. It goes to the person's social network, but also to whomever else might be interested. It is a sentence or a headline that captures something of the moment for the individual sending it, and it invites interaction. At the end of the first decade of the twenty-first century, there are fifty million of these being sent each day (Twitter blog, 2010).

Looking more widely at the online experience, there are more than twenty-four million Internet searches per day (The Nielsen Company, 2010), more than sixty million twitterers in the USA (Quantcast, 2010), and more than five hundred million Facebook users worldwide (Facebook, 2010). The majority of online users connect daily, with the use of the technology much higher in the rapid growth markets of emerging economies than in the mature economies. Mobile online users accelerate this use in all of these markets, with blogging and the use of social networks increasing the most in the rapid growth markets (Digital Life, 2010). In the midst of all this, online use by children shows the extent of the move away from reading books. A study by the Kaiser Family Foundation found that children in the US between the ages of eight and eighteen were using their phones, computers, televisions, and video-game systems for more than fifty hours each week (Barovick, Fitzpatrick et al., 2010). Reading, something done without interacting with others, was the only thing they were doing less.

With all this interaction comes a tension between personal privacy and the individual's wish to be found by others, apparent in the recent concerns over the way the Facebook platform used personal data (*The Economist*, 2010). But the continuing growth in online use suggests that managing this tension between privacy and the wish to be found by others cannot be without benefits. From the perspective of businesses, a recent McKinsey report on the networked enterprise found that highly networked organizations were fifty per cent more likely to have both market share gains and higher profit margins against their less networked competitors (Bughin & Chui, 2010). The growth in online use by individuals suggests that something similar is happening for them too. Taken overall, this explosion in online social connectivity indicates that something more than an information revolution is taking place (Drucker, 1999).

A social network is something more than the network itself

The explosion in online connectivity cannot be explained by the direct use of the links themselves, even though these are, of course, valuable. Thus, whether or not we approve of the particular form the online experience takes, the overall scale and scope of its impact is unprecedented. If we consider its effects on commerce, we see it leading to changes both in the economics of the enterprise, for example through the uses of mass collaboration (Tapscott & Williams, 2006), and in the structure of industries themselves, for example in the way they reflect changes in the way we use print, music, and pictures (Tapscott & Williams, 2010). And the social networks emerging from this online connectivity are of course valuable to businesses wishing to target potential customers. The value of such targeted advertising forms the very foundations of Google's success (Levy, 2009).

It may be the intention of the Google, Facebook, or Twitter platforms to support the emergence of social networks, but the networks that do emerge form not just around people, but around specific issues too. Examples of specific issues giving rise to networks include the blog in China commenting on a Japan-China incident involving a fishing boat (Link, 2010), the role of Twitter in the Iranian protests following their elections (Grossman, 2009), or twitters in Thailand following the protests in Bangkok (Sambandaraksa, 2010). The issues may not even be real, as in the networks forming around multiplayer online role-playing games such as the World of Warcraft (Wikipedia, 2010a), or around virtual worlds such as Second Life (Wikipedia, 2010c).

These social networks exist at all scales of social activity. Within the context of the single enterprise, such networks have been studied before in the guise of "sentient" groups (Miller & Rice, 1967). A sentient group is a group with which human beings identify that is distinct from task groups, and in which what is being shared is a particular way of sensing and responding to the world. The health of an enterprise depends on understanding how sentient groups and task systems interact.

At local civic and national scales, Theodore Roosevelt identified "fellow-feeling" between citizens as an equally important factor in producing a healthy political and social life, even though the technologies then available for their realization as social networks took a very different form (Roosevelt, 1900). More recently, this fellow-feeling was mobilized successfully by Barack Obama in the US presidential election (Wagner, 2008). Currently, the Tea Party movement in the US (Montopoli, 2010) is a social network that embodies such fellow-feeling far more than representing a coherent policy response to the current challenges facing US society (Ungar, 2010). As such, it is nevertheless credited with mobilizing the landslide movement against the Democrats in the US mid-term elections (Thompson, 2010).

Social networks may not always emerge for reasons that everyone would approve of, or even that other individuals would approve of, as in the cases where partners track the interests of their spouses (Leake, 2010). For example, the Google chiefs found themselves in court for not being fast enough in suppressing a YouTube video of bullying (Pisa, 2010), while the Chinese censors suppressed details of unrest in Xinjiang inconsistent with Chinese sensibilities for social harmony (*The Telegraph*, 2009). WikiLeaks recently provided us controversially with insights into the conduct of the war in Afghanistan (O'Loughlin, Witmer, et al., 2010). And the responses to their more recent release of documents on the conduct of US foreign relations have spawned yet further networks, including "hactivists" intent on taking action against those who disapproved (Watkins & Bradshaw, 2010), provoking yet further responses from Facebook and Twitter (Bradshaw, 2010).

Whatever the reason for their emergence, however, these social networks create affective networks based on fellow-feelings glimpsed along a kaleidoscope of different dimensions. These networks are based on some shared feeling, but they also provide something more than a feeling, enabling the person to celebrate something of themselves in the networking process (Dean, 2010): this something reflected by the network is something of the individual's experience of themselves. See also Chapter Six on the psychodynamics of fashion by Anna König in this volume.

We are all potential markets now

This focus on the subjective experience of the customer makes potential markets of each one of us. And it demands "agile" enterprises (Goldman,

Nagel, et al., 1995) that can organize themselves around the quality of the customer's experience (Prahalad & Ramaswamy, 2003). Instead of "pushing" products and services, these enterprises must be shaped by the "pull" of their customers (Hagel III, Seely Brown, et al., 2010). Thus looked at from the perspective of the enterprise, the Internet has changed the economics of distribution, enabling the enterprise to target markets containing very small numbers of customers (Anderson, 2006). For example, iTunes enables its users to buy only those individual tracks that appeal to their personal tastes. The effect of this is that the enterprise need not compete just on the basis of the products and solutions it supplies to markets, but on the basis of the support it can provide to the subjective experience of the customer (Zuboff & Maxmin, 2002). For example, the traveller who wants to use a travel service need only be offered services that fit with the way he or she likes to travel. In this environment, markets are "co-produced" by the relationship between the enterprise and its customers (Prahalad & Ramaswamy, 2004), enabling what the traveller wants to shape the travel experience he or she gets. Of course, enterprises have been doing such things for industrial customers for a long time. What is new is the ability to do it for the individual.

"Pull" markets may still be in the early stages of becoming viable. An example is the case of Microsoft providing personal health-care records in the US (Charette, 2010). Or it may not be the market itself that is what is of value, as in the case of the way voting was organized in "Dancing with the Stars" (Roach, 2010), or the way mobile phones are given away for "free" (Evans, Hagiu, et al., 2006). Indeed, the "market" may not even be one that we would recognize as such, as in the case of the Al Qaeda market for "open source jihad", aimed at disrupting the economics of US systems (Robb, 2010). But the direction is one of innovation at the edge of the enterprise where it meets its customers, leading the enterprise ultimately to the particular demands of the individual customer (Hagel III & Seely Brown, 2005).

And for all that is written about the effects of this focus on the individual customer, it is true that most suppliers still adhere to the "push" model when dealing with individuals—they do what they do, and the rest is up to us to sort out, including all those hours wrestling with the computerized menus of call centres! But the research nevertheless shows that over the last forty years, while large enterprises have become more efficient, their returns have dropped by seventy-five per cent in the face of intensifying competition, while their dependence on physical assets to generate profits has dropped forty per cent (Hagel III, Seely Brown, et al., 2010). And now we find ourselves in the midst of a jobless recovery from the Great Recession of the last few years. The recovery is jobless because so much more can be done using information technology, so that the only recourse is to innovate if we are to generate growth in employment (Peck, 2010).

So the change may not be rapid, but it is inexorable. It leads the enterprise in but one direction, towards every affective network being a potential market, at the limit creating potential markets of each one of us.

What are the consequences for us as individuals?

At the levels of both employment and the state, the contract with the individual will no longer support a through-life dependency. Rather, we must compete with each other in seizing what opportunities we can find in a world that appears to have become all markets, in which the most that can be expected from the state is that the individual should be provided with opportunities (Bobbitt, 2002). What are the consequences for us individually if we are each to become potential markets for ourselves and each other? To eBay, it may mean that we are now all potential sources of revenue for each other. But revenue for what? Are we to be markets despite ourselves (Harvey, 2005), subject to subconscious manipulation in a throwback to our worst fears in the 1950s (Packard, 1957)? Or are we newly liberated in this twittering age, enabled by the new technologies to know what we want in ways that were previously unthought-of (Baumann, 2009)? Our subjective experience is one of encountering an increasingly fragmented plethora of sources on what is right, what is true, and what is necessary for us. How are we to know where to turn in order to find what we want, whether we are looking for an education, a spouse, a job, or even just a meal? What can be considered authoritative in a world where every icon can be proved to have feet of clay (Boxer, 1994)? The individual faces risks all around them as they are faced with having to make choices for themselves, giving rise to new communities of interest based on shared anxieties (Beck, 1992).

A psychoanalytic perspective provides us with useful insights into our experience of these risks. The very technology through which we pursue our truths renders truth itself questionable. To address this, we need to consider both sides of it: what is happening to the technology, and what is happening to the way we can establish truths for ourselves within it. And to do that, it is helpful to look back to a time when all this happened before, although on a different scale.

The Printing Revolution: technology's impact on the social

The invention of the printing press had an impact on society that is comparable to the impact of the information revolution. Gutenberg assembled the first mechanical printing presses in 1440. Within a few decades, printing had spread across Europe. By 1500, more than twenty million volumes had been printed, and during the course of the sixteenth century, this rose to over two hundred million. At the present time, Google estimates that there are about one hundred and thirty million printed and bound unique books. It seems appropriate to quote from Wikipedia (Wikipedia, 2010b):

> The ready availability and affordability of the printed word to the general public boosted the democratization of knowledge and laid the material basis for the modern knowledge-based economy. In Renaissance Europe, the arrival of mechanical movable type printing introduced the era of mass communication which permanently altered the structure of society: the relatively unrestricted circulation of information and (revolutionary) ideas transcended borders, captured the masses in the Reformation and threatened the power of political and religious authorities; the sharp increase in literacy broke the monopoly of the literate elite on education and learning and bolstered the emerging middle class.

Two different kinds of change were happening. The first of these was a change in the "material basis" of what could be read, that is the technology used for reading changed, so that what previously had only been accessible in hand-written form became widely available in printed form. Just as with the impact of information technology, however, this brought a second kind of change in the people who were writing, reading, and publishing. At the beginning of the sixteenth century, these people were mainly members of the clergy, but by the middle of the sixteenth century, the balance was shifting towards the students of the humanities, extending to the "natural philosophy" of science in the seventeenth century (Burke, 2000). This change in who could be well read began to become apparent inside a period of sixty years, comparable to the length of time the information revolution has been with us.

The first impact was on who could be well read

To understand the impact of the change in the "material basis", we need to consider the nature of the institutions using the texts. The previously hand-written and hand-printed texts were used primarily by members of the clergy. From the Middle Ages, the Universities within which they worked as teachers were enterprises that had establishing strategies of monopolization of knowledge and exclusion of those not qualified, in the same way as the professions of law and medicine. But the Universities were still embedded within the much older institution of the Catholic Church.

The trial of Galileo as a heretic made it evident where the power lay in this world. Galileo was forced in 1633 to recant his reasoning that the Sun was at the centre of the Universe, supporting the work of Copernicus with his observations of the movement of heavenly bodies. The Church required this of him because it was against its teaching that the Earth was at the centre of the Universe. Galileo had been disrupting the received wisdom, and the Establishment was seeking to defend itself then, just as the censors do now.

The heretics were a different kind of community. They were held together by their discussion of the ideas to be found in books and letters, and not by their allegiance to a higher authority. They formed affective networks cutting across the communities working under the aegis of the Universities. The hundred-fold increase in the rate of production of printed books made new ideas accessible to a greatly enlarged community of writers and readers that was increasingly outside the traditional knowledge communities. The printing technology thus changed the balance between the Universities and the heretic communities, creating a material basis on which it was much easier to form new affective networks of shared interest. True, these networks were on nothing like the scale of today's networks, but they laid the foundations for the emergence of science in the seventeenth century and the Enlightenment in the eighteenth century, in which the locus of innovation moved decidedly beyond the Universities (Burke, 2000). In the same way, the current rapid increase in the accessibility of online textual material brought about by the information revolution has changed the balance in who can know what.

The second impact was on what was considered authoritative

This change in the balance of who could know what was enabled by the printing revolution, but it was the social revolution that began to emerge during the course of the sixteenth century that is the equivalent of today's Twitter Revolution. This revolution was in the basis of what could be said to be true, and two aspects to this social revolution appear relevant.

The first aspect involved the emergence of the Protestant movement. Luther argued for the importance of reading the texts themselves, and not depending on the clergy's reading of the texts passed on by the clergy's word of mouth. A key argument made by the Church against Luther was that his approach would lead to religious anarchy. Luther was able to counter this by establishing a social movement through communicating directly with the people in their own language on an unprecedented scale. To do so, he relied on being able to mass-produce pamphlets, over three thousand being written by him during his lifetime, creating circulations of hundreds of thousands. The result was a change in the basis of what was authoritative. This moved from being based on the spoken word of those in positions authorized by the Church, to being based on the reading of the texts themselves by men of letters and members of academies. It wasn't until the Enlightenment in the eighteenth century that this shift in the basis of authority began to be taken up by the Universities themselves (Burke, 2000).

Luther's criticism was of the basis on which religious truths were authorized by the Church. Rather than being based on the spoken word of the clergy, it should come directly from a reading of the texts themselves. His argument was nevertheless that religious truths could be established on this basis with certainty. The truth was there in the texts to be read.

The second aspect can therefore be identified with Erasmus's difference with Luther. Erasmus argued that no-one could claim to have found the true meaning of a text, so that it was therefore most important to treat any claim over the truth with scepticism. Both modern scientific method and Biblical criticism can be traced back to this second kind of shift, in which direct consideration is given to the effects of the text on the reader (Popkin, 1979). With scepticism, it was not so much one form of authority (the received truth of the Church) being replaced by another form (truth emerging from a reading of the texts themselves). Rather, it was the nature of what authorized the truth itself that was called into question. From today's perspective on the Enlightenment, scepticism remains an attitude of mind to be applied to the thinking process itself, rather than becoming a movement *per se* (Popkin, 1979).

We can observe both aspects of what can be said to be true in the current controversies surrounding global warming and its probable causes. The reader is referred to the chapter in this volume by Paul Hoggett on this very subject. If we take the establishment view to be that man-made greenhouse gases are the primary cause of global warming (*New York Times*, 2010), then the Lutheran equivalent would be to argue that this view is a grand conspiracy serving (for example) the interests of scientists (Dimiero, 2010), which can be overturned by examining the evidence itself. The Erasmian equivalent would be to argue that to make man-made greenhouse gases the primary cause is too simple an explanation for something much more complex that we do not yet fully understand (United States Environmental Protection Agency, 2010). It is this second aspect that best captures the attitude of inquiring from which affective networks emerge.

The impact depended on the relationship to the text

Both aspects of change depended on the new relationship to the text made possible by the revolution. In contrast, the earlier authority of the Catholic Church rested on the effectiveness of the words spoken by the clergy. The concept of the "speech act" describes how the act of speaking made things happen in the world through the effects it produced on the listener (Austin, 1962). Thus the efficacy of a statement such as "I pronounce you man and wife" depended very much on the circumstances surrounding its enunciation. Prior to being able to read the Bible for themselves, people depended on the speech acts of clergy for their understanding of what faith meant to them. The Church provided the circumstances in which these speech acts could produce their effects.

The new relationship to the text depended on individuals being able to read for themselves. The concept of the "script act" is based on reading rather than listening. It assumes not only that no work is ever read as a whole, but also that any given text is at best a partial representation of a literary work. A literary work therefore becomes an assemblage of read fragments that come together in a way that is particular to the reader (Shillingsburg, 2006). Script acts are the particular way in which the individual reads, and the circumstances surrounding the way script acts come together are the circumstances in which the reader reads. In these terms, reading a literary work in such a way as to grasp its author's meaning is at best a special case, and perhaps even a fantasy entertained only by the author.

The impact of Gutenberg was therefore to make the education of the reader the determining factor in how truths were located, rather than the circumstances surrounding the speaker. The Enlightenment saw newly authorized readings emerge that were equal to the authority of the Catholic Church's spoken truths, including those truths authorized by the state itself (Burke, 2000). And the institutions of education eventually expanded to provide individuals with the education they needed to read in this way, even today, when these authorized readings have become established truths.

The early fears for the information revolution in the 1960s were that it would further consolidate the authority of these truths, heralding an age of centralization and standardization based on the ability of the technology to process large quantities of data. In fact, the reverse happened, and it became increasingly apparent that the meaning of information depended on the particular social circumstances in which it was both created and subsequently used (Brown & Duguid, 2002).

The Twitter Revolution takes this further by enabling individuals to replace the "whole" texts of authors with the particular assemblages of text fragments that emerge in response to their online searching. In this environment, the blog serves as a representation of the assemblages that emerge as a result, creating the modern equivalent of the pamphlet. And the individual's affective networks assume a new importance, since it is they that inform which text fragments are considered. So how does the individual create truths in this environment? From where do truths emerge? The difference between the perspectives of the Catholic Church, Luther, and Erasmus provide us with a way of thinking about what happens at the level of the individual.

Identifying truths: recognizing what we want

The information revolution captures something of the technological impact which parallels that of the printing revolution. But the Twitter Revolution captures more of its social impact. The fragmented nature of the interactions reflected by twittering makes explicit the challenge the individual faces both in choosing what to read, and assembling what they do read into meaningful wholes. A glimpse of this could be seen in one person's assemblage of online reports detailing chaos and deaths in Tunisia (Carvin, 2011). It was not that the use of these media were themselves a cause of events, their part at best allowing individuals to catch glimpses of others' experiences (Allnutt, 2011). But following the Twitter feeds for #Egypt nevertheless altered what was present for the individual affected in a way that the authorities saw fit to suppress (Kravets, 2011). The multiple affective networks intersecting in the individual illuminates the challenge the individual faces. What does he or she make of so many disparate sources? Using the examples of Tunisia and Egypt, these sources clearly reflect affective networks across which individuals are making meaning, but how are we to understand the ways these meanings are being made?

The individual in the midst of the printing revolution could rely on the authoritative voices of the Church, or learn to read. And in learning to read, he or she could assume with Luther that truths were to be found in the texts, or, like Erasmus, assume that the truths he or she read were in some way shaped by his or her own interest. The Twitter Revolution presents the individual with these same choices today in the way he or she identifies truths. A psychoanalytic perspective expresses these choices in terms of how the individual creates and sustains their own identity through the way he or she identifies truths. The revolutions in Tunisia and Egypt have shown us that real consequences can follow from being able to share such truths across affective networks in ways unmediated by the state's authorized truths.

In his work on group psychology (Freud, 1921c), Freud distinguishes between identifying with someone, in the sense of wanting to be them themselves ("I want to be you"); and identifying with someone in the sense of wanting to have that person's way of organizing the way they are ("I want to learn how to be like you"). Here, we have the difference between identifying directly with the speaker, and learning to read like the other reads. The first of these two forms of identification are distinguished by the primary processes associated with establishing a "perceptual identity" corresponding to the individual's relations to pleasure and pain; and the second by the secondary processes associated with establishing a "thought identity" through which the individual's relationships to the world are organized (Freud, 1900a).

We see this distinction in Bion's work, between the manifestation of basic assumptions below the surface of the individual's working relationships, and the working relationships themselves, organized by a shared sense of purpose and outcome (Armstrong, 2005c). The primary processes and their manifestation as basic assumptions are always there, the issue being the extent to which they are in support of or in conflict with the secondary processes appearing as ideals shared in working together (French & Simpson, 2010). Together, however, primary processes subordinated to secondary processes form the warp and weft of any social endeavour in which there is shared purpose and outcome, constituting for the individual an "organization-in-the-mind" that reflects in some way the emotional experience of the endeavour itself (Armstrong, 2005a).

We can recognize in Luther's objections to the institution of the Catholic Church a rejection of the privileging of the voices of its clergy, and the particular forms of identification this supported. The Printing Revolution made it possible not only for new networks to be formed on a scale that could challenge the Church's own following, but also created the conditions in which different institutional forms could be established on the basis of a direct reading of the text. The same thing happened with the information revolution, enabling each one of us to read what had been previously hidden from us by the interests of scientists, corporations, and states. Except that this time the variety of institutional voices being put in question is much larger, and, as we saw earlier with WikiLeaks, what is true is not always immediately apparent. So what happens in the spaces between and beyond those institutional voices? How does the Erasmian perspective of the sceptics emerge?

It's a matter of attitude

The Twitter Revolution is enabling the emergence of affective networks, challenging the basis of the authority of scientists, corporations, and states (as, for example, in the case of global warming). To understand what happens between and beyond these institutional voices, we need to consider the process by which affective networks emerge, on what basis they form, and under what circumstances they might be said to be a good thing.

When the way an individual has learnt to be fails, they experience ambivalence about what is true which places their secondary processes at risk (Beck, 1994). They no longer know for sure what is true, exposing themselves to traumatic anxiety in which their very sense of themselves is at risk (Freud, 1926d). A psychic retreat is a particular type of defensive organization by means of which a person hopes to avoid such intolerable anxiety, for example taking the inter-personal form of a business organization, a religious sect, or a Mafia-like gang (Steiner, 1993). We have seen examples of this in fundamentalist networks, for example relating to *jihad* (Robb, 2010), in which the individual surrenders their identity to a larger system that absolves them of the question(ing) of their personal identity (Hopper, 2003). The opposite extreme is also possible, in which the individual withdraws from any inter-personal form of working, cutting themselves off from any interaction with others who might threaten them (Armstrong, 2005b). An example of this would be in the way avatars can be used in multiplayer online role-playing games (Wikipedia, 2010a), in which whatever happens, it happens to the individual's avatar and not to him or her!

If the basis of an affective network is the attitude that it enables the individual to share with others, then there is a quality of mindlessness in these two extreme responses, fitting with the loss of "thought identity". But if the basis of the extremes is a defence against traumatic anxiety, then there is a wide range of possible attitudes in between these two extremes in which new forms of truth can be established. It is this third possibility that constitutes the third form of identification distinguished by Freud. This is an identification formed not by identifying with someone, but rather with a situation that engenders a particular affective relation to themselves. The story used by Freud to distinguish this third form is as follows:

> Supposing, for instance, that one of the girls in a boarding school has had a letter from someone with whom she is secretly in love which arouses her jealousy, and that she reacts to with a fit of hysterics; then some of her friends who know about it will catch the fit, as we say, by mental infection. The mechanism is that of identification based upon the possibility or desire of putting oneself in the same situation.
>
> (Freud, 1921c, p. 107)

This third form of identification can describe, for example, the experience of joining football crowds or political movements. It also describes the basis for the affective networks so easily formed online, falling between the two extremes supporting psychic retreat.

To understand this third form of identification, the use of the word "desire" in the quote above needs to be examined more closely. Whether or not the affective networks formed by this third identification are a "good thing" depends on understanding it as the link to the Erasmian perspective on truth, in which truth is in some way shaped by the individual's own interest.

Attitude toward the Real

Lacan distinguished Freud's first two forms of identification as imaginary and symbolic identifications (Lacan, 1988). By "imaginary" identification, Lacan meant identification in terms of the reality within which the individual encountered an image of himself or herself. And by "symbolic" identification, he meant an identification mediated by the effects of language: the individual could say something of who s/he was, while always experiencing himself or herself as being something more than that. The single trait of which Freud spoke became the "unary signifier" in Lacan, which represented for the individual the symbolic identification that was the organization of that individual's way of being (Lacan, 1961).

As with Freud, taking up this organization involved subordinating primary process to a particular way of being, resulting in a loss arising from the repression of primary process involved. But understanding this as a symbolic identification, in which an organization of signifiers stood in the place of primary process, also enabled Lacan to speak of what was left out by that organization. What was left out was what could not be said or what was in some other way untranslatable in the individual's experience. This was the lack that gave rise to desire, forming the basis of the third identification. Desire was that which remained left out, constituted by the lack which was structural to the symbolic identification. For Lacan, the third identification was a Real identification. Desire reflected what the individual wanted, or rather found wanting, in their current way of being. This is the way the environment shows itself to the individual, showing what goes beyond the individual's own psychic boundary.

The "Real" was for Lacan that which could not be articulated within the symbolic, so that in pursuing their desire in this sense, the individual was pursuing something of what they lacked in their current way of being. In a Real identification, the individual exhibited an attitude toward the Real in the way they formed affective networks in pursuit of their desires.

Recognizing a beyond

Lacan draws together the three identifications in terms of three kinds of moment, representing the different ways in which the individual is able to know what s/he wants (Lacan, 1945). The first moment involves immediately recognizing what is wanted, literally seeing it. Much of online shopping tries to operate in this way.

The second moment only comes when it is not possible to find what is wanted in this way because it is not directly available. Instead, what is wanted has to be researched and uncovered. This second moment can take a long time as knowledge is acquired, opinions sought, and possibilities examined. Such researching may be limited by our knowledge, in which we can continue searching deeper and wider. But we may also reach the conclusion that there is no answer to what we want. It does not exist. It is also this limit to what currently can be known which creates the possibility of a beyond, the possibility of something more. The information revolution makes it much easier to discover this limit.

The third moment arises when the individual concludes that this is indeed true, and no answer will be found. Instead, the individual has to make a choice on the basis of what feels right in the situation that involves creating an answer. It is in this third moment that desire comes into play. The end of the second moment comes with recognizing what is lacking, what is wanting. The affective networks which then form around this recognition support this relationship to the "something more" that motivates them. This is the dynamic that is made so much more accessible by the Twitter Revolution. It is also the way objects in the individual's environment are experienced as independent of their own psychic phenomena.

Social consequences

The sceptics were motivated by the limits they recognized in their reading, and their social effectiveness was mobilized through the affective networks that they formed. These networks were considered heretical in their time, and the establishment response included the inquisition to which Galileo was subject. Even though many of these heretical networks were shut down or led nowhere, their legacy is nevertheless to be found in the aftershocks of the Printing Revolution that led to the Enlightenment and beyond. Today, we can draw on this history to anticipate some of the consequences of the Twitter Revolution.

The word "heretic" comes from the Greek, meaning "able to choose". The object of the inquisition was to ensure that this ability was exercised by the individual in the right way, just as scientific communities still tend to impose right ways of doing "normal" science (Kuhn, 1962). Today, the Twitter Revolution is greatly emancipating this ability to choose.

The information revolution started to change the balance between the supplier and the customer by making it easier to supply the individual customer. The Twitter Revolution represents the further impact of this revolution in the individual's ability to form networks: networks in which he or she can say what he or she wants both from the others in the network and from the suppliers to the network. As such, these networks represent a means by which individuals can defend themselves from anxiety through the alliances made possible with like-minded people sharing common attitudes. And they are also a means by which individuals can form alliances based on a shared recognition of the limits of what is currently possible for them. Such networks, like those of the sceptics, raise at least the question of what might be involved in going beyond those limits. And to the extent that individuals act on the basis of such questioning, they change things for themselves.

They change things for suppliers too. The markets formed by these affective networks present challenges to their suppliers as they exert "pull" (Hagel III, Seely Brown, et al., 2010), expecting whatever services are provided to be dynamically aligned to the individual's experience (Zuboff & Maxmin, 2002). And in order to respond in this way, suppliers have to adopt a different kind of organization of industry in which competition is subordinated to the need for collaboration within business ecosystems (Moore, 1996), in which the vanishing hand of the enterprise (Langlois, 2003) seeks to dominate the way collaborations are organized (Iansiti & Levien, 2004).

But these markets, however they are brought into existence, do not serve everyone's interests (Stiglitz, 2002). They can inflate themselves into bubbles that are dangerous for us all (Soros, 1998), and may produce unwelcome side-effects whether left free or regulated (Kay, 2003). It does not follow, therefore, that the Twitter Revolution is a good thing if the markets emerging from its networks are only to be re-colonized by the interests of their suppliers. But this is not the only possible outcome, as the history of the sceptics has shown.

American Federalism was a response to States' rights being suppressed by the colonizing interests of the British Imperium (LaCroix, 2010), leading eventually to the most successful of the market States (Bobbitt, 2002). Something similar is happening today at the level of the individual's rights subject to corporate interests. In the private sector, the shift in competitive dynamics from protecting markets to disrupting them (Christensen, Johnson, et al., 2002) speaks of a new level of dynamism and turbulence emerging in direct response to new forms of demand (Hagel III & Seely Brown, 2005). In the public sector, the same effects lead to a questioning of what constitutes public value in a way that insists on building directly from the citizen's interests (Moore, 1995). And in the not-for-profit sector, they lead to a need for generative forms of governance that are capable of continuous innovation in order to keep good works alive (Chait, Ryan, et al., 2005). Greater responsiveness to the individual demands new institutional forms, and it is these new forms that are emerging, fed by the effects of the Twitter Revolution. We do not yet know what new forms of governmentality this will require of us in the twenty-first century.

References

Allnutt, L. (2011). http://www.rferl.org/content/tunisia_can_we_please_stop_talking_about_twitter_revolutions/2277052.html
Anderson, C. (2006). *The Long Tail: Why the Future of Business Is Selling Less of More*. New York: Hyperion.
Armstrong, D. (2005a). The analytic object in organizational work. In: R. French (Ed.), *Organization in the Mind: Psychoanalysis, Group Relations, and Organizational Consultancy—Occasional Papers 1989–2003* (pp. 44–54). London: Karnac.
Armstrong, D. (2005b). "Psychic retreats": the organizational relevance of a psychoanalytic formulation. In: R. French (Ed.), *Organization in the Mind: Psychoanalysis, Group Relations and Organizational Consultancy—Occasional Papers 1989–2003* (pp. 69–89). London: Karnac.
Armstrong, D. (2005c). The work group revisited: reflections on the practice of group relations. In: R. French (Ed.), *Organization in the Mind: Psychoanalysis, Group Relations, and Organizational Consultancy—Occasional Papers 1989–2003* (pp. 139–150). London: Karnac.
Austin, J. L. (1962). *How To Do Things with Words*. Oxford: Oxford University Press.
Barovick, H., Fitzpatrick, L., Silver, A., Altman, A., Suddath, C., Fetini, A., Romero, F., Oloffson, K. & Webley, K. (2010). The couch potato generation. *The World* 1 February 2010, from http://www.time.com/time/printout/0,8816,1955582,00.html#
Baumann, P. (2009). 140 health care uses for Twitter. Retrieved 28 December 2010, from http://philbaumann.com/2009/01/16/140-health-care-uses-for-twitter/
Beck, U. (1992). *Risk Society: Towards a New Modernity*. London: Sage.
Beck, U. (1994). The reinvention of politics: towards a theory of reflexive modernization. In: U. Beck, A. Giddens & S. Lash (Eds.), *Reflexive Modernization: Politics, Tradition and Aesthetics in the Modern Social Order*. Stanford: Stanford University Press.
Bobbitt, P. (2002). *The Shield of Achilles: War, Peace and the Course of History*. London: Allen Lane.
Boxer, P. J. (1994). Intent and the future of identity. In: R. Boot, J. Lawrence & J. Morris (Eds.), *Creating New Futures: A Manager's Guide to the Unknown*. London: McGraw-Hill.
Bradshaw, T. (2010). Facebook and Twitter remove hackers. Retrieved 9 December 2010, from http://www.ft.com/cms/s/0/9eb16378-0380-11e0-9636-00144feabdc0.html#axzz17j9Jpi8u

Brown, J. S. & Duguid, P. (2002). *The Social Life of Information*. Cambridge, MA: Harvard Business School Press.

Bughin, J. & Chui, M. (2010). The rise of the networked enterprise: Web 2.0 finds its payday. *McKinsey Quarterly*, December.

Burke, P. (2000). *A Social History of Knowledge: From Gutenberg to Diderot*. Cambridge: Polity Press.

Carvin, A. (2011). Online reports detail chaos, deaths in Tunisia; add yours. *The two-way*. Retrieved 26 January 2011, from http://www.npr.org/blogs/thetwo-way/2011/01/13/132888992/tunisia-protests-social-media

Chait, R. P., Ryan, W. P. & Taylor, B. E. (2005). *Governance as Leadership: Reframing the Work of Nonprofit Boards*. Hoboken, NJ: Wiley.

Charette, R. (2010). Microsoft abandons hope of making profits on its healthvault personal health record product in US. Retrieved 22 November 2010, from http://spectrum.ieee.org/riskfactor/computing/it/microsoft-abandons-hope-of-making-profits-on-healthvault-personal-health-record-product-in-us?utm_source=feedburner

Christensen, C. M., Johnson, M. W. & Rigby, D. K. (2002). Foundations for growth: how to identify and build disruptive new businesses. *MIT Sloan Management Review*, 43(3): 22–31.

Dean, J. (2010). *Blog Theory: Feedback and Capture in the Circuits of Drive*. Cambridge: Polity Press.

Digital Life (2010). Global "Digital Life" research project reveals major changes in online behaviour. Retrieved 29 December 2010, from http://discoverdigitallife.com/global-digital-life-research-project-reveals-major-changes-in-online-behaviour/

Dimiero, B. (2010). FOXLEAKS: Fox boss ordered staff to cast doubt on climate science. Retrieved 15 December 2010, from http://mediamatters.org/blog/201012150004

Drucker, P. F. (1999). Beyond the Information Revolution. *The Atlantic*, 284(4): 47–57. Washington, October.

Evans, D. S., Hagiu, A. & Schmalensee, R. (2006). *Invisible Engines: How Software Platforms Drive Innovation and Transform Industries*. Cambridge: MIT Press.

Facebook. (2010). Facebook statistics. Retrieved 28 December, from http://www.facebook.com/press/info.php?statistics

French, R. B. & Simpson, P. (2010). The "work group": redressing the balance in Bion's *Experiences in Groups*. *Human Relations*, 63(12): 1859–1878.

Freud, S. (1900a). *The Interpretation of Dreams. The Standard Edition of the Complete Psychological Works of Sigmund Freud* (Vol. 5). Ed. J. Strachey. London: Hogarth and the Institute of Psycho-Analysis.

Freud, S. (1921c). *Group Psychology and the Analysis of the Ego. The Standard Edition of the Complete Psychological Works of Sigmund Freud* (Vol. 18, pp. 65–143). Ed. J. Strachey. London: Hogarth and the Institute of Psycho-Analysis.

Freud, S. (1926d). *Inhibitions, Symptoms and Anxiety. The Standard Edition of the Complete Psychological Works of Sigmund Freud* (Vol. 20). Ed. J. Strachey. London: Hogarth and the Institute of Psycho-Analysis.

Goldman, S. L., Nagel, R. N. & Preiss, K. (1995). *Agile Competitors and Virtual Organizations: Strategies for Enriching the Customer.* New York: Van Nostrand Reinhold.

Grossman, L. (2009). Iran protests: Twitter, the medium of the movement. Retrieved 30 December 2010, from http://www.time.com/time/world/article/0,8599,1905125,00.html

Hagel III, J. & Seely Brown, J. (2005). *The Only Sustainable Edge: Why Business Strategy Depends on Productive Friction and Dynamic Specialization.* Boston, MA: Harvard Business School Press.

Hagel III, J., Seely Brown, J. & Davison, L. (2010). *The Power of Pull: How Small Moves, Smartly Made, Can Set Big Things in Motion.* Philadelphia: Basic Books.

Harvey, D. (2005). *A Brief History of Neoliberalism.* Oxford: Oxford University Press.

Hopper, E. (2003). *Traumatic Experience in the Unconscious Life of Groups: The Fourth Basic Assumption: Incohesion: Aggregation/Massification or (ba)I:A/M.* London: Jessica Kingsley.

Iansiti, M. & Levien, R. (2004). *The Keystone Advantage: What the New Dynamics of Business Ecosystems Mean for Strategy, Innovation, and Sustainability.* Boston: Harvard Business School Press.

Kay, J. (2003). *The Truth about Markets: Their Genius, Their Limits, Their Follies.* London: Allen Lane.

Kravets, D. (2011). Amid street protests, Twitter shuttered in Egypt. *Threat Level.* Retrieved 26 January 2011, from http://www.wired.com/threatlevel/2011/01/twitter-revolution/

Kuhn, T. S. (1962). *The Structure of Scientific Revolutions,* Chicago: University of Chicago Press.

Lacan, J. (1945). Logical time and the assertion of anticipated certainty: a new sophism. In: *Écrits: The First Complete Edition in English.* Translated with Notes by Bruce Fink in collaboration with Héloïse Fink and Russell Grigg. New York: W. W. Norton, 2006.

Lacan, J. (1961). *The Seminar of Jacques Lacan, Book IX: Identification.* London: Karnac.

Lacan, J. (1988). *Book II: The Ego in Freud's Theory and in the Technique of Psychoanalysis* 1954–1955. Cambridge: Cambridge University Press.

LaCroix, A. L. (2010). *The Ideological Origins of American Federalism.* Cambridge, MA: Harvard University Press.

Langlois, R. N. (2003). The vanishing hand: the changing dynamics of industrial capitalism. *Industrial and Corporate Change, 12(2):* 351–385.

Leake, J. (2010). Suspicious wives make the best internet spies. Retrieved 23 May 2010, from http://technology.timesonline.co.uk/tol/news/tech_and_web/article7134060.ece

Levy, S. (2009). Secret of Googlenomics: data-fueled recipe brews profitability. *Wired Magazine, 17(6)*.

Link, P. (2010). A message too powerful to stop. Retrieved 29 September 2010, from http://www.nytimes.com/2010/09/30/opinion/30ihtedlink1.html?_r=2

Miller, E. J. & Rice, A. K. (1967). *Systems of Organization: The Control of Task and Sentient Boundaries*. London: Tavistock.

Montopoli, B. (2010). Tea Party supporters: who they are and what they believe. *Political Hotsheet*. Retrieved 14 April 2010, from http://www.cbsnews.com/8301-503544_162-20002529-503544.html

Moore, J. F. (1996). *The Death of Competition: Leadership and Strategy in the Age of Business Ecosystems*. New York: Harper Business.

Moore, M. H. (1995). *Creating Public Value: Strategic Management in Government*. Cambridge, MA: Harvard University Press.

New York Times (2010). Global warming. Retrieved 13 December 2010, from http://topics.nytimes.com/top/news/science/topics/globalwarming/index.html

O'Loughlin, J., Witmer, F. D. W., Linke, A. M. & Thorwardson, N. (2010). Peering into the fog of war: the geography of the WikiLeaks Afghanistan War Logs, 2004–2009. *Eurasian Geography and Economics, 51(4)*: 472–495.

Packard, V. (1957). *The Hidden Persuaders*. New York: Pocket Books.

Peck, D. (2010). How a new jobless era will transform America. *The Atlantic, 305(2)*: 42.

Pisa, N. (2010). Google executives convicted in Italy of violating privacy laws over bullying video. *Technology*. Retrieved 24 February 2010, from http://www.telegraph.co.uk/technology/google/7305616/Google-executives-convicted-in-Italy-of-violating-privacy-laws-over-bullying-video.html

Popkin, R. H. (1979). *The History of Scepticism from Erasmus to Spinoza*. Berkeley, CA: University of California Press.

Prahalad, C. K. & Ramaswamy, V. (2003). The new frontier of experience innovation. *MIT-Sloan Management Review, 44, 4*: 12–18.

Prahalad, C. K. & Ramaswamy, V. (2004). *The Future of Competition: Co-Creating Unique Value with Customers*. Boston: Harvard Business School Press.

Quantcast. (2010). Twitter.com. Retrieved 28 December 2010, from http://www.quantcast.com/twitter.com

Roach, J. (2010). How the "Dancing" vote was hacked. *Cosmic Log*. Retrieved 10 November 2010, from http://cosmiclog.msnbc.msn.com/_news/2010/11/19/5495782-how-the-dancing-vote-was-hacked

Robb, J. (2010). Open source Jihad. *Global Guerillas*. Retrieved 21 November 2010, from http://globalguerrillas.typepad.com/globalguerrillas/2010/11/note-on-innovation-in-warfare.html?utm_source=feedburner&utm_medium=feed&utm_campaign=Feed:+typepad/rzYD+%28Global+Guerrillas%29

Roosevelt, T. (1900). *The Strenuous Life: Essays and Addresses*. New York: The Outlook Company.

Sambandaraksa, D. (2010). Twitter sees red and yellow. Tech news. Retrieved 17 March 2010, from http://www.bangkokpost.com/tech/technews/34572/twitter-sees-red-and-yellow

Shillingsburg, P. L. (2006). *From Gutenberg to Google: Electronic Representations of Literary Texts*. Cambridge: Cambridge University Press.

Soros, G. (1998). *The Crisis of Global Capitalism: Open Society Endangered*. London: Little, Brown and Company.

Steiner, J. (1993). *Psychic Retreats: Pathological Organizations in Psychotic, Neurotic and Borderline Patients*. London: Routledge.

Stiglitz, J. E. (2002). *Globalization and Its Discontents*. London: Allen Lane.

Tapscott, D. & Williams, A. D. (2006). *Wikinomics: How Mass Collaboration Changes Everything*. New York: Portfolio.

Tapscott, D. & Williams, A. D. (2010). *MacroWikinomics: Rebooting Business and the World*. New York: Portfolio Penguin.

The Economist (2010). Lives of others. *Privacy and the Internet*. Retrieved 20 May 2010, from http://www.economist.com/node/16167766

The Nielsen Company (2010). Top U.S. search sites for July 2010. *nielsenwire*. Retrieved 25 August 2010, from http://blog.nielsen.com/nielsenwire/online_mobile/top-us-search-sites-for-july-2010/

The Telegraph (2009). China riots: Twitter and YouTube frustrate "censorship attempts". *China*. Retrieved 6 July 2010, from http://www.telegraph.co.uk/news/worldnews/asia/china/5756766/China-riots-Twitter-and-YouTube-frustrate-censorship-attempts.html

Thompson, D. (2010). The Tea Party used the Internet to defeat the first Internet President. *Business*. Retrieved 2 November 2010, from http://www.theatlantic.com/business/archive/2010/11/the-tea-party-used-the-internet-to-defeat-the-first-internet-president/65589/

Twitter blog (2010). Measuring Tweets. Retrieved 29 December 2010 from http://blog.twitter.com/2010/02/measuring-tweets.html

Ungar, R. (2010). What does the Tea Party really want? *The Policy Page*. Retrieved 15 April 2010, from http://trueslant.com/rickungar/2010/04/15/what-does-the-tea-party-really-want/

United States Environmental Protection Agency (2010). Past Climate Change. Retrieved 30 December 2010, from http://www.epa.gov/climatechange/science/pastcc.html#ref.

Wagner, M. (2008). Obama election ushering in first Internet presidency. *Government*. Retrieved 30 December 2010, from http://www.informationweek.com/news/government/showArticle.jhtml?articleID=212000815

Watkins, M. & Bradshaw, T. (2010). Hacktivists take revenge for WikiLeaks. US Politics and Foreign Policy. Retrieved 9 December 2010, from http://www.ft.com/cms/s/0/ee014b5e-02cd-11e0-a07e-00144feabdc0.html#axzz17j94k8oz

Wikipedia (2010a). Massively multi-player online role-playing game. *Wikipedia*. Retrieved 25 December 2010, from http://en.wikipedia.org/wiki/Massively_multiplayer_online_role-playing_game

Wikipedia (2010b). Printing Press. Retrieved 26 December 2010, from http://en.wikipedia.org/wiki/Printing_press

Wikipedia (2010c). Virtual World. Retrieved 30 December 2010, from http://en.wikipedia.org/wiki/Virtual_world

Winnicott, D. W. (1969). The use of an object. *International Journal of Psychoanalysis, 50*: 711–716.

Zuboff, S. & Maxmin, J. (2002). *The Support Economy: Why Corporations Are Failing Individuals and the Next Episode of Capitalism*. New York: Viking.

CHAPTER EIGHT

What are we celebrating in the celebrities?

Richard Morgan-Jones

Introduction

So what might be the fascination with celebrities really be about? What might attract to celebrities the role-model status that appears to become such a cause for celebration? How is it that public consumption of the media fuels and finances hypnotic fascination with the romances, weddings, scandals, births, separations, betrayals, divorces, fighting with the bulges, addictions, and ageing bodies, losses and illnesses, and deaths, not to mention the final testaments? And what does this "frieze of life" represent to us, beyond the vicarious sufferings and successes that can be distanced by being vicariously watched in others?

In exploring psychoanalytic reflections on the modern world, this chapter now turns the reader's attention to a specific aspect of the media. In exploring the phenomenon of celebrity, as with so many aspects of this book, and with the media as but one aspect of such socio-analysis, there is a central ambiguity. Is the phenomenon under observation, reflection, and discussion the product of internal psychological forces whose driving force can be analysed? Or are such phenomena produced as the result of the way the media manipulates them? Between these two possibilities lies a third, namely that it is the media that plays the part of a transitional "mediating" space which is neither the fan, nor the celebrity, but transforms the one to the other like a kind of go-between. Can psychoanalytic reflection on such interconnectivity that we observe in this phenomenon be the alternation between grandiosity and humiliation? Could this phenomenon belong to the small child's negotiation out of its own narcissistic wounds of let-down by mother, which becomes the model for self-esteem and the humiliations of shaming experience in later life? Such a transitional space might emulate and echo the transitional space of which Winnicott wrote, suggesting a means whereby a child could practise in safety independence from mother, through a first discovered toy, blanket, or plaything (Winnicott, 1971).

This chapter will provide some reflection on this thorny issue in trying to extrapolate a phenomenon that is perhaps best described as co-created by numerous forces of interconnectivity, only some of them describable in psychoanalytic terms.

It will in particular take up the dimension of shame, shaming, and shamelessness as a key feature of the reproduction of fame and celebrity in the media. It will also explore the symbolic aspect of these dimensions of living in order to see what they might represent unconsciously. Such representations are not made conscious in the minds of fans as they borrow temporary identities without becoming aware of their use of the other person for their own processes of identity formation and developmental conflict across emotionally charged life transitions. The absence of such awareness, working-through, and personalizing of symbolic meaning is shaped by the vicarious aspect of this phenomenon. It is much easier to see others suffer the experience of being idealized and lifted above human status, followed by losing such a position and reputation, than for individuals to experience their own ordinary ups and downs of everyday life. Fans revel in stars revealing themselves as mere mortals whose fall from being super-heroes we have contributed to by buying voyeuristic scandal-based media or voting them out with a click of the voting button on some celebrity performance show. This failure in realizing the symbolization at work renders the very process of symbolic relating null and void by turning it into concrete, literal, and thus psychotic thinking and behaving that alienates people from their own capacity for relating and from their own humanity.

This chapter will explore these themes from a number of psychoanalytic, group-analytic, and socio-analytic perspectives. But first,

I want to delve into the meaning and use of the terms "celebrity" and "celebrating".

The celebrity phenomenon: cult or a new religion?
The inherited meanings of celebrity and celebration down the ages

Language reveals in its usage both truth and meaning prevalent within a current social and historical context and yet at the same time also draws upon their past. The contemporary *Collins English Dictionary* defines the noun "celebrity" as "a famous person", and the adjective as "fame or notoriety". Its *Thesaurus* adds meaning to the word "celebrated" to include: "well-known, acclaimed, distinguished, eminent, glorious, lionized, revered". Its antonyms include: "dishonoured, forgotten, insignificant, obscure, trivial, undistinguished". Already we can see the shape of a binary either/or that separates the celebrity from the others. This chapter will argue that these are opposite extremes of ordinary self-esteem are dramatized across the dividing boundary of shame.

An older dictionary, the *Shorter Oxford English*, includes solemnity, a solemn ceremony, before turning to more modern meanings to include notoriety. To celebrate means originally to publicly perform a religious ritual, to observe with solemn rites, to proclaim publicly, or to honour with festivities. This original meaning belongs to a more dependent culture that managed its differences and uncertainties with religious practice, a more structured society and a sense that everybody knew their place with dignity. The Irish poet Cecil Alexander who wrote the well-known nineteenth-century Christian hymn "All things bright and beautiful", includes the following verse:

> The rich man in his castle,
> The poor man at his gate,
> God made them high or lowly,
> And ordered their estate.

(Oxford Dictionary of Quotations, 1992)

With all its benefits, this historical change in social structure, heralded by political and social revolution, and characterized by secularization and economic mobility, appears to have created a society where all are equal under the law. And yet there remains no obvious mechanism for dealing with how to process socially and emotionally large differences in wealth, fame, and fortune that contemporary society promotes. Additionally, there are few processes to recognize and contain the emotional experience of provoked and innate envy. My hypothesis is that the cult of celebrity fuels and is fuelled by this dynamic, whilst at the same time safely contains and neutralizes this process.

Celebrity worship syndrome: cult or religion?

The following of celebrities as an activity of fans is often described as a "cult". This suggests some form of possibly primitive religion of the sort that the mainstream religions demean by describing it as idolatry, whereby people and the symbols that represent aspects of them are equated. This is what psychoanalyst Hanna Segal describes as the symbolic equation of equivalents, whereby in place of developed object-relating between sentient beings, psychotic thinking mistakes a representation for something concrete (Segal, 1957). In this way, the artefacts of celebrity are mistaken for the person themselves, and the identity represented by the celebrity is taken for the possession that fills the empty space left where a person has evacuated any identity of their own. Such artefacts include the music, personal details, often web- or media-based, and rituals representing a celebrity's life that are ecstatically adored and hyper-valued, and an almost hysterical compulsion to have experiences of being in the real presence of the idolized figure as if they are a demi-god to be worshipped.

It could be argued that such cults and cult figures are the secularized version of the expression of meaning left by postmodern societies no longer held together by the dependency culture of institutional religion. It is striking that in the USA, the cult of the personality, wealthy, talented, or star-struck, co-exists with the majority of the population engaged in institutional religion. Perhaps it might be more accurate to say that pop cults scoop the psychic energy that once cathected people to the ordinary idealization and identification processes of family, school, and community life that were integrated by national religion. Returning to the idea of the celebrity as the expression and use of a transitional object, might there be a more appropriate analogy than the religious idea of a demi-god? Might it not be more appropriate to use the electronic analogy of a semi-conductor, that acts as a channel of communication both screening some currents such as the exposure of personal and individual narcissistic wounds, while allowing others to be expressed vicariously on the celebrity stage?

Before going further with this social analysis, I first want to go deeper, using psychoanalysis, to explore what might lie behind such dynamics in the nature of the process of forming identity that is thrown up by this discussion.

Identity and identification

The concept of identity can be elusive. In the context of a child psychoanalytic psychotherapy session, an emotional need for ordinary identification and introjection is poignantly described by child psychotherapist Anne Alvarez. A girl raised in a Third World orphanage is deeply distressed. After twenty minutes of desperation, the girl has calmed.

> … she asked musingly and tensely of the therapist, "Why are you called Jane?" A little later, she briefly stroked the fuzzy shoulder of the therapist's cardigan and asked, softly, "Why is it so fuzzy?" The language she was using and the question "why" was that of a 10-year old, but in reality I think she was doing what the baby does when it explores its mother's face with its eyes or hands, getting to know, reflectively and cognitively, as well as emotionally, not the why-ness of his parents, but the what-ness, the is-ness.
>
> (Alvarez, 2010, p. 15)

An ordinary aspect of family development involves the disillusionment of early identifications with parental figures. This is a feature of adolescence worked out in the swiftness of the shifts of loyalty among fans when a celebrity disappoints. We can see in this process what psychoanalytic thinking describes as an unconscious split between seeing one part of a relationship projected as idealized and the other as denigrated. When the star disappoints, it reverses the process from the fan denigrating what they are and have in idealization of the star, and instead denigrating and monsterizing the star for their inevitable failure to live up to a perfect image. What Alvarez points to is the vulnerability to being seduced by the need to borrow an identity from the other for this process. It as if the celebrity provides the sought-after emotional experience that was insufficiently provided by parental figures when family life has not provided secure earlier identifications through the kind of ordinary explorations of identity such as described above as "is-ness".

Celebrity worship: a pathology?

Psychologist John Maltby and colleagues have analysed the findings from the "Celebrity Attitude Scale" and propose three types of attitude that fans develop towards the celebrity:

Entertainment-social: Attraction, gossip, stories about the celebrity, joining events, or the virtual experience of socializing with friends via shared enthusiasm or curiosity about a particular figure. It is the large group aspect of this everyday phenomenon that is distinctive in fiercely felt but fleeting allegiences.
Intense-personal: The intensity, compulsion, and identification with the object adored is the feature of this dimension. Good or bad things that happen to the idol are felt to happen to the fan. Following the dress style, likes and dislikes, even tattoos and piercings, identify a fan with their idol.
Borderline-pathological: In this dimension, the compulsion becomes more intense, as does the identification. Thoughts, dreams, and fantasies become compellingly distracting, as does impersonating the celebrity in dress and style of speaking and dressing. At an extreme end of psychotic pathology, there is the stalker who cannot bear to be separated from the embodiment of their idol, or indeed the murderer who cannot live with the reality of not being them (Maltby, 2005).

Celebrity as a group phenomenon

Diana at a Palace garden party

England. The green manicured lawns and gardens. The scudding clouds that cool a perfect summer's day. Cucumber sandwiches, tea, and cake. The daffodil-yellow sleeveless summer dress, matching the buttercup-yellow stilettos and clutch bag toned perfectly with the wide-brimmed hat held discreetly by the lady-in-waiting so that the two or three being presented could receive the full benefit of the tall, toned, and athletically trained body. A picture of beauty and loveliness. The voice inside spoke forbidding words: "Look but don't touch". Was I a stalker to be shamed?

For the children, the perfect drop of a half knee to arrive at their level and forge a relationship born of attention to some detail or folly of the occasion: "I expect you always look so clean, especially on a football field after a game—do you like bikes? I like roller-skates. Palace corridors are just great!" Her face angled in sympathy, eyes alert to engage, tease, seduce, voice timbred delicately with deep notes of compassion or a tinkling laugh; how could she not be adored and admired by one and all? A people's princess. Her task in life? Well, some of the press declared her the royal family's brood mare to produce an heir. Hers was the genetic role of the aristocracy to keep the lineage going. And yet she was a star, a celebrity, a princess with a common touch, an ordinary intimacy that brought her close to strangers and yet not to the family she represented and reproduced, except perhaps her much-loved boys.

My own acceptance of my work organization's annual invitation to the Palace was born of voyeuristic curiosity. What was this royal family under whose spell for centuries we had been held as subjects rather than becoming citizens? How did they manage to command such loyalty and dependency in a democratic state, when clearly not being blessed with contemporary intellectual, commercial gifts or the tradition of their Dutch or Norwegian counterparts who are more humanly accessible? It was when I was approaching, even straining to catch more of the sight and sound of the encounter with a celebrity royal, that I felt on my elbow the firm hand of a gentleman of the entourage, nudging me gently but firmly beyond the invisible three-yard line it was his, and I noticed later, his six colleagues' task to police. Adrenalin rushed, anger and fear, fight or flight. I observed his groomed appearance, immaculate morning suit tails, the pin-striped trousers, the umbrella that he carried appearing somewhat heavier than most, indicating perhaps a concealed weapon and the tell-tale bulge at rear waistband level suggesting military and security training.

For Freud, one of the keenest sexual pleasures is in voyeurism and its potential to satisfy the fetishized replacements for what was forbidden (the "no" of the father), lost or inaccessible in a mother's body. This was the pleasure of taking in and imagining what could be done or felt if closeness were possible. For him, the sexual sublimation of such a pleasure evoked guilt and shame. For Klein, it evoked primitive and regressive desires for part-objects, parts of a mother's body that were the very sustenance of life in infancy, the breast, the nipple, the womb.

Freud had traced the evolution of the child's developing desire for an intimacy he called sexual, from the physical satisfaction at the breast, through the pleasures of restoring equilibrium through evacuation. Such promises of satisfaction, Freud traced in the stirrings of genital desire brought on by awareness of the difference between the sexes and feelings and fantasies of what one had got and had not got as body parts and the desire for penetrating or being penetrated to recover physical unity with the lost (m)other.

But psychoanalysis has been less forward in taking up the social dimension of survival by belonging to the group and that is what I want to explore in this chapter. In the experience described above, are these primitive feelings not related to human survival? Are they not related to dependency on royalty, promise of intimacy, anger, and fear? Psychoanalyst Wilfred Bion suggested that each of these primitive patternings of emotion, shapes each of three different ways in which people behaved in groups dominated by overwhelming emotions when their identity was threatened. He called these shared basic assumptions that enabled individuals to club together to borrow a group identity and defend themselves against maddening fears and anxieties of a catastrophic kind. He also suggested that they had a shared matrix that shaped them where what was physical and what was emotional could not be distinguished, and this he called the protomental system (Bion, 1961, p. 102; Torres, 2010).

In the observation of a social scene recorded above, each of these emotional patterns was evoked: the desire to depend, fascination with the pair that would produce an heir, his majesty the child, and the need for flight or fight. These, Bion suggested, were the group manifestations of the psycho-physical experience of succour (dependency), creative intimacy (pairing), and aggression (fight-flight).

He also suggested that individuals were drawn to particular kinds of groups with their own emotionality, and he used the word "valency" to describe the way people appeared to borrow from the group an identity in order to vicariously deal with emotional and physical aspects of experience that they needed to suppress. One way of putting this is to suggest that individuals borrow an identity from the skin of the group, and that maintaining that identity is their devoted desire (Anzieu, 1989). At the opposite pole, individuals may use the group to establish precisely what they are in no way any part of, repudiating and rejecting its demands, even its right to be a group. As Bion put it: "the group is often used to achieve a sense of vitality by total submergence in the group, or a sense of individual independence by total repudiation of the group" (Bion, 1961).

Shame, shamelessness, and the skin game[1]

It might be argued that shame as a concept no longer exists in contemporary society, as social flaunting of traditional values and behaviour is widespread. Stars and media collude to reveal glimpses of flesh, and the sexual parts of their bodies, that a previous generation concealed behind a veneer of dignity. People in the public domain, like artists, politicians, or bankers who have transgressed an important norm do not automatically disappear from public view as would have been the case in the past. Instead, they often return, reinvented and reinvigorated, and still command and demand social attention. But I would argue that the experience and awareness of shame and shamelessness and its significance is suppressed and denied by the celebrity culture among other social contexts.

The shame barrier is the description given to the physical, sexual, and emotional boundary that is developed by the individual through a sufficiently robust yet protected childhood that builds self-esteem and identity and can discern what is enjoyable self-expression, and what belongs to the privacy of intimate relationships.

When a celebrity attacks or transgresses such a barrier, demeans human dignity and morality, and attacks the values and coherence of the human group, there is shamelessness. Shame is experienced when the individual realizes that this barrier has been transcended. Shame is exported into another person when a shameless act shocks a person into feeling shame on behalf of a celebrity. Shameless acts reveal a deep unconscious split in the psyche between denial of shame, on the one hand, and felt shame, on the other. Normally, it is felt shame that modifies impulsive and unconscious behaviour. However, when the tension between these two states of mind is denied, it can be externalized, with the celebrity behaving shamelessly and the fan suffering the manic excitement of belittling shame. This splitting process may, of course, go the other way, where it is the fan who behaves shamelessly and the celebrity who feels shame and shock on their behalf. This is illustrated in the comparison between sportsmen David Beckham and Jonny Wilkinson below. Each party can be either shocked or excited without either owning the opposite feeling that might moderate both behaviour and the emotional painfulness of the experience.

In searching for ways to describe the physical nature of social identity, anthropologist of the body Terence Turner (2007, p. 83) describes the social skin:

> Decorating, covering, uncovering or otherwise altering the human form … seems to have been a concern of every human society of which we have knowledge. This objectively universal fact is associated with another of a more subjective nature—that the surface of the body seems everywhere to be treated, not only as the boundary of the individual as a biological and psychological entity, but as the frontier of the social self as well.

In a paper exploring the nature of shameless violations to human dignity and identity, Nuno Torres and I described the way individuals deal with and process potentially disturbing emotions through vicarious use of belonging to a group using Bion's idea of valency (Morgan-Jones & Torres, 2010). We develop this idea of Bion's by suggesting that individuals are drawn to borrow from groups an identity beyond their own that serves to help them manage having to face both ordinary and disturbing emotions that belong to the existential truth and loneliness of being an individual. We argue that social dynamics somatically regulate psycho-physiological phenomena of the bare skin via the emotions of the individual as a social actor. It is as if the individual borrows from the social skin that holds the group together rather than to live through an experience in their own skin. More than that, we suggest that it is the image of skin and how it is treated that comes to represent the social skin of the group.

In relation to the group of fans who worship a celebrity, the body of the celebrity represents the embodiment of the group, held together by their skin. The sound skin provides an envelope of music and words, the fashion and tattoos used to decorate and shape their skin become the protomental shapes that forge the group identity (Anzieu, 1989; Bion, 1961; Torres, 2010). The shameless ways in which bare skin is exposed provides a sexualized form of attachment marked by a fusion of identity and a frenzy of ecstatic sound that merges the group with its leader. In short, we are dealing with the dynamics of oneness, incohesion, and massification described by psychoanalyst Pierre Turquet and group-analyst Earl Hopper (Hopper, 2003; Turquet, 1974).

In my work with Nuno Torres, we wanted "to explore the hypothesis that there is an even deeper layer and a more elemental and literal link between the three related elements of 1) the social sphere, 2) the feelings and mentality of the individual, and 3) his/her somatic skin" (Morgan-Jones & Torres, 2010). In short, this is the matrix of often encapsulated psycho-physical-social experience that can only be gleaned by intuition of sensation and which Bion defined as protomentality. Another way to describe it is to say that it provides the very conditions for group belonging to exist at all because it is of the essence of the human survival instinct of belonging to a group (Morgan-Jones, 2010[2]; Torres, 2010).

Bion goes on to suggest that, "It is these proto-mental levels that provide the matrix of group diseases. These diseases manifest themselves in the individual but they have characteristics that make it clear that it is the group rather the individual that is stricken" (Bion, 1961). From a group perspective, then, could we see the celebrity cult as recycling not just individual but also group pathology.

It would, however, be wrong to think that such a fascination with the lives, body, and skin of the celebrity is only pathological. Some stars have pioneered self-sacrificing charitable work such as singer-songwriter Bob Geldof's work for famine crises in Africa. Likewise, Australian performer Kylie Minogue has championed awareness of the need to screen, research, and treat breast cancer after she courageously went public by continuing to perform when stricken with the disease. In addition, British actor, comedian, and critic Stephen Fry, and North American comedian Ruby Wax, have encouraged a large number of fellow sufferers of depression and mental illness, by describing their own struggle. The influence of these celebrities can be seen as far more powerful and significant than the representative attempts by the body of politicians to address and seek support for similar causes and issues.

The positive role of celebrities and stars supporting humane social movements is traced and explored in Stephen Huddart's paper from Canada. In particular, he takes up the history of actors and musicians in fostering social causes. The clearest recent example is the development of Martin Luther King's vision of a non-racist America that inspired musicians Joan Baez, Harry Belafonte, and Bob Dylan to write and perform protest songs as part of the civil rights and anti-war movements.

In particular, he points to the creative potential for mass movements to be influenced subliminally through the sound envelope, or surrounding skin of music, that creates neural pathways that musicians have always exploited to get their message across. He points to the way "… it is sufficient to discern in medieval song two possible models of music as precursor to social innovation—one structural, consisting of rhythm, tone scale and harmonics and the other expressive, comprising language and melody" (p. 12). Historically, this links to the social critics down the ages from the Troubadors, to the civil rights and anti-war movements, as well as the Band Aid movement to address the economic plight of starving Africans by Bob Geldof and collaborators. In the terms of this chapter, this points to the positive use of subliminal techniques to create large group dynamics, in this case loyal to positive and humane social causes.

TV fandom in Brazil

The cult(ure), texture, or social skin of celebrity is well illustrated in the group dynamics of fandom as described by Maria Coelho. The major Brazilian television network *Rede Globo de Televisio* in Rio de Janeiro is the media hub for Brazilian music and drama. In 1991, a pop group appealed deeply to the life of poor people with lyrics that included the line: "I belong to the people, I'm just a John Doe". Performances included the lead singer inviting a member of the audience to sing the line solo on stage amid a frenzied response from the audience to the singling out of the chosen one. Fifteen seconds of national broadcasting fame. As Coelho puts it: "… it always struck me because of its power to synthesize what I suggest to be the essential paradox of the experience of fandom: the wish to have singularity recognised, but however expressing this wish as part of the crowd" (Coelho, 2005, p. 97).

In pursuing this psycho-social analysis, social researcher Coelho examines the mail of fans, given to her not even opened by the singers. This in itself reveals their scorn for their admiring following, treated as inferiors. She quotes from a letter, characteristic of many: "I know it is hard for you to answer these letters, for there are many of them. But, please, take just five minutes TO ANSWER MINE" (p. 102).

This analysis echoes the ideas of group relations pioneer and psychoanalyst Pierre Turquet when he describes large-group dynamics and the move between being a singleton (alone in the crowd) to becoming an individual member (with an identity formed by others) to becoming a membership individual (who can retain identity while still belonging) (Turquet, 1974). He also outlines an idea developing Bion's basic assumptions to include oneness to describe what joins members as an individual member (Turquet, 1975).

It is significant that in producing a selected fact (Bion, 1962) to organize this complex group dynamic, Coelho uses as her title: *Experiencing Television Fandom: Notes on the Tension between Singularization and Massification*. This model of thinking closely resembles Earl Hopper's development of Turquet's theory of basic assumption oneness when he describes the functioning of traumatized systems that produce the narcissistic dynamic of group incohesion: aggregation/massification (Hopper, 2003). What Hopper adds to the situation is the idea that such extremes of crowd or large-group social phenomena are expressions of the referred pain of trauma that is being suppressed. In the case of Brazilian society, it is the pain of the dispossessed identities of impoverished groups in society who are fed "bread and circus" entertainment to keep the peace as surely as the Roman emperors provided similarly entertaining distractions for their populace to keep social order.

Celebrity performers across the world attract fans to their cult following. The screaming girls who mobbed the Beatles when they arrived in the USA in the 1960s, the scores who flock to television talent competitions to demonstrate that they are the one who has something special, the families who groom their daughters into little princess belles and future talented celebrity models, even sportsmen and women, politicians, evangelists, and news commentators, all have to deal with some aspect of the projected power of the felt inferiority of others that proclaims upon the celebrity their charismatic status. Each of these artefacts of the social skin evoke visceral responses that might be described as hysterical for the volume of emotion and the capacity it holds for suppressing real pain, trauma, and loss of identifications that are more humanely enduring and fostering of intimate social and romantic relations.

Unconscious phantasy as a defence against social anxiety

Menzies Lyth developed Melanie Klein's idea of the role of unconscious phantasy that is representative of primitive instinctual desire (Menzies Lyth, 1959). She took Eliot Jacques' idea that social systems act in a particular emotionally defensive way to protect themselves from anxiety. In the phenomenon of fandom and celebrity, the question remains: what comprises the primitive phantasy of fame? On the one hand, there is the pairing and intimacy of the admiring crowd with the celebrity. This even prevails for the fifteen seconds of fame described on

Brazilian television, repeated elsewhere. On the other hand, there is the phantasy of getting in on the act of some intimate relationship between ordinary person and a celebrity. This is suggested by the fan mail that is at once seductive as an attempt to be more interesting for however brief a moment than other fans, or indeed other intimacies in the fan's life. As a footnote to Menzies Lyth's pioneering work, we could suggest that modern social networks like organizations, particularly in government finance and the media function as social systems that export anxiety into its stakeholders, whether citizens, employees or in the case of celebrity into merchandised fans with their fetishized commodities.

It is this, I would suggest, that made Diana the star she was, the princess with the common touch whose presence was given exclusively and compassionately to a singled-out individual. Along with such an experience comes a barely concealed and sexualized seduction, and the replication of the phantasy of the deeply loving and attentive mother whose child has no rival. This at last is the imagined cure for all narcissistic wounds. As one fan put it: "She touched me on the arm and I am not going to wash that arm for a month ... maybe never." Perhaps it was this too that touched so many tuning in across the globe for her son William's Royal Wedding to a non-Royal, Kate, with whom people could identify. Could this perhaps be seen as a hoped-for renewal through pairing of a more dependable contract between the powerful and traditional leadership of the celebrity British monarchy and the nation of common people whose faith in love and conception for the future is hungry for representation?

Psychoanalyst Ron Britton has suggested that one of the unconscious desires of the hysteric is somehow to get in on the act of the intimacy between others (Britton, 1999). This suggests the primitive Oedipal phantasy of the primal scene where the child wishes to be between the parents in their intercourse as if this might be a way of having both, being both or either, and sealing the loving identification of their own conception eternally, beyond all fear of losing this valued and feared internal object.

Exploitation of the desire to be in on the act: public image and politics

There is, however, a further insidious development in the manufacture of celebrity. If part of the contributory dynamics of celebrity phenomenon is the disposed, unidentified aspect that proliferates the massification of popular culture, then this provides an arena for exploitation. Here, I want to use two examples from among many. One is from the deliberate development of celebrity status among television stars in order to accelerate the success of a BBC soap opera. The other is the political exploitation of a media image that was an aspect of George "Dub-ya" Bush's success in becoming a United States President for two terms.

The eventual establishment and success of a soap opera on national television typically takes at least two years to become popular and established, the sort of reputation that makes people arriving at work say, "Did you see last night's episode?" When, in February 1985, the BBC launched *EastEnders*, it was not only written in a way that created and reflected archetypal roles in the East End of inner-city London with its community loyalty and questionable ethics of street traders. Publicity for the programme also provided details of the lives of the real-life actors who had been deliberately chosen for the way their life experience was close to the culture and events that were dramatized in the soap. The tabloid media grasped on these details and magnified a following that was titillated with gossip and scandal in the past and present lives of the cast. In short, the tabloid world of star-creation did the work of the channel's publicists for it. The show was widely popular within a year, faster than any other similar media output. These minor actors became, in consequence, influenced by publicists, fixers, agents, as if they became their own merchandised products for the show itself. As McNicholas puts it, "Now they go where the media expects them to go, they wear what the media expects them to wear, they behave how the media expects them to behave ... it is clear that, the surrender of the right to a life which is in a way private seems a fair exchange for even a fleeting moment of that old imposter, fame" (McNicholas, 2005, p. 53)[3].

If exploitation and manufacture of identity exploits both exploiter and exploited, it is now possible to see the political exploitation of an image through the lens of this same dynamic. In a paper entitled: "Brand 'W' and the Marketing of an American President: Or, Logos as Logos"[4], Jeremy Hockett describes the way the image and media creation of a logo with the single capitalized letter "W", with the words "The New President" underneath, created a brand image for a politician. Hockett describes the way, "the semiotic and symbolic messages contained within a variety of Brand W campaign merchandise (can be) analysed and discussed as "meaning systems" that target emotional rather than rational political reaction" (Hockett, 2005, p. 72). The image of ordinary "Dub-ya" (how Texans pronounce the letter "W"), with local Texan Southern American drawling speech and phrasing appealed to ordinary voters who felt dispossessed by the intellectual image of leading politicians. The image worked. For the seduced voter, it was the very ordinary identity of the great leader, the presidential image that incarnated the American dream from log cabin to White House. As a phenomenon, this illustrates the range of media-based political interventions shaped by "spin", image consultants, presentation coaches, and the rest of the media circus, that divert politicians and their fans from political policy and message to the manufacture and exploitation of an image. (See also Chapter Nine, on the new unconscious and the manipulation of voters, in this volume.)

Psychoanalytic commentary: shameless violations

A striking comment by French people coming to England is the shock at the invasion of privacy that is permitted and encouraged by the tabloid press in the UK. In France, there are strong laws against invasion of privacy. It is not that the press in that country are devoid of interest in celebrities. *Paris Match* has carried articles on international celebrities, the wealthy, the famous, the royalty of Europe for over eighty years. However, the press's right to intrude is strictly regulated. By contrast, this leaves the English press with few mechanisms for managing shamelessness. Celebrities are vaunted as much for their creative endeavours as for their failings. But it is their failings that have become open sport for the press and enable celebrities to play up to their bad image.

Exhibitionism and voyeurism: the skill of managing privacy/ public exposure alongside other values—David Beckham v. Jonny Wilkinson

Sportsmen and sportswomen often thrive on the support of the crowd for their performance or their team. They like to use it to perform for the crowd and are pleased to share their victories and successes with the crowd, signing autographs, supporting young people who want to take up sport and do well. And yet they also attest to the pain of intrusion that fame brings. Jonny Wilkinson was the England Rugby fly-half who kicked the winning drop goal in extended time in the World Cup in 2003. A shy man who takes his practice and perfectionism more seriously than most, he has come back with resilience from many injuries. He describes having to deal with the shamelessness of people selling his autograph on an England shirt on E-Bay while distracting from the many good causes for which people use such trophies. He admires England footballer David Beckham for the way he handles the whole media circus. "Accepting it will always be part of his life, he is more pro-active and uses it to his advantage … . He doesn't allow himself to be distracted despite all the madness around him" (Wilkinson, 2004, p. 104).

Beckham himself likes to use his celebrity status to offer private encouragement to people who suffer. About his fan mail, he writes:

> The ones I like to respond to are the genuine ones from people who are ill or have something in their family who is ill. We pick a few out and I'll give that person a ring at home. You hope it will raise their spirits a bit as they try to deal with their problems … . If I did it as part of a big campaign I would spend half my time dealing with the publicity. That is no good for the people you are trying to help … and sometimes parents of sick children don't want themselves all over the papers.
>
> (Beckham, 2000, p. 80)

What is striking from the books of both men, each entitled *My World*, is that they both dislike the intrusion of publicity and long for more privacy. However, in the context of their game, and for the benefit of sport, they both try to use some of their celebrity status to do some private good. They also admit to getting a buzz from all the attention, but try to moderate its effect. We could ask if their views are genuine. Beckham is very well paid, better than Wilkinson by a large factor. He also has a wife who, once a pop star, now has a successful fashion business sold on the image she and her husband have created. Perhaps for the purposes of this chapter, we can see the struggle of dealing with the fundamental exhibitionism and voyeurism that is at the heart of performing a sport in front of a gathered crowd. Such performance and the aggressive battle between teams representing loyalty, to club, region, or nation, evokes the primitive dynamics of warfare between rival groups, particularly among English football fans, who have attracted a sometimes shameless and drunken reputation for enacting violently such partisan conflicts off the sports field. It may be that such performance of necessity invites the sportsman to split himself off from the pain of the body assisted by the notion of taking a role for others rather than being his own person. And yet, at the same time, individual skill and the capacity to be a generous and shrewd team-player is of the essence of an individual style of play and ability, both on the pitch and in how the sporting hero responds to the hungry mob of admirers.

Conclusion

In the classic Greek myth of Narcissus, the hero falls in love with his own image in a pool and, ignoring the claims of love from the voice of Echo, drowns in the pool. Freud used this story to describe the archetypal way people chose attachment figures who mirror some aspects of their own idealized image of themselves. The narcissist fails to identify the symbolic meaning of the other who has become a representation of a desire that cannot be fulfilled and in the light of which the emotions of loss, lack, failure, and mourning cannot be endured. In the face of such dynamics and their blind shamelessness, celebrity cults are provided with emotional fuel on which to thrive, amplified by media attention.

Notes

1. For further discussion, see Morgan-Jones (2010, chapter 8): "Shameless violations: can restorative justice meet the case?".
2. See especially chapter 4: "Group body, group skin".
3. This paragraph draws largely on McNicholas's research.
4. First "Logos", first syllable pronounced with long "o", signifying a designed symbolic image representing a brand. Second "Logos", first syllable pronounced with short "o", signifying verbal reasoning (in Greek and philosophy).

References

Alvarez, A. (2010). Melancholia and mourning in childhood and adolescence: some reflections on the role of the internal object. In: E. McGinley & A. Varchevker (Eds.), *Enduring Loss: Mourning, Depression and Narcissism through the Life Cycle* (pp. 3–18). London: Karnac.

Anzieu, D. (1989). *The Skin Ego*. New Haven, CT: Yale University Press.
Beckham, D. (2000). *My World*. London: Hodder and Stoughton.
Bion, W. R. (1948–1952). *Experiences in Groups and Other Papers*. London: Routledge, 1961.
Bion, W. R. (1962). *Learning from Experience*. London: Karnac.
Britton, R. (1999). Getting in on the act: the hysterical solution. *International Journal of Psycho-Analysis, 80*: 1–14.
Hockett J. (2005). Brand "w" and the marketing of an American President or Logos as Logos. *Westminster Papers in Communication and Culture, 2(2)*: 72ff. University of Westminster, London. Accessed 21 April 2010, from http://celebrity-culture.blogspot/comtroversy
Hopper, E. (2003). *Traumatic Experience in the Unconscious Life of Groups*. London: Jessica Kingsley.
Huddart, S. (2002, revised 2005). Do we need another hero?: understanding celebrities' roles in advancing social causes. Accessed 2 December 2010, from: http://www.cvsrd.org/eng/docs/MMP/Do%20 We%20 Need%20 Another%20Hero%204.pdf
Maltby, J., Giles, D., Barber, L. & McCutcheon, L. E. (2005). Intense-personal celebrity worship and body image: evidence of a link among female adolescents. *British Journal of Health Psychology, 10*: 17–32.
McNicholas, A. (2005). EastEnders and the manufacture of celebrity. *Westminster Papers in Communication and Culture, 2(2)*. Accessed 21 April 2010, from http://celebrity-culture.blogspot/comtroversy
Menzies Lyth, I. (1959). The functioning of a social system as a defence against anxiety. Reprinted in: *Containing Anxiety in Institutions*. London: Free Association Books, 1988.
Morgan-Jones, R. J. (2010). *The Body of the Organisation and its Health*. London: Karnac Books.
Morgan-Jones, R. J. & Torres, N. (2010). Individual and collective suffering of organisational failures in containment: searching for a model to explore protomental dynamics. *Socio-Analysis, 12*: 57–75. [Previously presented as a paper entitled: Under the skin of the organisation: violation and shamelessness—searching for a model to explore protomental dynamics. Paper given to ISPSO Symposium, "Differences at Work: Towards Integration and Containment", Toledo, 26–28 June.]
Segal, H. (1957). Notes on symbol formation. *International Journal of Psychoanalysis, 55*: 515–519. [Reprinted in *The Work of Hanna Segal* (pp. 49–65). New York and London: Jason Aronson, 1981.
Torres, N. (2010). Social stress related epidemic diseases: failures in emotional containment. In R. J. Morgan-Jones (Ed.), *The Body of the Organisation and its Health* (chapter 6). London: Karnac.

Turner, T. (2007). The social skin. In: M. Lock & J. Farquhar (Eds.), *Beyond the Body Proper: Reading the Anthropology of Material Life*. Durham, NC: Duke University Press.

Turquet, P. (1974). Leadership: the individual in the group. In: G. S. Gabbard, J. J. Hartman & R. D. Mann (Eds.), *Analysis of Groups*. San Francisco, CA: Jossey-Bass.

Turquet, P. (1975). Threats to identity in the large group. In: L. Kreeger (Ed.), *The Large Group: Dynamics and Therapy*. London: Constable.

Wilkinson, J. (2004). *My World*. London: Headline.

Winnicott, D. W. (1971). *Playing and Reality*. London: Methuen.

CHAPTER NINE

The new unconscious: opening wider perspectives on society

Kenneth Eisold

The unconscious has had a robust and lively history—and it is still being written. Today, its scope is widening, and the evidence for its reach into every corner of society is being gathered from new domains.

Freud is generally credited with "discovering" the unconscious, but his achievement was to put it into scientific language and use it to account for neurotic behaviour. He postulated that the mind banished irrational and socially unacceptable thoughts from conscious awareness, thoughts that resurfaced as symptoms. Subsequently, he linked up his explanation of symptoms with a theory of dreams, and he conceived of an extensive netherworld below the surface of consciousness that was ruled by a logic of its own, what he called "primary process". Shortly afterwards, his explorations of infantile sexuality in *Three Essays* described the sexual motives that essentially mandated the existence of that unconscious world, the repressed impulses and thoughts generally unacceptable to civilized society. At that point, psychoanalysis had a coherent theory of a dynamic unconscious (Ellenberger, 1970; Makari, 2008).

A second modern attempt to delineate the unconscious, what I call "the new unconscious", began about twenty-five years ago. A loosely assembled group of philosophers, cognitive scientists, neurobiologists, and information theorists interested in AI (Artificial Intelligence), began to explore the limitations and flaws of consciousness itself. The key players in this new movement were philosophers like Daniel Dennett and Robert Searles, neurobiologists like Antonio Damasio and Joseph LeDoux, neuroscientists like Gerald Edelman, Walter Freeman, and Eric Kandel, and cognitive psychologists such as Jerome Bruner and Howard Gardner.

These men worked largely without reference to psychoanalysis, convinced that Freud's view of the unconscious was inaccurate. Indeed, to maintain the legitimacy of their project, it often seemed to them necessary to put a wall between their findings and the unsubstantiated assertions of psychoanalysis. For them, the ingenious account that Freud put together at the turn of the century had not been validated by research. Moreover, psychoanalytic sectarian battles had made it seem dogmatic and arrogant, belief systems rather than legitimate theories.

Far more important to them, was the fact that there were a number of significant problems with consciousness itself, problems that had become increasingly apparent over the course of the twentieth century. No longer could consciousness be considered a reliable guide to reality. Not only did it vary among cultures, it varied significantly from person to person. Increasingly, it was shown to be quirky, inconsistent, subject to the influence of many factors. But, then, what purpose *did* it serve? How did it work? Why had it developed over the course of human evolution?

John Searle, the philosopher, noted that when he first became interested in the subject, now about 30 years ago, "most people in the neurosciences did not regard consciousness as a genuine scientific question at all". He recalled a renowned neuroscientist telling him "It is okay to be interested in consciousness, but get tenure first" (Searle, 1997, p. 193).

This work was aided considerably by new research into the anatomy and functioning of the brain, and more recently by neuro-imaging, ways of detecting neural activity as it occurs. No longer was the mind a black box, impervious to investigation. Thanks to such new technologies as PET scans and electroencephalograms, hard data gradually became available to researchers.

In a remarkably short amount of time, a set of answers began to emerge. I give a fuller account of this new consensus in the first chapter of my book, *What You Don't Know You Know* (Eisold, 2010), but let me quickly review the chief points here.

Philosophers have called the common sense picture of external reality we see in our minds the "Cartesian Theatre", as if we were seated in our brains, looking out at the world through our senses. We believe we see what is actually out there. But apart from the dualism about two kinds of substance that Cartesian theory implies, there are several difficulties with this conventional view.

Consciousness presents an essentially seamless view of reality, a consistent picture in which the gaps and inconsistencies have been edited out. In other words, it deceives us by eliminating vast stores of information that do not fit, as well as smoothing over inconsistencies, creating a superficial coherence at the expense of accuracy.

It also edits out unwanted painful or embarrassing perceptions, generally colouring what we see to enhance self-esteem and advance our psychological wellbeing.

It supports our view of ourselves as the agents behind our actions, sustaining the illusion that we are deciding to respond to events and implementing our intentions. Now, however, there is substantial agreement that our bodies and brains construct responses to stimuli that are already set in motion by the time we become aware of them. Antonio Damasio puts it this way: "We are always hopelessly late for consciousness and because we all suffer from the same tardiness no one notices it."

Our perceptions and responses are layered, built up over time. New neural circuits build on old circuits, bundling together overlapping responses to similar categories of stimuli. The mind is not inherently logical. It is built up by associations and past connections. So the pictures we see are highly idiosyncratic.

Why, then, did consciousness evolve in us? If we don't need consciousness in order to decide to flee danger or seek shelter, if it doesn't present us with a fully reliable picture of reality, if it flatters us and induces us to believe that the world hasn't changed much over time, what is it good for?

The consensus on this that has emerged is that consciousness gives us the opportunity to *re*consider our actions. It enables us to inhibit our initial, automatic reactions, to talk among ourselves about alternative responses, to pool information, and discuss different explanations for what we see and jointly to consider different plans. Consciousness, then, is linked with our social life, important to the coordinated and interdependent demands of our evolving communities. As individuals, our innate processing of information might be sufficient for survival. As societies, we needed more complex and reflective ways to work together.

This new body of research and synthesis has not easily linked up with psychoanalysis. For their part, as I said, the new researchers and theorists kept their distance. For psychoanalysts, on the one hand, the new research confirms so many key ideas that it has often seemed like a vindication. Yet it also challenges the theoretical autonomy and "splendid isolation" of the psychoanalytic profession. For a serious synthesis or integration of psychoanalysis and neuroscience to work, the cherished and heavily defended theories of its different schools would need to become subordinate to experimental findings. If confirmation for those theories is not forthcoming, psychoanalysts would have to modify or relinquish concepts that have become integral to their identities. The response has been equivocal. Let me give an example. Repression is a key concept in Freud's unconscious, referring to the disappearance of ideas threatening to emotional stability. For Freud, repression is what pushes or pulls thoughts and perceptions into the dynamic unconscious. Heather Berlin in a review of relevant neurological research notes how much of it supports traditional psychoanalytic concepts: "Studies on unconscious affect provide persuasive evidence that people can feel things without knowing they feel them, and act on feelings of which they are unaware; an idea that has guided psychoanalytic clinical practice for a century." But, then, she acknowledges that while there is robust neurological evidence supporting the existence of the defences of suppression and dissociation, "the existence of repression is contentious" (Berlin, 2008, pp. 27–32).

It may well be worth noting that, among psychoanalysts today, there is considerable renewed interest in dissociation as the mind's primary defence. It links up with growing interest in different self-states, and the spaces between them into which memories and links disappear. But if, lacking unambiguous empirical evidence, psychoanalysts are forced to abandon the concept of repression, what will those who have relied on the concept to account for Freud's dynamic unconscious replace it with? Clinically, this may not be such a problem, but it is an ideological challenge (Westen, 1998).

I have already touched on another problematic theory: "primary process". Existing evidence now suggests that there are far more than two systems of mental processing. To be sure, there is growing evidence for earlier non-verbal and sub-symbolic forms of processing that are similar to Freud's "primary process", but it is more complex and multifaceted than he believed.

This is only one example of the problems lying ahead for the synthesis of the new unconscious with the old. One can anticipate that several key concepts might not find the empirical support required to carry them forward. Evidence for psychic energy has been seen as shaky for some time now. The idea of a psychotic core is problematic. Will new findings support the theory of depressive and schizoid positions? Infantile sexuality is well established, but does it have the ongoing impact on individual development as Freud initially claimed? I mention these examples only to suggest the magnitude of the issues. It will take years for more neurological evidence to accumulate, and for psychoanalysts to develop their responses.

On the other hand, our understanding of the scope of unconscious behaviour is expanding dramatically. We know now that groups and systems are pervaded by unconscious dynamics, and a vast literature has grown up about the value of exploring them. A significant number of consultants use this perspective in their work. To be sure, Freud also wrote about unconscious aspects of historical and social issues, using the lens of his metapsychology. But his work was admittedly speculative and exploratory. Today's practitioners are more pragmatic, less inclined to draw large inferences. Their work is driven by specific problems and focused on seeking solutions to concrete problems.

It should be acknowledged, of course, that the information we have is far from definitive. There are serious methodological—as well as ethical—problems in studying the mind in stress. But as techniques and technologies improve, increasingly we will have more clear choices.

Before going on to describe this expanded scope, let me clarify that I think all unconscious processes work through individual brains, brains that are integral parts of their bodies. Group dynamics, for example, operate on individual, embodied brains, brains that are situated in groups, receiving all the clues that other group members provide, whether consciously or unconsciously registered. Individual minds are highly motivated to achieve the security of belonging to larger wholes, or to avoid the terror of exclusion, but it is individual brains that process those hopes and fears and the information that is relevant to monitoring them. Similarly, widespread social forces such as prejudice also work through individual brains, even though the information that provides the stimulus for individual acts of prejudice is widely distributed and is not the possession of any one brain.

Thus, even though we understand that the mind is distributed, pervious, and highly social, the neural activity that leads to each individual response so far appears to be bounded by the body. (To be sure, chaos theory does open the possibility that collectives of brains may self-organize, but as of now, to the best of my knowledge, there is no real evidence for this.) The legitimacy of our work with organizations, with culture, politics, and the economy, developments I want to focus on now, has to be grounded on the firm basis of the existence of such individually motivated neural activity.

I have identified seven domains of research where important work is being done to extend our understanding of unconscious influences on behaviour. The first three domains—the autonomic nervous system, the cognitive unconscious, and the emotional unconscious—are the domains that operate directly within individual minds and account directly for our behavioural responses. The other domains of investigation involve the information and signals that derive from our social and community lives, that shape our integration into larger systems.

I will not describe these seven domains here in any depth. But some brief account is needed to be able to describe new work that is expanding the boundaries of these domains.

The first domain, the autonomic nervous system, is about the regulation of bodily processes essential for maintaining life, such processes as breathing, blood pressure, digestion, and so on. These processes are homeostatic, normally functioning entirely without conscious awareness, but they can be affected by outside stimuli, and they can be manipulated through feedback mechanisms, meditation, and other techniques.

The second domain, the cognitive unconscious, as the psychologist Timothy Wilson put it, "gathers information, interprets and evaluates, and sets goals in motion, quickly and efficiently".

A major part of this scanning consists of perceptual categorization, whereby the objects or events we encounter are continuously classified into familiar categories, and appropriate responses are set in motion. That makes our world recognizable to us—but it also leads to the discarding of information that doesn't fit existing categories (Edelman, 1992; Wilson, 2002).

Emotions also shape our behaviour, but our awareness of them, like our awareness of our actions, is largely retrospective. As Joseph LeDoux put it: "The mental aspect of emotion, the feeling, is a slave to its physiology; not vice versa." For that reason, he and others claim, we have an "emotional unconscious", sets of established physical responses to events. These set responses are partly shaped by our emotional histories and become activated unconsciously in response to cognitive clues, but they are also shaped by emotional systems and some rudimentary plotting of such systems has occurred. Clearly, the cognitive and the emotional unconscious can overlap. Indeed, it is probably rare for one to operate entirely without the other, but they appear to be quite distinct systems. One does not require the other (Kihlstrom, Mulvany, Tobias & Tobias, 2000; Ledoux, 1996).

There is a fourth domain, closely associated with these, what I call the domain of self-esteem. Anything that threatens the stability and consistency of the cognitive and emotional categories that we have established and upon which we rely to live in the world will arouse anxiety because it forces us to acknowledge that we do not understand things as well as we thought, that we are not as much in control of events as we had believed, and that we cannot be sure of what we are currently planning to do. For the American psychiatrist Harry Stack Sullivan, there were different intensities of threat. On the routine level of everyday experience, we simply "selectively inattend" information that is inconsistent with what we want to continue to believe about the world and ourselves. (This is somewhat similar to the social psychologist Leon Festinger's concept of "cognitive dissonance".) More dangerous threats bring about dissociation, blanking out the information entirely. But this monitoring of experience is a continuous and largely unconscious activity.

It's worth mentioning here that early in his career, Freud stressed our powerful need to ward off awareness of motives damaging to self-esteem. He and Breuer used the concept of "censorship" to account for hysterical symptoms, and, as late as his dream book, censorship was a central concept in explaining the need to exclude certain thoughts from consciousness. With his theory of infantile sexuality, he moved into exploring what he took to be deeper motivations.

With the domain of self-esteem, we are moving closer to our participation in the social world, as threats to self-esteem largely originate there. The final three domains of the unconscious I describe are more directly about those social relations themselves. They are the domains of language, group cohesion, and politics.

The tool of language is not neutral. The primary medium we use to communicate, is also the best means we have to conceal and deceive. It is infiltrated with unconscious processes in two ways: language frames discourse, so that our social conversations are structured in ways of which we are usually unaware; and language confers meaning on our private acts, meaning that inevitably and invisibly suggests, as well as excludes, other meanings.

Both the cognitive and emotional unconscious, as we have seen, are based on our ability rapidly to discriminate and categorize perceptions. We often do not know what defines these categories, since we have to infer them from the behavioural responses they elicit in us as well as others. However, when it comes to behaviour, the categories appear to possess neuronal consistency. Researchers in this field express this in the slogan: "Neurons that fire together wire together."

Eskimos are reputed to have seventeen or eighteen terms for snow, because their ability to discriminate among different categories is important to their very survival. On another level, Foucault has made us aware of the political power of controlling a discourse. And there are stories and myths that guide our actions without out knowing. The intergenerational transmission of trauma is a good example of the power of stories to affect subsequent generations.

George Lakoff has argued that the Democratic and Republican parties in America offer competing metaphors of the family. The Democrats favour the metaphor of the nurturing family, concerned to protect and foster the development of its members, while the Republicans see the family, particularly the strong father, preparing its members for a tough and unforgiving world. In the light of these underlying metaphors, their differing social policies are more coherent than they might otherwise appear: the Republican vision of the family is characterized by the need for a strong national defence, firm law enforcement, a reduced emphasis on social insurance programmes and entitlements, a strict moral code. The Democrats, on the other hand, come across as more maternally oriented, trying to lend a helping hand to the disadvantaged, promoting social justice, offering insurance, and so on. Lakoff has offered his services as a political consultant based on his ability to decode such myths (Lakoff, 1999).

The next domain, unconscious belonging, is perhaps the least recognized and appreciated in our culture. Our historic, embedded focus on the individual has meant that we idealize and reward our leaders, our winners, our geniuses and heroes. It is a widespread conviction among us that groups thwart the individual, impede action, waste time. On the other hand, working together, group members can be creative and productive, achieving far more collectively than they possibly could working as separate individuals.

But what is the motive for belonging? Darwin argued in *The Descent of Man* that if members of a tribe were always ready to aid one another, sacrificing themselves for the common good, they would inevitably be victorious over other tribes. He believed that such a social instinct aided natural selection, especially when operating within the family unit. We are less likely to accept that there is such an instinct. But what gets individuals to cooperate or, at least, coordinate their actions?

I think it is fair to say that we can generalize two kinds of motives arising in individuals that profoundly influence group processes. One set is about anxieties over being included or accepted in the group. Bion postulated that this process was based on a primitive need to be accepted at the maternal breast, activated by our participation in complex and confusing social settings. That's one possible explanation for this anxiety. A second set of motives has to do with the anxieties that arise from failing at the task the group has come together to perform.

The desire for inclusion and approval is likely to be stronger among members of a teenage clique or gang, but we are well aware that no one is immune to the pressures of feeling accepted or, probably more importantly, to the danger of being extruded. A related set of individual motives has to do with identity. More adult or sophisticated group members may not be satisfied with mere inclusion, requiring recognition for their specific identities in order to feel secure. This is related, no doubt, to the anxieties of group dysfunction or failure, effects that not only threaten the stability of the group but also the livelihoods and reputations of its members.

The last domain, politics, has to do with the processes that affect society as a whole. This is probably less known than any other domain, but writers like Vamik Volkan have been working not only to understand the motives and dynamics around such issues as ethnic conflict and genocide, but also developed strategies to lessen or resolve them. (See Volkan, 2006.)

I think we do understand now that prejudice is a universal process, rooted in normal development. On the simplest level, it stems from the ways in which our brains create categories as part of our adaptation to reality; we cannot stop ourselves from doing it. It is based on our early ability to discriminate strangers from caregivers, those we know and have come to rely upon from those we don't. The normal two-year-old in our culture will cry in the presence of a stranger; the adult will simply stiffen or become more reserved. But as Peter Fonagy and Anna Higgitt have observed in their studies of normal attachment: "however socially noxious the strategies adopted by some individuals may be, prejudiced responses are basic to coping with insecurity in attachment" (2007, p. 71).

Prejudice, then, will never be done away with. Those who claim to be free of prejudice can only be speaking a half-truth, at best. The most they can validly affirm is that they do not act on their prejudices. This is clearly a place where consciousness needs to intervene, to help us suppress or reformulate our automatic reactions and chart alternative courses of action.

"Malignant prejudice", when normal processes of discrimination lead to splitting and active discrimination, often occurs when group identity is involved. Erik Erikson coined the ungainly term "pseudospeciation" to describe the all too familiar process through which we come to believe we are members of a different species, apart from other groups of human beings, whose different racial, religious, or ethnic communities no longer deserve our respect or understanding.

Prejudice is just one example of large-scale social processes based on unconscious motivations, though perhaps the most urgent for us to work on understanding. Terrorism can perhaps be thought of as an aspect of this process, but what other motivations does it rely upon—or stimulate in others? What is the effect on us of our increasingly ubiquitous digital communication or social networking? (See Chapter Seven by Philip Boxer in this volume.) What about the erosion of traditional identities? The long-term effects of the destabilization of gender differences or acceptance of differences in gender orientation?

On the other hand, there are idealizing effects of prejudice as well. Our entertainment and advertising industries are based upon the manipulation of such perception and feelings, creating celebrities and stars, trusted brands, strong candidates, and television series that inspire identification and loyalty. This is inevitable in a consumer-oriented society, where those who have products to sell seek out the means to manipulate perceptions and create positive prejudices, otherwise known as brands. (See Chapter Eight by Richard Morgan-Jones in this volume.)

This is a quick summary of what I call the "new unconscious". I don't claim that these seven domains of inquiry are definitive. They are what I see now—and they will inevitably change as our knowledge expands and new problems present themselves. Even now, we can begin to discern where these fields are moving—and the new problems that understanding the unconscious can illuminate.

There is some important new research on the question of how new ideas arise and how old ideas can be changed. The new unconscious, like the old, tends to be conservative, illustrating the sway of past learning over the present. But, clearly, new ideas cannot be impossible to generate. Nor can it be impossible to alter or extinguish old ideas.

One of the most fascinating areas of current research is into what is called the "default network", the brain systems that are active when the brain is not engaged in focused, problem-solving actions. Understandably, researchers first studied the brain functions underlying cognition and motivation. But evidence began accumulating around the edges of that research showing that the brain was highly active in "default mode". According to researchers, default activities include: reminiscence of past experiences based on episodic memory, recalling autographical incidents, day-dreaming, and planning for the future (see Mazoyer et al., 2008).

These "stimulus-independent thoughts" (or SITs, as researchers call them) seem to correspond to what psychoanalysts mean by free association, "free-floating attention", or reflection, the state of mind that facilitates new connections and new thoughts. Although it is too early to decide on the evolutionary value of these functions, some researchers have suggested it is crucial to planning the future.

A related area of research focuses on insight, the process by which new ideas suddenly appear, like revelations. The brain systems involved in insight are thought to be "at rest", somewhat different from the "default system" in that different areas of the brain are involved (see Kounios et al., 2008).

Experimentally, it is relatively easy to distinguish the flash of sudden understanding characterizing insight from the problem-solving that comes from the methodical cognitive work of comparing or analysing data. Moreover, techniques have been developed to observe the brain engaged in both activities. Insight is accompanied by a dramatic spike in gamma rhythms, the highest electrical frequency generated by the brain.

One researcher noted the drawback of the cognitive approach to problem solving: "Concentration comes with the hidden cost of diminished creativity." That is, determined efforts to come up with the solution to cognitive puzzles can work, but they do that by blocking out information and forestalling approaches other than the method the brain is resorting to at the moment. He tells the story of a Zen monk who could not use insight to solve any of the puzzles he had devised in his experiment, concluding that the Zen master was too intently focused. But then, suddenly, the master got it. He learned to focus on not focusing, and the solutions came, one after the other (Lehrer, 2008).

Tracking brain activity revealed that insight involves the right brain, where neurons with longer branches and more dendrites collect information from larger cortical areas. They are less precise but better connected. But, first, the brain has to be primed by left-brain cognitive efforts to engage and direct attention. In other words, we have to struggle to engage the problem we are seeking to understand; then we have to let go and let the brain do its work without pressure. "If you are in an environment that forces you to produce and produce, and you feel very stressed", says John Kounios, co-author with Mark Jung-Beeman of many of the key articles describing this work, "then you are not going to have any insights" (2008, pp. 281–291).

A sceptic might well ask, "What does this add to what we already know intuitively?" There are two answers. That fact that there is empirical data for unconscious processing can help convince others that we do know what we are talking about. It is also likely that experimental research will uncover new strategies to promote insight. Kounios & Jung-Beeman have reported on their research to DARPA, the research arm of the military that has been responsible for such revolutionary practical developments as the Internet. Given the strategic and competitive advantages of insight, we can be sure that they are working to find ways of promoting it.

Let me conclude by shifting our attention away from the brain to two areas of research that are receiving more and more attention: the behaviour of voters and the making of financial decisions. In both areas, the role of unconscious motivation is becoming increasingly apparent, and understanding that role can have substantial economic payoffs.

Earlier, I touched on George Lakoff's theory about the opposing family myths that underlie democratic and republican politics in the US. Lakoff set up a research institute to provide help to liberal politicians. Others have followed, but I think it fair to say that much of this work is not publicly disclosed. Politicians not only want to protect their competitive advantage, but they are also reluctant to be seen as "manipulating voters".

Drew Westen, a clinical psychologist who has written extensively on links between brain research and psychoanalysis, in his recent book draws on neurobiological research. He describes an experiment in which the brains of subjects during the 2004 election were scanned while they were exposed to conflicting statements by the candidates they favoured.

He found that, faced with the contradictory information, initially the brains showed signs of conflict and distress, but they rid themselves of the distress by quickly disposing of the troubling information. This is consistent with the work being done in the domain of unconscious efforts to maintain self-esteem. More surprisingly, he found: "not only did neural circuits involved in negative emotions turn off, but circuits involved in positive emotions turned *on*. The partisan brain didn't seem satisfied in just feeling *better*. It worked overtime to feel *good*, activating reward circuits to that give partisans a jolt of positive reinforcement for their biased reasoning" (Westen, 2007).

Westen has also set up a consulting firm to attempt to capitalize on his findings about politics and the emotional unconscious, and no doubt increasingly others will as well. The equipment is expensive, and much of the theorizing is speculative, based on how the emotional unconscious is thought to function. But it's not hard to imagine a time in the near future when teams of neurologists and psychologists will routinely advise and vet political campaigns.

The second area of great potential growth is economic behaviour. The recent credit meltdown has discredited the inadequate motivational concepts that underlay classical economic theory and created an unprecedented opportunity for new thinking. Classical theory was based on two ideas: rational decision-making based on individual's self-interest, and efficient markets that optimized all the information available, the idea that markets are "perfect". For many years, these ideas were virtually dogma in the world of economists, and traditional risk management was largely based on them.

Behavioural economists were standing in the wings to suggest other motivations grounded in a more sophisticated psychology. But it wasn't until the recent credit crisis and the failure of economic policies based on classical theory that they have been getting the attention they deserve. A key idea for them is that investors are not merely motivated by self-interest, but that they are also "loss averse", that is, often, they will not sell in a market to maximize their gains because they shrank from experiencing a loss. Behavioural economists have promoted other psychological principles about investor irrationality: ninety per cent of people overestimate their abilities and indulge in wishful thinking about their prospects; they persist in holding certain beliefs, reluctant to look for evidence that disconfirms them, and misinterpreting the evidence when forced to face it; their judgements about probability are skewed by the availability of relevant memories. But as two authors put it recently: "behavioural models often assume a specific forms of irrationality". That is, far from providing a flexible and comprehensive theoretical framework, they are linked to very particular, concrete forms of behaviour (see Barberis & Thaler, 2005).

Let me give a small example. The chief financial correspondent for *The New York Times* recently commented on how victims of fraud have often refused to accept the settlements they have been offered. He gave the example of how many of Ponzi's investors would not accept the government's offer of 30 cents on the dollar, continuing to believe that Ponzi would make good on his original promise, even though he was in jail at the time, having been convicted of fraud. The *Times'* correspondent invoked the new behavioural finance explanation: they declined the real if lesser gain of the settlement because they could not bring themselves to accept the loss. But it is at least equally plausible that they refused to accept the humiliating conclusion they had been duped. Far more than the mere loss was at stake. Behavioural explanations often do not take us deep enough into the realm of motivation.

Accounts of financial bubbles often acknowledge the importance of "herd behaviour", markets being driven by a kind of contagion that, in effect, compromise their rationality. But so far, few have tried to systematically link up sophisticated theories of group membership with market behaviour. This remains a promising area for exploration. It is not difficult for us to imagine how an understanding of defensive operation triggered by anxiety could be brought to bear on understanding markets, or how a deeper understanding of unconscious conflict might illuminate investor behaviour.

A few psychoanalysts have started to enter the dialogue. David Tuckett has interviewed a number of fund managers and developed the theory that the excitement generated by the prospect of great economic gains, especially in financial bubbles, overrules the normal and appropriate anxieties associated with potential losses (Tuckett & Taffler, 2008). He has also included references to basic assumption behaviour.

There are other promising signs, stimulated by the recent collapse of the credit markets and the subsequent recession from which we are still struggling to emerge. Much as the 1929 crash of the stock market and the subsequent worldwide depression required a profound re-evaluation of economic theory, this crisis presents a unique opportunity to re-examine the assumptions underlying our economic behaviour.

Perhaps there is an analogy here for us. Just as research into brain function gives us an opportunity to re-examine our psychoanalytic beliefs about the ways in which the unconscious works, social failures open up new vistas and fresh opportunities for social psychologists and psychoanalysts seeking new insights into political and economic motivation.

The new unconscious is grounded on empirical research, as well as a wide variety of empirical practices. That's the good news. The black box of the mind is no longer opaque. We can now see it as translucent, if not transparent, lit up by powerful flashes of mental activity, revealing mechanisms of coordination, driven by consistent needs. It sheds more and more light. As we grope our way through the tangled underbrush of old, familiar thoughts and the thickets of conventional expectations, increasingly it will help us to find our way.

And as we clear paths, others will follow.

Note

This is an expanded version of a paper presented as keynote speech at the Annual Symposium of the International Society for Psychoanalytic Study of Organizations (ISPSO) in Copenhagen, Denmark, in June 2010.

References

Barberis, N. & Thaler, R. (2005). A survey of behavioral finance. In: Richard H. Thaler (Ed.), *Advances in Behavioral Finance*, Vol. II, Chapter 1. Princeton, NJ: Princeton University Press and the Russell Sage Foundation.

Berlin, H. (2010). Neurological explanations of the dynamic unconscious. *Impulse: Journal of Psychology, I*: 24–51.
Edelman, G. M. (1992). *Bright Air, Brilliant Fire*. New York: Basic Books.
Eisold, K. (2010). *What You Don't Know You Know*. New York: Other Press.
Ellenberger, H. F. (1970). *The Discovery of the Unconscious*. New York: Basic Books.
Fonagy, P. & Higgitt, A. (2007). The development of prejudice. In: H. Parens, A. Mafouz, S. Twenlow & D. Scharff (Eds.), *The Future of Prejudice*. Lanham, MD: Jason Aronson.
Kihlstrom, J. F., Mulvany, S., Tobias, B. A. & Tobias, I. P. (2000). The emotional unconscious. In: E. Eich (Ed.), *Cognition and Emotion* (pp. 30–86). New York, Oxford: Philosophy in the Flesh.
Kounios, J., Fleck, J. I., Green, D. L., Payne, L., Stevenson, J. L., Bowden, E. M. & Jung-Beeman, M. (2008). The origins of insight in resting-state brain activity. *Neuropsychologia, 46*.
Lakoff, G. (1999). *Philosophy in the Flesh*. New York: Basic Books.
LeDoux, J. (1996). *The Emotional Brain*. New York: Simon and Schuster.
Lehrer, J. (2008). The Eureka Hunt. *The New Yorker*, pp. 40–45.
Makari, G. (2008). *Revolution in Mind: The Creation of Psychoanalysis*. New York: Harper Collins.
Mazoyer, B., Zago, L., Mellet, E., Bricogne, S., Etard, O., et al., (2001). Quoted in R. L. Buckner, J. R. Andrews-Hanna & D. L. Schacter, The brains' default network. In: A. Kingstone & M. B. Miller (Eds.), *The Year in Cognitive Neuroscience, Annals of the New York Academy of Sciences* (p. 38). Boston, MA: Basil Blackwell, 2008.
Searle, J. R. (1997). *The Mystery of Consciousness*. New York: New York Review of Books.
Tuckett, D. & Taffler, R. (2008). Phantastic objects and the financial market's sense of reality: a psychoanalytic contribution to the understanding of stock market instability. *International Journal of Psycho-Analysis, 89(2)*: 389–412.
Volkan, V. (2006). *Killing in the Name of Identity*. Charlottesville, VA: Pitchstone Publishing.
Westen, D. (1998). The scientific legacy of Sigmund Freud: towards a psychodynamically informed psychological science. *Psychological Bulletin, 124(3)*: 333–371.
Westen, D. (2007). *The Political Brain: The Role of Emotion in Deciding the Fate of the Nation*. New York: Public Affairs.
Wilson, T. (2002). *Strangers to Ourselves: Discovering the Adaptive Unconscious*. Cambridge, MA: Harvard University Press.

PART IV

PSYCHOANALYTIC REFLECTIONS ON THE WORLD AROUND US

CHAPTER TEN

Psychoanalysis of a cityscape: a case of post-traumatic stress disorder—the city of Warsaw[1]

Andrzej Leder

Introduction

Before a psychoanalytical case study is presented, it is necessary to provide a brief description of the physical aspects of the patient and the most salient facts in their history. In particular, this applies to the character portrait that remains hidden to the majority of readers. Let me then share a brief history of our patient—the city of Warsaw—with the readers who might not be so familiar with its dramatic past.

Warsaw through a kaleidoscope of history

In the sixteenth century, Warsaw became a "royal" city, the capital of the Polish Lithuanian Commonwealth that stretched from the Baltic to the Black Sea. This royal heritage was decisive in dictating the constructs of the urban grid, stretched along a north–south axis along the Wisła River dissecting the Mazowiecka Lowland, between the Royal Castle as the seat of political power and the king's summer residence in Wilanów.

At the close of the eighteenth century, Poland lost its independence. Three empires—Prussian, Austrian, and Russian—grabbed the opportunity to divide the territory of Poland at a moment of political crisis. Warsaw suffered a fall from the status of a royal city to that of a provincial capital of a region in the Russian empire—and afterwards, after unsuccessful uprisings, lost even that status. In the nineteenth century when capital cities of independent states were modernizing at a dramatic pace, Warsaw was mired in apathy and any development that occurred was ad hoc and chaotic. The eastern and western boundaries were areas of dire poverty, and there, especially in the west, most of Warsaw's heavy industry was concentrated. At that time, about twenty-five per cent of the city's population was Jewish.

Poland's return to independence in 1918 was a true miracle for Warsaw. In the space of twenty years, up to the outbreak of war in 1939, the city was transformed into a small Central European metropolis—the "Paris of the north" as it was sometimes referred to, with approximately 1.2 million inhabitants.

And then came the Nazi occupation. Already the battle over Warsaw left the first scars, a result of bombing—on a scale with that of the air raids over London in the early 1940s. Then began the murderous and harrowing occupation. Over three hundred thousand Jews were crammed into a penned area, which became the Ghetto. Most of the Jews were deported to the death camp of Treblinka and murdered in gas chambers. In April 1943, several dozen survivors of the Jewish Combat Organisation and other soldier formations began an uprising in the Warsaw Ghetto, which was inevitably overpowered by the Nazis. Afterwards, on the orders of Hitler, the German Wehrmacht levelled the entire Ghetto to the ground.

In 1944, due to the impending arrival of the Soviet Army from the east, the Polish government in exile in London decided to start an uprising, which was to liberate the remaining areas of Warsaw—thus opening them for the Soviets. At the same time—as the capital city was liberated by the Polish resistance army—it also confronted the Russians with the issue of Polish sovereignty as an fait accomplis. About fifty to sixty thousand regular Polish soldiers, previously in hiding, took up arms. Almost all of Warsaw was initially liberated but Stalin held the Soviet army back, and for the next two months after heavy fighting the Nazis systematically won back suburb after suburb. Approximately two hundred thousand Varsavians died, mostly civilians. After the 1944 Uprising was put down, Hitler ordered a total destruction of Warsaw, which was systematically carried out up to January 1945, when the Soviet Army entered Warsaw along with the new Polish Army that had been formed in Russia.

Up to seventy-five per cent of the city's substance was destroyed. Early on, thought was given to moving the capital to the nearby industrial centre of Łódź—in the end, this plan was abandoned and it was decided to rebuild Warsaw. This process of rebuilding Warsaw was completed at a time of increasingly totalitarian subjugation of Poland by the Soviet Union—the growth of Stalinism in Poland, which left an important mark on the character of the city raised from rubble and ashes.

One characteristic anecdote is relevant here: in the 1950s, Stalin offered the Polish authorities Soviet help in rebuilding the city. He gave them a choice of building a metro or a huge Palace of Culture. The Polish President at the time, Bolesław Bierut, chose the Palace, a symbol of Soviet domination—though no doubt most of all the city needed a metro.

After the death of Stalin, the "Real Socialism", as it was known, as a political form lost its totalitarian character, though it remained crude and primitive, disorganized and at the same time repressive. All this came to bear on the development of Warsaw, which was subject to the plans of subsequent Polish Communist leaders, in particular Władysław Gomułka, in the 1960s.

The Solidarity movement of 1980 to 1981—the beginning of the fall of the Soviet Empire—deeply changed the mood and the spirit of Varsavians. Crushed after the martial law which was introduced in the end of 1981 by General Jaruzelski, Solidarity movement didn't leave material traces, but prepared the mental change, that occurred in 1989.

After the "People's Autumn" of 1989, Warsaw became a city of the most dramatic transformation—a vacuum drawing people and capital into its vortex, to become the Central European centre of consumption. These changes, however, could not erase the very character of Warsaw, one formed over time in the preceding two centuries.

Psychoanalysis of a cityscape: Warsaw

"A Condition has long been known and described which occurs after severe mechanical concussions, railway disasters and other accidents involving a risk to life; it has been given the name of 'traumatic neurosis'" (Freud, 1920g, p. 11), writes Freud. No doubt Warsaw was subject to "severe mechanical concussions", and threats to life certainly took place. We have every reason to suspect that in this system, symptoms of post-traumatic stress disorder shall occur. More than that: in the essay on *Civilization and Its Discontents*, the father of psychoanalysis formulated the hypothesis whereby it is possible to imagine that the city "… is not a human habitation but a psychical entity with a similarly long and copious past—an entity, that is to say, in which nothing that has once come into existence will have passed away and all the earlier phases of development continue to exist alongside the latest one" (Freud, 1930a, p. 69). If we were to conduct a psychoanalysis of urban space, in accordance with this "wild" hypothesis, then Warsaw from the very first encounter will appear as a traumatized being, psychical entity subject to past shocks and then one attempting to come to terms with them.

It is important to state that the city is foremost a combination of images; it is formed out of shapes and structures. Just as the consciousness, the city is its own image. That is why the job of the analyst is made easier. In fact, the psychoanalysis of urban space is similar to the research of sleep. The system of architecture or even urban landscape share with sleep the same characteristic feature—"their ideational content [is] being transformed from thoughts into sensory images, to which belief is attached and which appear to be experienced", as Freud remarks incisively in *Traumdeutung* (Freud, 1900a, p. 534). We wish to observe these images, more—we want to live in them and touch their hard texture. Thus there is a need for such interpretations, ones that take into consideration the change of how time and narration proceed in a spatial arrangement—its shapes, colours, or their lack.

It would seem therefore that simply walking along the street, ingesting the usual cityscape, and suddenly we are transported to …

Ruined walls and apartment blocks

… the ruined walls of the late bank that used stand in the square, today overgrown with the odd clump of grass and weeds. A splendid right angle where the main wall was, against the open sky, for all to see, from the street—a miracle! From the inside through brick, shining red against sun and classical arches of empty windows. A marvellous ruin of a building, one whose impossible outlines are only caught because trauma is recorded, a painful blow that came to form Warsaw.

Someone though could say: If only the bare, yet-to-be rebuilt walls were to be the symbol of this city! Walking under the bare arches, Warsaw could be read as if a town of the ancient world—full of ruins.

Almost like Freud's Rome, where "... the castle of S. Angelo would still be carrying on its battlements the beautiful statues which graced it until the siege by the Goths, (...)" (Freud, 1930a, p. 69). This comparison of Warsaw with Rome though is absurd—maybe only beyond the breaking point, a trauma that for both towns is the siege by the Goths. Today, after the hasty reconstruction, along Marszałkowska Street there are no arches, and the cityscape is—well everyone knows, drab and insipid.

However, even if preserved ruins are only a tiny element of the city's image, we shall remember, that not even the most minute of details should be ignored in the process of diagnosis. The father of analytical technique is clear on this point: "... precisely the most trivial elements of a dream are indispensable to its interpretation and that the work in hand is held up if attention is not paid to these elements until too late" (Freud, 1900a, p. 512). The analyst's comment therefore must be open in fact to these minor and hidden traits. As a consequence, they seem to "illuminate" what stands out most; they are a medium of meaning's "weightedness". It is thus that the above mentioned ruins in Hypoteczna Street initiate the process of interpretation surrounding its grey concrete apartment blocks that everybody inevitably looks at.

Such blocks are a recurring element of Warsaw's cityscape. Seemingly swathed in over-proportion but in fact, rather shaky in their economy of materials. They sprout like grey, coarse stains over the entire fabric of this city. A reminder: "By its death, the outer layer has saved all the deeper ones from a similar fate—unless, that is to say, stimuli reach it which are so strong that they break through the protective shield" (Freud , 1920g, p. 26). What fate though, does Freud really have in mind?

Therefore the question can be put—what in fact do these blocks block out? If it were not for them a void would fill the metropolis— estranged, open hills of rubble with the odd isolated surviving edifices. Three-quarters of its substance levelled with the surface of the earth. Alas, Warsaw then would no longer be a living city. Thus would look its remains, had in 1945 the plan gone ahead of moving the capital to Łódź and leaving Warsaw-the-Brave for dead; an immortalized pang of conscience.

After the hit, the ruined capital nonetheless was revived. Thus a mass of grey housing fills the massive space of trauma. Repeating this a thousand-fold, a monotonous pattern separate from the unbearable experience of loss, creating some lacunae for life—even if this life is closed in appallingly repetitive and claustrophobic stairwells and kitchens. After breaking the resistance to stimuli, as Freud comments: "Cathectic energy is summoned from all sides to provide sufficiently high cathexes of energy in the environs of the breach. An 'anticathexis' on a grand scale is set up, for whose benefit all the other psychical systems are impoverished, so that the remaining psychical functions are extensively paralysed or reduced" (Freud, 1920g, p. 29).

These apartment blocks witness "that the remaining psychical functions were extensively paralysed or reduced". Many of these buildings—ideas "transformed from thoughts into sensory images"—are produced by the anal desires of the party chief Gomułka. Dwarf-like, they appear as if someone had laboriously spat them out, though at the same time, thanks to the repetition compulsion, they are able to fill the void of trauma with their unchangeable aspect. They exist thanks to the obsessive obligation to repeat, tied to the loss of libidinal energy and simultaneously, to a great extent, consuming the remains of it. The very same stairwells, row after row of windows, balconies in vertical stripe and satellite antennae in their thousands.

Traffic jams as the symptom of melancholia

Not only permanent elements of cityscape, however, such as various constructions, lend themselves to investigation. The city's integral variety is always subject to a hidden form that defines the place where all phenomena arise. As in the case of traffic jams. In this instance, Freud's assertion appears particularly insightful: "even thought-structures so extraordinary as these and so remote from our common modes of thinking are nevertheless derived from the most general and comprehensible impulses of the human mind" (Freud, 1911c, p. 17).

It should be noted that boredom and a sense of powerlessness are characteristic for certain connections in the network of a constant flow. Lacan's psychoanalysis would claim that metonymic movement, from signifier to signifier, is being interrupted. Streets are like traces of understanding; movement of thought in some areas flows and is clear, in others it is mired in melancholy and poisonous dead ends. Such in fact, is the traffic jam.

The environs of the South Station, where Niepodległości Boulevard meets Puławska and Wilanowska streets, are like an unsolved problem. Once at the boundaries of the city, today are a failed locus, a bridge between two town suburbs. Movement, only a moment ago dynamic, dries up and thoughts circle around angry fantasies or sail away into disconnected delusions. Helplessness. Boredom.

And suddenly a collision. *Raptus melancholicus*. A sudden, often bloodied eruption of spirit on the surface of events. Equally often caused by anger, as by absent-mindedness. Collisions recur regularly in particular places, at particular times, changing the capital cityscape into human misfortune. As in negative thoughts that can change an ailing structure of awareness into terrible deeds—were they to flow out of dark abysses and dominate consciousness.

Where do these places come from in which stagnation, traffic jams and collisions occur? It could be said, from the stupidity of urban planners. But not so—for the structure of urban space is only to a small degree shaped by a rational plan. Structure is rather the fruit of a slow process of grafting. After all, this also likens it to consciousness. A product of time where every event leaves a trace, defining forever the possibility of other events arising. It organizes them, lays down paths, and fences off impossible areas. The appearance—some time in the seventeenthth century—of an axis joining the Old Town and Wilanów, determined the linear, rather then spherical, growth of urban space. Elsewhere, organized as in Mazowsze villages, stretched along the road. Everything that is important in Warsaw stretches north–south, forcing one to constantly wander along this axis. This oscillation can never be fluid, constantly breaking—into traffic jams and stops. Just as the thoughts of a melancholic who constantly oscillates from sadness to excitement, seemingly embracing the great gamut of meaning—though we know after all from *Mourning and Melancholia*: "the content of mania is no different from that of melancholia, that both disorders are wrestling with the same 'complex', but that probably in melancholia the ego has succumbed to the complex whereas in mania it has mastered it or pushed it aside" (Freud, 1917e, p. 253).

This impoverishment of variety in meanings that encodes them into a monotonous oscillation was perhaps present already before the blow that altered the structure of the city, before the time of trauma. At that time, the movement of oscillation was connected to the lack of possibility to shake free associations into another sphere, a lack of alternative paths and connections, or maybe rather the subjection of all routes to the dominant, one full of hubris and scorn. For the thoughts that wander along the Royal Route north–south axis—one that always defines the Warsaw ego—east and west boundaries of the city are not present, have not been given cathectic energy, are not taken into consideration. In the east and west, the unattractive is turned away, the poor, the shameful, ones who "have for other reasons aroused strong aversion" (Freud, 1911c, p. 66), as Freud describes in the analysis of the Schreber case.

The Russian governate of yesteryear Warsaw, the orthodox church, small bazaars, pushed out into Praga, right bank Vistula. Working class toiling earth substance packed into the western suburb of Wola. Sudden advance of village poor from north-east Mazowsze, inhabiting Targówek on its boundaries. And threatening spots of brutality—hamlets at the foot of the capital, with their menacing names of Ząbki (Jaws) or Wołomin (Angry Stag). Everything—a sphere of matters repressed and concealed. After all, though, at the same time it is integral to the whole, to the nature of the metropolis. Reluctance and indifference to all in the east and west of the city centre, manifests itself in neglected communication links; too narrow arteries leading to the central and dominating boulevards. The deep, however, organic interdependency of all districts of the city arises in the form of enormous traffic jams exactly on these arteries linking east and west with the city centre.

Thus traffic jams occur on the east–west axis—an entirely different phenomenon than those in the north–south. Events seemingly mutually similar, in different parts of the structure, apparently tell a different story, carry another meaning. For "either the affect remains, wholly or in part, as it is; or it is transformed into a qualitatively different quota of affect, above all into anxiety; or it is suppressed, i.e., it is prevented from developing at all" (Freud, 1915e, p. 177). Apparently similar expressions of anger as shouting, pithy vulgarities, and waving of fists in one place of the structure can be seen as the result of long-term humiliation and, elsewhere, violation of the desire for omnipotence.

The blow, the dream, and the bucolic green

Yet, once more, today's Warsaw is not anymore determined by its royal history. Today, it is a self-awareness after trauma. Structure of two axes, though still important, is no longer the core of its nature, as was the case a hundred or even seventy years ago. Today, we can only speculate about it. Or develop fantasies. For all that came before the blow is like a dream in Warsaw—scraps of images and recollections out of the dim past.

Not even the blow itself, the one that caused the initial contusion, is in fact any longer present. And the process of reparation "happens silently; we receive no intelligence of it, but can only infer it from subsequent events" (Freud, 1911c, p. 70). To this very day, this reflection by Freud sends a cold shiver. The trauma itself is no longer there—the aftermath of effort—never benign—can be seen though, placed in containing it.

And this defines our metropolis. Discreetly growing over in the verdure of parks, squares and paths. Surprisingly bucolic green say those who visit here during the summer. A green valley in front of the monument to the 1943 Ghetto Uprising, the much smaller of two uprisings that took place during the time of trauma. On the monument, black figures attempt to free themselves from the granit relief and once and for all, flee from this God forsaken place. This valley is un-filled by the un-presence of the museum of the un-remembered. The Jews. The meadow is surrounded by green hills on which stand the new houses of Muranów. Covering over cellars filled with the rubble of a people slowly strangled.

The Jew forgotten, does not even bestow ghosts onto neighbouring residents. The un-memory of this place resides side by side with an exceptionally overstated form of massive apartment blocks—known as The Estate Behind The Iron Gate—as if suddenly the compulsion to repeat had to overcome an especially painful boil.

Freud's formula, however, can be applied more kindly in stating "The delusional formation, which we take to be the pathological product, is in reality an attempt at recovery, a process of reconstruction" (Freud, 1911c, p. 70). Today, impoverished flats in identical blocks are rented by families of new immigrants, representatives of another Asian race that came here to do business. Vietnamese replaced the Jews. With ease, they fill all lacunae—this time in the very fissures of culture—opening shops, warehouses and shanty take-away stands, for which there is always demand. And for which there will always be a need in this dead-end place, Masovian plane, natural habitat for farmers, deprived of Jews, late quick-silver merchants, now long dead. Regarding this succession of immigrant peoples, Freud's commentary may seem rather scathing:

"the truth is rather, as we now see, that what was abolished internally returns from without" (Freud, 1911c, p. 70).

A "meta-traumatic" reflexion on the process of reparation

Usually trauma is thought of as something concrete. A blow, wound, excess—all have their palpable meanings only when it comes to language. Though—to repeat—for a traumatized consciousness, a blow is foremost an interruption that requires subsequent joining. An artefact that in its irritating un-presence forces a frenetic completion of work, grows over with unwieldy phenomena that are to join its nothingness with the surrounding structure. Modelling what is preserved therefore enables a successful remedial process. However, in Warsaw, the surrounding structure is dramatically fragile. As a result, it is not this but phenomena that have grown out of a post-trauma, post-war fever that mark out the nature of urban space. They are the encasement—in a literal sense—of trauma's concealed memory.

An important trait of such raised consciousness is in fact the singularity of its phenomena. On account of the fact that they destroy the past, and because they bloom in formlessness for the majority, the metapsychological assertion is true that "It proliferates in the dark, as it were, and takes on extreme forms of expression" (Freud, 1915d, p. 148). The breaking of continuity in every dimension of the urban space and resulting lack of context means that what is created is monstrous, hideous—corresponding to a chaotic nexus of intentions. A scar formation, growing into proud flesh, over and above the original tissue.

The enormous, stalinian lump of Palace of Culture. Extending over entire quarters of the former town centre—absurdly reaching skywards with thousands of rooms, stairwells and corridors that in fact should fill buildings standing along these very streets. A negative of an empty square that stretches all around. A narcissistic false ego puffed up in a void. "From this it may be concluded that in paranoia the liberated libido becomes attached to the ego", would say Freud "and is used for the aggrandizement of the ego" (Freud, 1911c, p. 71). The Palace, testimony of history's twists and turns is a reminder that history itself is after all, the tug and pull of continuity and at the same time, its lack. The Palace arose where trauma—or void—appeared not only as the material destruction of city substance but the complete severing of political continuity. The former backbone of authorities, "personnel resources" was destroyed, one producing political elites throughout the entire period between the First and Second World Wars. In its place entered a misshapen will, wounded by repeated blows, terrified and masquerading fear with ebullient shouts of triumph. Desperate voice of No-Go-For-Metro Bolesław Bierut. After all, he could have had a metro. But he didn't vote for it—for looming above all he saw was the terrifying shadow of the Kremlin. And it is this shadow to this very day that puffs its chest out in triumph over and above the very fabric of Warsaw. A narcissistic phallus of cowering mediocrity.

On the peripheries of the city, a mirror reflection of this disintegration of thought-process are the hideous shacks, squares with fences strewn-full of rubbish, workshops constructed out of sheets of metal sitting cheek by jowl with walls plastered in ceramic debris, behind which lie pretend-villas. The impermanence of attention defines the character of the place, a nipping off—one point from another. As if they were mutually imperceptible, one for another, as if a mutual unseen, as if their "mutualness" did not exist. In this manner, consciousness after trauma separates particular spheres of difficult experience from itself, lays the world out into fragments out of which everyone is on their own in their own self, looking inwards. Every fragment, introverted, closed, meets the description of a psychotic person, as put by Freud: "The patient has withdrawn from the people in his environment and from the external world generally the libidinal cathexis which he has hitherto directed on to them. Thus everything has become indifferent and irrelevant to him, and has to be explained by means of a secondary rationalization as being miracled up, cursorily improvised" (Freud, 1911c, p. 69).

This ruination of character in the suburbs is in fact typical for all modern cities. They are not content within a set of walls but greedily devour the surrounding agrarian substance, lose sense of measure and proportion, as in a dream. However, the usual castle-in-the-sand dreaming that at first light extends to the extremities of body and mind has no entry to the core of oneself. Here, in Warsaw though, it is the opposite. The chaos of the peripheries breaks out into the centre of this living entity itself. In Warsaw, the peripheries are not eccentric—they arise as sheds and ungainly courtyards in the scars of the city centre. They become blind neighbours of the obsessive attempt at coming to grips damned in apartment blocks, along with the remnants of former city substance. In this being-for-self, every detail may begin to inflate and be sated with what appears to be a vision of sense and assumes a monstrous importance. An ordinary House of Culture turned into a Palace. Or repeated indefinitely—the mantra of nondescript high-rise housing estates.

Mania—the way to deny depression

It is possible to believe therefore that a freedom that allows to think honestly opens the way to reparation, as a process that returns coherence to the traumatized sphere. Even if evidence of this reparation has taken on already a hallucinatory nature, it is after all in accordance with psychoanalytical pathomorphology: "Here once more we may regard the phase of violent hallucinations as a struggle between repression and an attempt at recovery by bringing the libido back again on to its objects" (Freud, 1911, p. 76). At the same time, however, its limitations should be remembered: "Such a reconstruction after the catastrophe is successful to a greater or lesser extent, but never wholly so" (Freud, 1911c, p. 60).

The first sign of entering the free market was thus a change of the symptom, a means of filling the void after trauma. Among the tottering suburbs overgrown with the grey mould of high-rise apartment blocks, skeletons of unfinished factory sheds and empty buildings taken over by weeds, there begun to grow monstrous embodiments of malls and shopping centres. Vibrant colours, poignant smells, delectable shapes offer respite from deep-seated hunger and promise some partial satiation, as if giving lie to the dreams of a bulimic patient. These gaudy shapes now in a form of a huge platter where a stack of shining hamburgers glistens, piled one on top of the other—with a mountain of golden French Fries splattered in bloodied ketchup. Or huge gateaux such as the Mokotów Mall, rising up from the centre of the not so long ago drab suburb of Służew.

Looks like somebody dreamt up a heavenly desert, sitting at a table covered with a stained newspaper, where a battered salt shaker stood. And then the gateaux unexpectedly materialized in all its glory. And it happened that all around stainless steel pot arose—office towers with out-of-this-world names such as the Cirrus or Mars Building. Nevertheless, as often in dreams, some reality shines through the dream—the table is still covered with a newspaper.

In the city centre, appetite is satisfied in another way. Up to now bereft of shape, "he builds it up by the work of his delusions"

(Freud, 1911c, p. 70). Clubs, small cafes, pubs, and nooks create a rather unified breeding ground for a varied though hungry form of human substance. In this nursery, mania is christened in the feverish, extended time of youth. It can be said to be "... an over-estimation of the power of their wishes and mental acts, the 'omnipotence of thoughts', a belief in the thaumaturgic force of words, and a technique for dealing with the external world—'magic'—which appears to be a logical application of these grandiose premises" (Freud, 1914c, p. 74).

Because the past has almost no certain memorabilia from its fathers, this human substance lives in an inflated present. Living energy that is not burdened with memory produces the Warsaw style, a "metropolis fusion" that is perhaps the first coherent—apart from Gomulka-period, 1960s-style high-rise blocks—stylistic form of this capital. Italian spaghetti, dried tomatoes downed with Żywiec beer, rucoli salad and ciabatta, chewed with radiating orthodontal braces.

A note of interest concerns the sexual life of the one, who experienced trauma and tried to forget it. Lapses into a particular form of excitation and then already "... the manic subject plainly demonstrates his liberation from the object which was the cause of his suffering, by seeking like a ravenously hungry man for new object-cathexes" (Freud, 1917e, p. 254). The emotional state of Poland's richest city frenetically orbits at night in taxis from club to club, gorging itself on the thunder of amplifier noise and energy-booster drinks poured into the interior of selves with pure vodka. As Freud writes: "They are plainly seeking themselves as a love-object, and are exhibiting a type of object-choice which must be termed narcissistic" (Freud, 1914c, p. 87). And copulate they do. Sex explodes into hundreds of cards showing Silvia and Tania in the buff. Falling from behind windscreen wipers, forming a solicitous carpet under pedestrians, giving life to the grey and crooked Gomułka pavement stones.

However, even in the manic phase of the process of healing, the traumatized mind does not like itself. And certainly never will. So as not to fall into the sphere of destruction that is the core of its organization, it has to keep an ironic distance in relation to its own self. If it were not to distance itself, it would fall into pathos—in the sense that the English offer the word pathetic, the subject of derision. This auto-irony, however, becomes addictive and deforms every thought, every spontaneous gesture. The form of monuments that attempt to patch abducted memory, unintentionally bear witness to this admixture of pain and derision. Warsaw statues are a static form of testimony that places layers of conflicting intentions; intentional that pays respect and unintentional that derides. The influence of the latter, capricious, manifests itself in the grotesque nature of the monument; akin to witticisms, which "… do in fact give this sort of sound-presentation of the word"—or physical aspect of the monument—"greater prominence than its meaning, and that sufferers in such states proceed in their speech on the lines (…) of the 'external' instead of the 'internal' associations of the word-presentation" (Freud, 1915e, p. 119). This explains why Warsaw statues are always grotesque in style. As the pathetic Warsaw 1944 Uprising Monument—composed of a huge number of bronze figures—an unsettling reminder of the film *The Night of Living Death*.

Warsaw—the metaphor of the postmodern world?

Consciousness subjects itself to analysis. The same as the psychological sphere, a city can also be interpreted, reveal its defence mechanisms, join what is cleaved open and show the meaning of denial. There is no one scheme of interpretation. A different town, a different worldview. Formed by the organization of urban space, the sign-laden gamut of the continuous and non-continuous—based on fundamental geometric forms.

The encrustation of concentric boulevards like in Vienna or Moscow, mesh of great arteries of New York or—as in past Warsaw—axes joining extremes. All this—populated by time—renders the town unique, just as the mind is. And every one of these forms has something to say. It is possible to deliberate over the narcissistic pedantry of elegance that continually strokes that same detail—if to take the example of the Parisian garret, repeated in a million ways. Or the maniacal extremes of American towns where downtown rockets vertically skywards only to a moment later dissipate moss-like out into the suburbs.

Today's Warsaw is all non-continuity and artefacts. Thinking about the Polish capital is a confirmation of how difficult post-trauma analysis is. The image of the whole continues to change, every subsequent entry into the field of understanding forces one to start afresh. Trauma, which organizes the whole, can never be identified. Its place is taken by bloated details of recollections, hurriedly glued together consolations—rituals that allow time to be made complete—and unrealistic plans for the future. Joined in a makeshift way, they create a chaotic image. In the past, someone arranged the rubble back together again—such that the town could live on. And so it does. Subsequent creations arise in new places, fulfil their functions in a pulsating fever and elbow each other, taking as much room as possible for themselves.

At times, this peculiar organism is pitied; at times, it causes embarrassment. Especially when returning from the beautiful cities of Central Europe, as in the case of Prague or Budapest. Though if it happens to draw affection—it's not difficult to do so if one has lived with it since time immemorial—then thought blunders along, searching for a formula that shall give it justice. And such a formula exists. It is so obvious, available within arm's reach, spread out across the surface of phenomena that it is, as a result, in fact unseen.

We all live after all in times of disintegration. Not only Warsaw wallows in chaos. The world is fatigued by chaos. One reads the world as a shattered, poured out form of debris where damaged treasures sit side by side with the embarrassing traces of intimacy, and dolls with twisted arms gaze out into empty cans. This rubbish tip sets the camp aesthetic. Incoherence has become the confession of faith.

An over-abundance of facts, images, and events changes the dominant structure of thought. Consciousness increasingly has to divert its attention. Forgets coherent metaphors that once for long periods organized thought. No circles, mesh, or axis. Bricolage dominates, allowing to answer the moment's needs. The world is post-traumatic and finds satisfaction, raising its wounded spirit skywards. Yes, it shouts exaltedly, this is how it must be. An end to order and peace!

If all were to fall into this madness then perhaps, paradoxically, might Warsaw become the most modern of European cities? Perhaps it is necessary to shout that—in fact, yes—it is deconstruction made permanent in urban space. The purest of Bricolage metaphors? A commonplace admixture today of ugliness and beauty that indeed here has gained its highest form. Let us be proud! Maybe in this post-traumatic world, at last we shall find fame, recognition, and love …

Put the dreams on hold

Rather, recognize along with Freud that "here once again, it will be well to call a halt and to postpone any further explanation of mania until we have gained some insight into the economic nature, first, of physical pain, and then of the mental pain which is analogous to it" (Freud, 1917e, p. 257).

Note

1. This is an expanded version of a Polish essay *Nerwica Miejska. Warszawa* by Andrzej Leder, first printed in *Res Publica Nowa* in 2008. Reprinted here with the publisher's permission.

References

Freud, S. (1900a). *The Interpretation of Dreams*. S.E., 4–5. London: Hogarth.
Freud, S. (1911c). *Psycho-Analytic Notes on an Autobiographical Account of a Case of Paranoia (Dementia Paranoides)*. S.E., 12. London: Hogarth.
Freud, S. (1914c). *On Narcissism: An Introduction*. SE 14. London: Hogarth.
Freud, S. (1915d). *Repression*. S.E., 14. London: Hogarth.
Freud, S. (1915e). *The Unconscious*. S.E., 14. London: Hogarth.
Freud, S. (1917e). *Mourning and Melancholia*. S.E., 14. London: Hogarth.
Freud, S. (1920g). *Beyond the Pleasure Principle*. S.E., 18. London: Hogarth.
Freud, S. (1930a). *Civilization and its Discontents*. S.E., 21. London: Hogarth.

CHAPTER ELEVEN

Panic and pandemics: from fear of contagion to contagion of fear

Mario Perini

From time immemorial, epidemics[1] threatened man's survival, mental peace, and the social order that man has come to create.

As Walter Pasini writes in his presentation of a recent Symposium on "old and new epidemics":

> Plague, smallpox, syphilis, cholera, tuberculosis, influenza have changed mankind's history for their impact on men's life and health, and their demographic, financial and social effects. The great epidemics created panic and anxiety as they decimated entire populations. If one single person's illness or death represents a tragedy for his/her family, the collective death adds on feelings of impotence and fear concerning men's fate.[2]

Besides being a haunting ghost, a terrible memory of the past, epidemics have recently also become a present nightmare, a source of individual and collective fears, so much harder to bear in that they symbolically represent all the unseen or disavowed insecurity, complexity, and vulnerability belonging to our current life, as well as the archaic anxieties and "nameless terrors" belonging to every human being's early childhood experience.

During the last decades on the stage of an increasingly globalized world—where everything, even risks, tend to happen on a worldwide scale—over thirty new infectious, epidemic or pandemic, illnesses appeared, the so-called "emergent infections": AIDS, SARS, Ebola virus, the H5N1 "bird flu", the "prions illness" ("Mad Cow"), and the new entry, the H1N1 A influenza or "swine flu", are only the best known among these new threatens, while the traditional ones (malaria, typhus, cholera, tuberculosis, etc.), although no longer feared in Western countries, are still going on and killing thousands of people within the poorest lands.

During 2009, the flu pandemic shook the world. While causing fewer casualties than expected it demonstrated the extent to which "the king was naked", namely, how vulnerable our social systems were and how inadequate our managerial, scientific, technical and communicational abilities have been shown to be. Above all, it highlighted how deeply unprepared the governments, technical bodies and mass media were when faced with the need to manage not just the virus and the illness, but also the spreading of fear amongst the populations.

In order to deal with present and future challenges—as Pasini outlines—we need to start by keeping in mind the lessons from the past, and the understanding of epidemics' history. To this relevant warning, I would also add one more: in order to deal with challenges involving anxiety, fear and panic for thousands or even millions of people, we also need to better understand these human emotions, the way they develop, what may enhance or mitigate them, what their psychological and social dynamics are, how do they impact on individual and group behaviour, as well as organizational functioning.

In what follows, I want to offer a contribution to this necessary process of understanding.

The centuries of fear[3]

Words like "epidemic", "infectious", "contagion" are still able to trigger fear by their mere sound, although the modern medicine has by now eradicated, at least from industrial societies, most of the infectious diseases which have been plaguing humankind for centuries.

The first evidences of an epidemic may be traced back to the Egyptian and the Babylon epochs, and terrible pandemic plagues devastated ancient China as well as the Mediterranean lands during the Troy war. Ancient and modern history describe all along the centuries cyclic periods of major plagues throughout the known world. In 430 BC, Athens falls prey of a plague, as Tukydides narrates in detail; the Western Roman Empire, just prior to being destroyed by the barbaric invasions, has already been weakened by plague and smallpox epidemics; the Eastern one, the Byzantine, during Justinianus is lashed by bubonic plague. In the Middle Ages, leprosy first and then tuberculosis adds to the plague. The greatest epidemic of the pre-modern era, the so-called Black Death, develops in central Europe by 1345: probably carried from Asia through the caravan routes, in a few years it spreads all over the continent, striking Constantinople in 1347; Florence, Marseilles, and Paris in 1348; and many other countries in the following years, until it came to an end in Russia in 1351.

With the great discoveries the sailors bring to Europe syphilis they have contracted in the Americas, while the natives are decimated by the illnesses exported by the conquerors: smallpox, measles, and even the ordinary cold. During the seventeenth century, thanks also to the Thirty Years War, the plague strikes again in Europe, spreading death in collaboration with other then endemic illnesses, like malaria and smallpox, and new killers like spotted fever.

In the following century, plague pays still a further visit to Europe, in Austria in 1711 and in the Balcanic area from 1770 and 1772, to reappear sporadically by the second half of the nineteenth century, on the edge of a big Eastern pandemic which lead to more than twelve millions of dead in China and India.

During the first half of the same century, cholera had struck Italy, while in England the new working class was paying to Industrial Revolution the heavy toll of thousands of victims for tuberculosis, which then would also hit France, Germany, and Japan. Furthermore, tuberculosis appeared to be a fatal gift of colonial expansion, which spread mainly in Africa and in the Southern Seas; smallpox, measles, diphtheria, and influenza over time also crossed countries and continents and became exported almost everywhere.

Influenza and viral illnesses were the absolute protagonists in the twentieth- and early twenty-first-centuries' epidemics and pandemics. The discovery of bacterial origins of many infectious diseases, an increased concern for the public health, the practice of vaccinations, and the new drugs, the antibiotics, allowed to eradicate nearly all the sources of the traditional plagues and epidemics, or at least to contain their diffusion. The last enemies, however, the viruses, appeared harder to fight against than bacteria, and from their ranks arose what may be considered the two most dreadful "plagues" of the contemporary age: AIDS and flu pandemics.

The first HIV epidemics—which presented the world with a new disease, AIDS—date back to the 1980s. Oddly enough, although this illness is still far from being defeated, and goes on bringing pain and death among the emergent and the poorest nations, people's fears and the mass media's attention massively moved away to focus on the flu.

Influenza viruses, always at the origin of large epidemic events, during the twentieth century have provoked three pandemics: the Spanish flu (1918–1920), which claimed approximately twenty millions of victims; the Asian flu (1957), which killed two million people; and the 1968 Hong-Kong influenza, which made one million of dead. In this first decade of the twenty-first century, influenza viruses spread panic within the globalized world on three occasions: the SARS in 2003, the "bird flu" in 2005–2006, and the last one, the A influenza, so-called "swine flu", in 2009.

Epidemics as psychosocial processes

The relation between epidemics and contagion has been taken for granted, but for a considerable time the science, the culture, and partly also people's opinion attributed them to other causes. Quite paradoxically, however, the concept of contagion—a transmission of some illnesses from a person to another person (or from animal to person)—is really a very old one[4], for centuries the official medicine has been supporting different explanations, adding to those coming from popular fantasies and superstitions, and from the religious doctrines.

Hyppokrates[5] believed that epidemics were provoked by seasonal changes and the action of "miasmata", that is, the air-polluting substances, while in *Oedipus Rex* Sophokles gives the miasma a religious meaning of impurity (and guilt) due to a bloodshed, which caused the plague afflicting Thebe. The "miasmatic theory" of contagion remained pivotal to Western medicine until the nineteenth century and the discovery of bacteria as infectious agents. From the Renaissance, however, this theory contributed, at least indirectly, to improve the struggle against epidemics and poor-hygienic living conditions. Measures such as safeguarding the purity of water and freshness of food, promotion of personal cleanliness, and responsible waste and sewage disposal protected the population from plagues as well as through quarantines and isolation of ill people in lazarettos.

However, the Catholic Church, from its very origins, during the Middle Ages, and, to an extent, to the present day, had been declaring that epidemics represented nothing but God's punishment for men's sins, drawing on the accounts of Biblical plagues and furnishing people's terrors with a reassuring cultural container based on the dynamics of guilt/punishment/penance. From this perspective, we could say that both the Church and medicine, by taking on the roles of "managers" of primitive fears of illness, contagion, and death, have established themselves as parallel institutions acting as social defences against such anxieties, and relying upon these "psycho-social" functions to increase their cultural and political influence and authority.

The modern institutions responsible for dealing with contemporary epidemics also inherited, to a great extent, the following functions: to anticipate the outburst of an epidemic, to identify its aetiological agent, to interpret its trend and dangerousness, and to make decisions on what and how things should be organized in order to face it. Besides their "rational" task, they are also expected to manage individuals' fears and mass panic amongst the populations.

Over such a terrain, where emotional, unconscious, and irrational aspects reign supreme, even amongst those charged with the task of governing the process, the logic of science, rationality, and critical reasoning will not have a sufficiently strong hold. Hence the great importance of a sophisticated social communication in situations of alert and panic; if not inspired by a deep understanding of personal and social aspects of human fear (and particularly the fear of contagion), such communication may boil down to a series of procedures and informational routines, and risks to be perceived by people as a superficial, bureaucratic, and self-absolving reassurance, inevitably turning into a source of mistrust and of further insecurity.

These considerations bring us directly to the core of the problem. Epidemics are not just a health problem, they also imply psychological, social, cultural, and political processes which require complex, multi-dimensional approaches. These should be focused on the individual–society interface and on the overlap between these two-way relational dynamics: one part of this is the way social order impacts upon individuals' behaviours and responses, the other refers to how people's mental functioning interacts with and gets to shape or change social systems, sometimes to a great extent.

Some authors, though not so many, and mainly following the shock of the discovery of AIDS, explored these specific aspects of epidemics. One of the most interesting contributions, from the perspective I wish to develop here, is an article by Philip Strong on "Epidemic psychology".[6]

Although his work is mainly sociological and intended to describe a general model of human behaviour during epidemics, in his analysis Strong pays a great attention to psychological elements and to individual and collective emotions, which are an integral part of the process and have a deep impact on the process itself and on the social order in a broad sense. He points out how an epidemic may become "a medical version of the Hobbesian nightmare—the war of all against all", and how the spreading of the biological disease may be followed by psychological epidemics of fear, suspicion, panic, and stigma, fierce moral and ideological controversies, veritable wars of religion around causes, responsibilities, and solutions to be adopted.

As Strong puts it:

> Epidemic psychology, indeed, seems to involve at least three types of psycho-social epidemic. The first of these is an epidemic of fear. The second is an epidemic of explanation and moralisation and the third is an epidemic of action, or proposed action. Any society gripped by a florid form of epidemic psychology may, therefore, simultaneously experience waves of individual and collective panic, outbursts of interpretation as to why the disease has occurred, rashes of moral controversy, and plagues of competing control strategies, aimed either at containing the disease itself or else at controlling the further epidemics of fear and social dissolution.[7]

Strong comes then to remark that, just like the infectious disease, the three "psycho-social" epidemics are able to infect almost everyone within the social system, individuals as well as organizations, and for this reason, they "simultaneously possess profound psychological and collective characteristics" (ibid.).

Another relevant consideration, though it might appear quite obvious, is that the epidemics of fear, interpretation, and action seem to be much more severe when the disease is new or strikes in a new way. Two aspects are relevant here: one relates to the way social systems are equipped with norms, routines, narratives, roles, beliefs, etc., in order to deal with novel and unknown issues; the other raises a difficult psychological question: whether fear is more triggered by what is completely unknown or by what is somehow deeply known but still unbearable and therefore impossible to think and articulate?[8]

For the purpose of this chapter, I will focus more on the first epidemic, the epidemic of fear, but keeping in mind the problems of both morality and action, as all three domains are profoundly intertwined.

On fear and its vicissitudes

I'd like to make some preliminary remarks on fear as an emotion and also as a related behaviour. Fear is a primary emotion which is aroused by a danger (actual or potential) and mobilizes bodily as well as psychic coping processes and fight/flight behaviours aimed at allowing the subject to escape from the danger or to suppress its source. Fear is thus necessary for survival, first of all, as it helps us to become aware of risks, but sometimes it may turn into a counterproductive or even damaging device, both for the individual and for the social system.

Fears may be inborn or learned. The first are part of the instinctual equipment and are triggered by:

- strong or unexpected physical stimuli like pain, light, noise;
- unknown[9] objects, people, or events, which the individual cannot face, like strangers or new diseases;
- risks for survival, like altitude, darkness, cold, lightening, aggression, illness, wounds and bleeding, abandonment by parents.

Learned fears come from the individual's personal (or sometimes ancestral) story and from the beliefs and the prescriptions held by his or her group or community concerning what should be considered dangerous or painful. They may sometimes turn into excessive or inappropriate fears—the phobias—through complex unconscious dynamics and social learning processes.

This leads us to the distinction between "normal" and pathological fears, the latter often being a disguised expressions of internal dangers based on unconscious fantasies, anxieties and related defences. What is important here is that, for this very reason, such pathological fears are rather inaccessible to evidence, reasoning, or reality testing.

If fear is useful when working for survival, it is admittedly such a painful emotion that, in order to be tolerated and allowed to exert this function, it needs psychic and social devices which would protect the individual and the environment from its potential damages, such as stress, mass panic, and social paranoia. Some of these defences are psychological and working on an individual basis, like repression, projection, or denial, while others are concretely embodied in social institutions, for example the police, whose task is to protect us from other people's (but also our own) antisocial behaviours. Like emotions, defences may also be relatively "normal" and adequate, as well as excessive and pathological, just as defensive social systems like police services might come to perform a socially destructive role when used by a totalitarian government. Denying one's own fear of an illness may expose an individual to fall ill or for a disease to become more severe if left untreated.

Fear may present different degrees both of strength and concerning the quality of emotional experience, from sustainable worry, awe, hesitation, disquiet, to heavy conditions of scare, anxiety, and terror, or even pathological states like distress, anguish, panic, and phobia.

Although individually perceived, some fears are less rooted in the individual than in the group to whom he or she belongs or is connected by means of identification: if a threat is hanging over the group, then all individuals are likely to feel menaced by it, even though they might not be actually in danger. These collective, social fears are enormously increased as a result of group or organizational dynamics, which may act as real emotional "amplifiers", as the recent market meltdown has shown eloquently.

The psychosocial roots of fear are to be found in the mix of primitive early anxieties and needs for safety present in the internal world of the child from the very beginning of life, and the sense of insecurity and helplessness stemming from our relationships with natural and societal environments. Naturally, what adults are afraid of is generally quite different from what scares the children, but there is evidence that adults' fears—and the consequent coping strategies—are largely modelled by those experienced during early childhood.

The first shield against all fears is the mother, later on the family or its social equivalents. But with growth, this protection appears increasingly defective, partial, and full of ambivalence, which enhances the role of individual and social psychic defences. Faced with unbearable fears, the mind may try to repress, displace, or deny them or the dangers, to project them unto others, to find reassurance in some rational explanation, or to split the reality into a bad, dangerous outside world to be warded off, and a good, safe, and idealized place—including legal and illegal drugs—where to withdraw in search of salvation.

Social defences[10] may also serve the purpose of avoiding fear: the social system itself, its institutions and politics may be involved in a defensive set of beliefs, actions, and organizational routines aimed at protecting their members from an experience of fear, provided the latter accept to live within a social bond essentially based on dependence, fidelity, obedience, and conformism, or on the splitting and projection of all responsibility for the danger into the demonized Other—the scapegoat, the enemy, which therefore has to be feared, excluded, blamed, or even destroyed. As a result, all theories and catch-phrases which sound reassuring and optimistic exert a strong seduction for the public opinion, even when apparently false or manipulated; another consequence is how rapidly and superficially do these defensive systems identify dangers, enemies, faults, unhealthy foods, causes of cancer, terrorists, and so on. Nothing would please us more than having a quick fix to heal most fears, to find a name for them, and to point a finger to a culprit: splash the monster across the front page, and people will resume peaceful sleep at night.

Another problem is the fact that these social defences are not just unconscious processes managed by individuals, groups, or communities searching for safety. As Freud pointed out in *Group Psychology and Analysis of the Ego*,[11] their capacity of convincing people, dragging them and blinding their critical functions, is well known to leaders and to anybody who wants to achieve or exert power over others. That's why occasionally "politics of fear" arise and develop, by riding or feeding collective anxieties and conflicts.[12] See also Chapter Nine in this book.

Fear of epidemics and epidemics of fear

The fear of contagion and infectious epidemics has some very specific characteristics. One is the fear of the invisible, something that is among us but cannot be seen, because it is too little (like bacteria and viruses), too big (like pollution, radioactivity, the stock market, or an epidemic process), or homely and familiar[13] (like air, water, food, the next-door neighbour, the members of our family). The core unconscious fantasy in the fear of epidemics is that "the enemy is among us or even one of us".

Its hallmark is a set of paranoid defences, involving split (between the guilty and the innocent, the pure and the contaminated) and projection of guilt and blame on individuals and groups supposed responsible for contagion.

As Strong points out "the epidemic of fear is also an epidemic of suspicion. There is the fear that I might catch the disease and the suspicion that you may already have it and might pass it on to me".[14] The central character of the drama is the "untore", a term used in seventeenth-century Italy to denote a plague-spreader, as vividly described in Manzoni's novel *I Promessi Sposi* ("The Bethrothed").

In our times of global connectedness, the role of plague-spreader has been extended from one single person to entire groups or even systems. During contemporary pandemics, one continues to be afraid of individuals, but the suspicion extends rapidly to embrace groups such as: strange people, foreign communities (like the Chinatowns), enemies (like Islamic terrorism), or large organizations, hidden powers, and obscure interests. This is the case with recent pandemics, when heavy doubts have been raised about the financial interests of some corporations (the food industry as well as pharmaceutical companies) or against the governments themselves, accused of playing with people's lives for politic reasons or even spreading new plagues through their secret laboratories for biological warfare.

Although in these suspicions, there is probably more truth than one could imagine or wish for,[15] undoubtedly they are right in the range of delusional persecution and magic omnipotent fantasy. Looking at this with the psychoanalytic lens, we could see how such paranoid transformation of mourning may well serve to fight the depressive view of human frailty,[16] and how conspiracy theories, involving the idea of malignant all-powerful organizations, are somewhat reassuring if confronted with the discouraging evidence that faced with pandemics even our highest powers appear substantially disarmed and helpless.

The use of epidemics as a social defence, displacing internal insecurities on an external bad object, allows individuals and societies to keep a fantasy of locking out dangers and fears, and making themselves immune against them. In this sense, epidemics appear not very different from wars.[17] The combination of a splitting of reality and a special mobilization of energies (including the crucial role of mass media) may help for a while to divert attention both from individuals' everyday problems and from governments' failures.

What makes the difference is the very nature of danger, which in epidemics is invisible and difficult to spot, which makes them more similar to terrorism than to war. Where the enemy might be "any one of us", including the family, no team spirit or social solidarity that are likely to work in wartime, can develop or survive. As Strong reminds us, this may turn into a war of all against all:

> A ... characteristic of novel, fatal epidemic disease seems to be a widespread fear that the disease may be transmitted through any number of different routes, through sneezing and breathing, through dirt and through doorknobs, through touching anything and anyone. The whole environment, human, animal and inanimate may be rendered potentially infectious. If we do not know what is happening, who knows where the disease might not spring from?[18]

As the core risk is contagion, namely contacts, relationships, empathy, and social interactions, the sole safety lies in isolation, not so much in a medical sense, as a means of preventing the transmission of infectious agents, but rather as an antisocial drive, leading first to withdrawal and mistrust, then to exclusion, ostracism, or even persecution of the scapegoated other.

These defensive dynamics are similar to those of social phobias: primitive anxieties from the individual's inner world, matching with everyday "endemic" worries and the global insecurity of present life, are fully displaced onto an external object perceived as bad, dirty, strange, and ill—the epidemic and the virus, first of all, and secondarily some kind of plague-spreader. In this sense, the "fear of contagion" rather than to dirt phobia or pathophobia appears closer to xenophobia, the fear of strangers.

The idea of epidemic as an exotic production and of strangers as typical "untori", vehicles of contagion, wards off the troubling evidence that the danger is with us, inside our family or in human nature. Immigrants, specially when illegal, are the best candidates for the role of plague-spreader: they are poor, not very clean, coloured, badly speaking, they steal (our jobs and our things), rape, peddle drugs, kill—surely they are the ones who brought this damn virus here?! They look like us, but actually they are different: in fantasy, "they are not what they appear", that is to say, they are kind of alien, unreliable objects, precisely dangerous as they seem familiar, just like air, water, daily bread, and next-door neighbours during an epidemic.

Again, in such gross biases there may be something true, and after all, most of infectious agents really do come from across the border; but this idea of illegal immigrants as potential plague-spreader essentially reassures us against further puzzling evidences:

- that we ourselves could be a vehicle of epidemics as tourists or business travellers or peace-keeping soldiers;
- that to some extent, the main "untore" is globalization, whose human, financial, and social costs are still far from being quite understood and mastered and contained.

Another link which could be explored is the one between infectious and mental diseases. This connection is somehow obvious if one thinks of how easily an epidemic might drive people crazy, or bring to mind what Foucault describes in his *History of Madness*,[19] namely how old lazarettos for infected people were being gradually transformed into asylums for "lunatics". But subtler links may be also found in certain persisting attempts to discover some infectious agent as a source of psychic disorders (jokingly called a "schizococcus theory"); and at least partly in the strong emphasis that some theories, even within the psychoanalytic field, place on traumatic events as the origin of mental diseases. It is as if there was a shared wish to ascribe madness to some external agent instead of having to acknowledge what Marion Milner called "the suppressed madness of sane men".[20]

What we need to be aware of is, as Bion suggested, the defensive meaning and use of theories, which basically protect us from facing a world so often uncanny, unknown, inexplicable, and unpredictable. In the case of epidemics, what is being avoided is the evidence that all the time we live among viruses and bacteria, which since time immemorial have been our constant "travel companions". Some of them may actually be useful, like intestinal bacteria, or the germs involved in the production of antibiotics or biological agriculture, but more often than not, they are dangerous, reminding us of what our technological hubris would sometimes try to make us forget: our human limits and our own vulnerability.

The last point I wish to discuss is how the fear itself may spread and act as a kind of epidemic. Let us consider an epidemic of fear following or concomitant with an epidemic illness as a social pathology overlapping the biological disease, the two being relatively independent from one another. A wave of fear and panic may explode among a population even when very few individuals have actually been infected. On the other hand, a society may come to adapt itself to periodic epidemic cycles, at least when the illness is known, so that epidemics may become "normalized and institutionalized", just as AIDS has by now become over the period of the last thirty years or so.[21]

When an epidemic of fear is under way, one can see panic and irrationality going well beyond the ordinary citizens, to strike even those who should be either best informed about the disease, like doctors, or well equipped to find the best solutions, like government bodies and officials. As mentioned above, this epidemic causes serious damages to the social order as a whole and particularly to social cohesion, solidarity, and collective ability to deal with the problems. The main symptoms of such social pathology seem to be confusion and stigmatization.

Confusion appears from the very beginning of epidemics as a collective process of "exceptionally volatile intellectual state",[22] an inability to decide whether the situation is serious or not, and a flood of explications on how it could be originated (sometimes hiding moral or ideological judgements), as well as of suggested strategies to solve the problem. This leads to a general disorientation that is usually amplified by mass media. People experience this as an evidence of profound disorganization of public authorities that as a result become more and more denigrated, their warnings and instructions increasingly ignored and unheeded.

Stigmatization is not a product of epidemics, as it is a permanent potential process in all societies, along with beliefs, stereotypes, biases, and myths. An epidemic may help underlying stigmata to surface, and to apply to the specific situation (as was the case of AIDS and homosexuals), resulting in what Strong calls an "epidemic of stigmatisation":

> the stigmatisation both of those with the disease, and of those who belong to what are feared to be the main carrier groups. This can begin with avoidance, segregation, and abuse, and end—at least potentially—in pogroms. Personal fear may be translated into collective witch-hunts. Moreover, so we should note, such avoidance, segregation and persecution can be quite separate—analytically at least—from actions aimed at containing

the epidemic. Such behaviour can occur with all types of stigma, not just with that of epidemic disease. We are dealing here with magic and taboo, not just with quarantine.[23]

Unveiling hidden social issues

It has been said that in extremely dangerous conditions such as epidemics or wars the human beings reveal its very nature, particularly the dark instinctual side hiding behind the well-mannered civilized façade. This is certainly true, but more than that, an epidemic may represent a powerful test for the social system itself. Experience shows that large-scale epidemic diseases (or pandemics) may deeply undermine the conventional social order, bringing about a collapse of its structure or a corruption of its culture, as well as highlight its hidden distortions, failures, and unresolved businesses. Strong gives a vivid description of the former process:

> All kinds of disparate but corrosive effects may occur: friends, family and neighbours may be feared—and strangers above all; the sick may be left uncared for; those felt to be carriers may be shunned or persecuted; those without the disease may nonetheless fear they have got it; fierce moral controversies may sweep across a society; converts may turn aside from their old daily routines to preach a new gospel of salvation; governments may panic. For a moment at least, the world may be turned upside down.[24]

The emergence of the shadow side of a social system seems very hard to recognize mainly because it's so easy to hold an epidemic responsible for anything that is going wrong; however, claiming that the plague has revealed such and such bad facets of our society also risks unveiling just that sort of crusade spirit and moralizing frenzy that is an integral part of the epidemic's social pathology.

It's certainly possible that inhuman behaviours of individuals or organizations portray the narcissistic decay and lack of solidarity of postmodern communities, that isolation and difficulty to work in groups is an expression of a growing liquidity[25] and a loosening of social bonds, that transgression and crimes may indicate a general crisis of leadership and authority. However, all these hypotheses would remain a vain intellectual exercise unless a collective mental space to work through them is offered at a proper time and provided with enough authority to promote an uncomfortable awareness and to inspire reasonable decision-making processes.

Otherwise, the place for thought is bound to be filled by action, namely the storm of control measures (not always so mindful) taken to contain the epidemic: a generally impulsive and mindless kind of action, driven by fear or its denial, or by the projection of vulnerability, impotence, and guilt.

If we agree that great epidemics and pandemics, when also studied by historians and social scientists, may enlighten not only the evolution of science and health care, but in particular the demographic, economic, structural, and cultural changes that have occurred in human societies, then we could assume that such exploration should result in increased understanding and awareness.

But here we close the circle by connecting back to the issue of fear, because it is well known—above all, from the psychoanalytic psychology—that fears and anxieties are major obstacles preventing us from both awareness and understanding of our external and internal realities.

How could we heal or at least contain collective fears or mass panic? You cannot just tell people: "hey, listen, you must not be afraid!", or spread clouds of Valium throughout the planet. Neither the politics nor the official medicine today seem able to create enough safety and trust to reduce such fear.

From this point of view, admittedly, even individual and social psychology are not likely to provide effective solutions for such unpredictable and uncontrollable phenomena. One can just reiterate the following common-sense points:

- that facing fears should be better than denying them or turning a blind eye to them;
- that putting them into words and creating reflective spaces for their exploration is already a good-enough way to reduce them;
- that experience shows us how the simplest solutions may be highly attractive but actually are often mostly deceptive.

Can psychoanalysis be of help?

Psychoanalysis also puts forward awareness as a good-enough antidote to fears saying that if adult people want to face their own anxieties as well as to consider real dangers, they should be able to match a mature vigilance of actual reality with the capacity to get in touch with their own "inner child" and early ways of experiencing fear, while at the same time giving up any pre-packaged, conformist, and mechanistic responses offered by the current culture.

As Gaburri and Ambrosiano point out:

> Strong emotions—and fear among them—require a response which is to be specific, namely the result of a work made by the adult in order to hold and to some extent share the child's point of view, finding a way to get through. Resorting to group prefab responses … only shows that adults cannot stand to let themselves to be infected by the child.[26]

The contribution of psychoanalysis might therefore be to enlighten the general picture in terms of developing or encouraging a "weak thinking" aiming to achieve a deeper understanding of a problem, rather than a strong set of "how-to" prescriptions. This is similar to what Bion intended when he spoke of a "negative capability"[27] to bear uncertainty for a while instead of rushing into action or explaining away what should be first tolerated and understood. Some authors[28] emphasized the use of such capability as a specific quality of leadership, particularly in turbulent conditions or environments, when mind, thought, and linking are under attack by the pressure of primitive anxieties.

The first pathway to try to face epidemic panic would therefore imply setting up a rather steady political as well as clinical governance of the phenomenon. Here, a psychodynamic approach may help the development of an appropriate "situational" leadership and support its capacity for keeping on thinking when things become tough.

Trying to work directly upon mass opinions and behaviours would be a sign of unforgivable omnipotence, if not arrogance and manipulation. What people need when facing real danger is feeling that they are in the mind of their leaders, and wisely and realistically conducted by them. They also need leaders who make them feel safe and prevent them from experiencing pain, often in a magic way, and this is what triggers omnipotence among those in charge of making crucial decisions.

But a good-enough leadership should be aware that when emotionally driven population must be respected and treated as reasonable adults, but also need to be understood as frightened children. That's why, in order to lead them towards a real safety and security, an authentic parental attitude and state of mind is generally required. Also in terms of neither pursuing popularity nor reassuring people by false and seductive solutions. Such qualities are to some extent intrinsic in some individuals' personalities, but they may even be inspired and fostered with suitable means, like psychoanalytically oriented in-depth coaching or role consultancy, organizational diagnosis, and group relations training to enhance both awareness and the exercise of personal and delegated authority.

As you also need to deal with day-to-day problems and emergencies while keeping in mind the overall frame, a systems psychodynamics consulting to the numerous bodies involved in emergency processes and related decision-making might help them to maintain the necessary "binocular vision": upon the here and now as well as the future; on both individuals and large groups and systems; considering rational, mature, and task-oriented functioning but also taking into account the primitive, emotional, basic assumptions dynamics.

One last point where psychoanalysis may give a contribution is after the storm, that is by helping to learn from the occurred experience, in order to be prepared to deal with future crises without repeating the same errors. Repetition compulsion is a general tendency of human mind, both in individuals as in population, and in some cases might even prove useful as a way of sparing energies and maintaining homeostasis. But it also represents a by-product of traumatic experiences badly worked-through, and the resulting stress disorder may thus obstruct the capacity for thinking and learning. The last "swine flu" pandemics expired unexpectedly, while people were prepared to see millions dead on the streets, and whilst the local authorities were holding emergency meetings to decide where to locate the necessary mass graves! A sigh of relief has been breathed worldwide, but two clouds are still hanging on the horizon: another pandemic wave is expected next year (the future is still uncertain) and no lesson has been drawn from the last events as yet (the past is still to be deciphered).

On such a large and complex scale, learning from experience is nearly a "mission impossible", but just by looking at what happened some elements are actually available for insight and reflection. The extraordinary level of panic which affected all the layers of our societies, individuals as organizations, powerful statesmen as well as ordinary citizens, scientists as well as uninformed people, shows the power of the global, overwhelming uncertainty that we continuously live under.

It warns us all of the urgent need to reduce the weight and the duration of widespread insecurities, to rebuild trust and a safer base for coexistence and cooperation, to restore more mindful authority and leadership structures, which may act as learning organizations, reflective spaces, and institutional containers capable of holding and transforming societal anxieties—as well their own worries—as a liable drive for action.

This obviously will not prevent epidemics from occurring, nor people from feeling scared by the last plague; but it may help to use an overcome (not just passed over) crisis as a tool to cope with the next one.

And, as somebody[29] argued with reference to the Lehman Bros.' bankruptcy and the past market meltdown, "A crisis is a terrible thing to waste".

Notes

1. The term "epidemic", deriving from the Greek ἐπιδήμιος (compounded of ἐπι, "upon", and δῆμος, "people"), describes an infectious illness which rapidly spreads around by means of contagion, directly (from an affected person or a healthy carrier) or indirectly (through infected objects), hits a large number of individuals in a more or less wide territory, and after a longer or shorter time span eventually comes to an end. An epidemic spreading over the population in a huge territory, like a continent, or worldwide, is called a pandemic (from the Greek παν, "all"). An illness, whether infectious or not, spreading over a region and keeping steady, as for onset and number of affected people, is defined as an endemic illness. The "A Influenza" of 2009, the so-called "swine flu", is a pandemic, while the common influenza is not, being instead endemic in Western countries, as well as AIDS in Africa.
2. Pasini (2010).
3. *Treccani Encyclopedia* (2009).
4. The Bible itself already mentions the leprosy as a contagious disease.
5. *Epidemics* (I & III Book) and the treatise *On Airs, Waters and Places*.
6. Strong (1990).
7. Ibid.
8. Cfr. Christopher Bollas's concept of "unthought known" (Bollas, 1987).
9. See the above paragraph.
10. Menzies (1961), Krantz (2010).
11. Freud (1921).
12. Perini (2010) in Brunning & Perini (Eds.).
13. See Freud's concept of *Unheimlich* (Freud, 1919).
14. Strong (1990).

15. As was the case of the "Anthrax envelopes" sent around by Al-Quaeda in 2001.
16. Like in Stanley Kubrick's movie *Dr. Strangelove*, where US General Jack D. Ripper launches a nuclear attack on the USSR, in his firm belief that Reds are trying to alter the "genuine body fluids" of the Americans by contaminating water.
17. Eisold (1991).
18. Strong (1990).
19. Foucault (1961).
20. Milner (1987).
21. The origin of the illness should trace back to the first half of the century, probably for a migration and transformation of a monkey virus, but the "appearance on the stage" dates around 1981, when in Atlanta, USA, many sudden cases of illnesses connected to "human immunodeficiency" were found among homosexuals.
22. Strong (1990).
23. Ibid.
24. Ibid.
25. Bauman (2000, 2005).
26. Gaburri & Ambrosiano (2003) [the author's translation from the Italian text].
27. Bion (1970).
28. French (2000); French, Simpson & Harvey (2002, 2009).
29. F. Guerrera (interview on "La Stampa", 16 September 2010).

References

Bauman, Z. (2000). *Liquid Modernity*. Cambridge: Polity Press.
Bauman, Z. (2005). *Liquid Life*. Cambridge: Polity Press.
Bion, W. R. (1970). *Attention and Interpretation*. London: Tavistock Publications.
Bollas, C. (1987). *The Shadow of the Object: Psychoanalysis of the Unthought Known*. New York: Columbia University Press.
Eisold, K. (1991). On war: a group relations perspective. *Psychologist-Psychoanalyst*, XI (Supplement): 32–35.
Foucault, M. (1961). *Madness and Civilization: A History of Insanity in the Age of Reason*. London: Tavistock, 1965 (In French as *Histoire de la Folie à l'âge classique*. Paris.)
French, R. (2000). "Negative capability", "dispersal" and the containment of emotion. Paper presented at the Symposium of the ISPSO, London, 2000. Published in *Bristol Business School Teaching and Research Review*, 3, Summer 2000.

French, R., Simpson, P. & Harvey, C. (2002). Leadership and negative capability. *Human Relations, 55(10)*: 1209–1226.
French, R., Simpson, P. & Harvey, C. (2009). "Negative capability": a contribution to the understanding of creative leadership. In: B. Sievers, H. Brunning, J. de Gooijer, L. J. Gould & R. Redding Mersky (Eds.), *Psychoanalytic Studies of Organizations*. London: Karnac Books.
Freud, S. (1919). *The 'Uncanny*. Standard Edition, 17 (pp. 217–256). London: Hogarth, 1955.
Freud, S. (1921). *Group Psychology and the Analysis of the Ego*. Standard Edition, 18 (pp. 67–143), 1955.
Gaburri, E. & Ambrosiano, L. (2003). Ululare con i lupi: Conformismo e rêverie. Bollati Boringhieri, Torino. ["Howling with Wolves: Conformism and Reverie"]
Kernberg, O. F. (1997). Ideology and bureaucracy as social defenses against aggression. In: R. Shapiro (Ed.), *The Inner World in the Outer World: Psychoanalytic Perspectives*. New Haven: Yale University Press.
Krantz, J. (2010). Social defences and 21st century organizations: a tribute to the contribution of Isabel Menzies Lyth. *British Journal of Psychotherapy, 26.2*, May.
Menzies, I. E. P. (1961). The functioning of social systems as a defence against anxiety: a report on a study of the Nursing Service of a General Hospital. In: *Containing Anxiety in Institutions: Selected Essays*. London: Free Association, 1988; and in: E. Trist & H. Murray (Eds.), *The Social Engagement of Social Science: A Tavistock Approach. Vol. 1: The Socio-Psychological Perspective*. London: Free Association, 1990.
Milner, M. (1987). *The Suppressed Madness of Sane Men: Forty-four Years of Exploring Psychoanalysis*. London and New York: Tavistock.
Pasini, W. (2010). Presentazione a "Vecchie e nuove epidemie". Convegno di studio, Bologna, 24 aprile 2010 ["Old and new epidemics": introduction to a Symposium, Bologna, 24 April 2010] http://scienzaonline.com/index.php?option=com_content&view=article&id=393:vecchie-e-nuove-epidemie-convegno-di-studio-sabato-24-aprile-2010-archiginnasio-di-bologna-ore-10–12-&catid=55:eventi&Itemid=70
Perini, M. (2010). Si vis pacem para bellum: psychoanalysis, peace education and conflict literacy. In: H. Brunning & M. Perini (Eds.), *Psychoanalytic Perspectives on a Turbulent World*. London: Karnac Books.
Strong, P. (1990). Epidemic psychology: a model. *Sociology of Health and Illness, 12(3)*: 249–259.
Treccani Encyclopedia online (2009). Epidemie e contagio: i secoli della paura ["Epidemics and contagion: the centuries of fear"]. www.treccani.it/Portale/sito/altre_aree/scienze_della_vita/percorsi/epidemie.html

CHAPTER TWELVE

Climate change and the apocalyptic imagination[1]

Paul Hoggett

Introduction

This chapter explores a key dilemma of political activism—how to combine thoughtfulness with conviction. This dilemma is particularly acute in facing up to climate change—where uncertainty is high but the stakes are huge. This article attempts an analysis of one form of "conviction politics"—the apocalyptic response to actual or imagined disasters—and traces two variants of this response, the redemptive and the survivalist. Whilst such responses appear radical, it will be argued that they are more a manic attempt to fend off despair. For scientists, activists, and policy-makers, the dilemma is how to avoid the Scylla of paranoia and the Charybdis of complacency (Hoggett, 2009, p. 171), that is, how to sound the alarm without being alarmist.

Paradoxes of activism

One of the paradoxes of political activism is that the passion required to sustain it—anger, grief, hope—is based upon a certain degree of splitting. Donald Meltzer (1975) noted how, when we decide to act, we necessarily have to suspend our belief in, or withdraw our commitment from, other perspectives or choices. According to Meltzer, "every decision involves the setting in motion of a single plan from among its alternatives: it is experimental (and) involves risk (and) a certain ruthlessness towards oneself and others" (1975, p. 241). Action therefore requires a capacity to use what the Kleinians call the paranoid-schizoid position in a creative way. Where action requires some cost or sacrifice to oneself, it is impossible to act decisively if one simultaneously acknowledges the equal validity of other points of view, particularly the points of view of erstwhile political opponents. The depressive position, with its openness and receptivity to other minds, with its commitment to toleration of uncertainty and doubt, therefore does not provide a firm foundation for action. Ideally, the activist needs to be able to move back and forth between certainty and doubt, "black and white" and grey, if her or his commitment is to be free of dogmatism. This back and forth movement is conceived by Ron Britton (1993) in terms of a necessary oscillation between the paranoid-schizoid and depressive positions. But this is no easy task, and requires quite a high level of individual emotional maturity, or a political movement which is tolerant, curious, and generous to dissident points of view. Because it is so difficult to hold the contradiction between doubt and action, the necessary and temporary suspension of doubt can so easily become a permanent stance, in which an internal establishment (Hoggett, 1997) decrees that dissident thoughts are no longer thinkable.

The motivational basis for action demands a sense of moral urgency, for example, that we should act now against human trafficking because it is an affront to our values. But moral urgency can so easily switch into something quite different, that is, into temporal urgency, the sense that if we don't act now, it will be too late. This then is the dilemma of alarmism, of "crying wolf". This dilemma is one that I believe has faced all radical movements of political protest. For much of the twentieth century, radical labour and anti-colonial struggles tended to draw upon a form of Marxist discourse which slipped imperceptibly from Marx's original thesis concerning the imm_a_nent nature of the contradictions of capitalism into a conviction concerning the imm_i_nent nature of capitalist collapse. Such catastrophist scenarios became just another, albeit contemporary, instance of that millenarian current that, in his fascinating book *In Pursuit of the Millennium*, Norman Cohn perceived as a recurring motif in European history from the Dark Ages onwards. As Cohn described it, "the tense expectation of a final, decisive struggle in which a world tyranny will be overthrown by a 'chosen people' and through which the world will be renewed and history brought to consummation" (1993, p. 285).

There are a number of interlinked themes here that I will explore in this chapter. I think the central theme is what I am calling "catastrophism" which I see encompassing subsidiary themes of apocalypse, survivalism, salvation, and redemption. The relevance to climate change is this. As Mike Hulme points out, climate change is a classic example of "post-normal science" where "facts are uncertain, values in dispute, stakes high and decisions urgent" (2009, p. 78). Lacking predictive powers, we simply do not know how objectively bad the situation is that we face, yet faced with what seems like cultural complacency the temptation for activists is to exaggerate, to fall into a politics predicated on the necessity to act and act now in the face of imminent catastrophe. This is a dangerous path, as I hope to show.

History and collective trauma

Each generation appears to have its own "looking into the abyss" moment. I was eleven at the time of the Cuban Missile Crisis in 1962, and it passed me by completely, but the period around the Iran Hostage Crisis in 1979 shook me to the core. At the time, I remember newspaper reports about schools in London that were struggling to provide effective reassurance for distressed pupils. And while money was to be made from the installation of reinforced concrete bunkers in suburban gardens, several close friends of mine actively contemplated moving to New Zealand as the one place in the world most likely to avoid annihilation. Moreover, like many others, my dream life was literally haunted by images of imminent atomic catastrophe. As global warming gathers pace and the likelihood of an effective international response seems to wither, we seem to be heading for another of those moments when we look into the darkness. The difference, of course, being that this time the threat is gradual, "the long descent" as some describe it (Greer, 2008).

Over the last hundred years, there have been repeated moments when citizens in Western democracies have had to face up to civilization's capacity for the utmost destructiveness. Freud's experience of the First World War convinced him to revise his theory of the human drive, to make space for a drive towards cruelty, aggression, and destructiveness alongside love (1930, pp. 45–53). Another of the previous century's great intellectual figures, Theodore Adorno, forced into exile in 1934 by the rise of Nazism, was to confront the catastrophe of the Holocaust in writings which had a profound impact on subsequent social thought (Adorno, 1951). Move forward another twenty-five years, and the capacity for Mutually Assured (Nuclear) Destruction in the context of the Cold War was casting its shadow upon a new generation of writers and activists, a shadow which seemed to be nursing a new structure of feeling (or, rather, non-feeling) that some called "bomb culture" (Nuttall, 1970). And now, today, faced with what some, like Jared Diamond, term "ecocide" (Diamond, 2005), civilization's destructive forces once more present themselves, this time in terms of potential environmental catastrophe. The point is, each generation tends to think of its times as unprecedented. In fact, we have been here many times before—facing the abyss, that is.

Interestingly enough, that "terrible war" (Freud, 1920, p. 9) also led Freud to reintroduce the idea of trauma, an idea that had tended to fade into the background after Freud had earlier abandoned the idea of "actual seduction" in his theorization of hysteria. As Freud puts it, "we describe as 'traumatic' any excitations from outside which are powerful enough to break through the protective shield" (1920, p. 35). Such excitations can belong to the realm of the real or of the psychic imaginary. The trauma that results from having one's foot blown off in war or from being sexually assaulted requires little or no psychic mediation. But the terror of nuclear destruction and the massive anxieties aroused by the prospect of climate change are wholly mediated by the psyche—nuclear war never came, but it was the thought of it that was terrifying. What cannot be thought about will be somatized, projected, or enacted, and Freud's exploration of trauma and people's difficulty in moving beyond such experience leads him to an investigation of our compulsion to repeat, and this in turn opened up huge areas for further work, including the transgenerational transmission of trauma (Fonagy, 1999; Volkan, Ast & Greer, 2002). The two world wars, the Holocaust, and the Cold War, with its attendant possibility of nuclear warfare, can be thought of in this light—each left an imprint on the collective psyche which in some way could not be assimilated. The growing recognition of the reality of anthropogenic climate change faces us with the same collective psychic predicament—how can we think in a realistic way about something whose implications are unthinkable?

Like nuclear war, climate change threatens the imagination with excess (Yusoff, 2009).

In this chapter, I will explore some of the ways in which we have responded to previous real and imagined social catastrophes in order to enable us to understand better some of the ways we may already be responding psychically to our present one.

Adorno: facing the Holocaust

Adorno's is a philosophy of despair. You get something of its quality from the following, written in the early 1940s while Adorno was in exile in the USA:

> The thought that after this war life could continue on "normally," or indeed that culture could be "reconstructed"—as if the reconstruction of culture alone were not already the negation of such—is idiotic. Millions of Jews have been murdered, and this is supposed to be only the intermission and not the catastrophe itself. What exactly is this culture waiting for anyway? And even if there was time left for countless people, is it conceivable that what happened in Europe would have no consequences, that the sheer quantity of victims would not recoil into a new quality of the entire society, into barbarism? As long as like follows like, the catastrophe perpetuates itself.
>
> (2005, section 33)

There is no hope to be found, certainly not in politics, not even in private life. Virtues like honesty and authenticity are no longer possible. The subtitle of these writings *Minima Moralia: Reflections from Damaged Life*, captures this well. In this work and later, in the *Dialectic of Enlightenment*, written with his collaborator Max Horkheimer, Adorno offers a totalizing critique of society. For Adorno, twentieth-century European civilization has no redeeming features, there are no progressive possibilities to be discerned within it. Civilization leads inexorably towards a world in which technology is used for the purposes of domination, man over nature, man over man, it leads inexorably to the camps. Faced with an irredeemable external reality, Adorno seeks internal, personal redemption in isolated intellectual critique—if the world is without hope, then at least in one's mind transformation is possible. Joel Whitebook argues that in this way Adorno was able to maintain a posture of ultra-radicalism "which remained confined to the theoretical and aesthetic planes" (1997, p. 86). As Adorno puts it in the closing paragraph of *Minima Moralia*, "the only philosophy which can be responsibly practiced in the face of despair is the attempt to contemplate all things as they would present themselves from the standpoint of redemption". But even this cannot succeed, and so he adds, "it must comprehend its own impossibility for the sake of possibility" (2005, section 50).

The theme of redemption here should give us pause for thought. This is, of course, from a much older Judaeo-Christian discourse, meaning to save or deliver from sin and damnation. There is a strong theme of salvation here and also of cleansing and purification. As we have seen, for Adorno this corresponds to a retreat to a place inside himself from where the world can be subject to contemplation and critique. I detect these themes in a number of parts of the climate change community who are on the brink of despair. Indeed, some former activists have already abandoned hope and seem to be engaged in the same kind of retreat, something exemplified by the Dark Mountain Project. Rejecting accusations of catastrophism aimed at them by John Gray (2010) and others, they argue in the editorial of their first book of essays:

> We are facing the end of the world as we know it; but this is not the same thing as the end of the world full stop. The decline or stuttering collapse of a civilization, a way of life, is not the same thing as an apocalypse. It is simply a reality of history. The Dark Mountain Project, in other words, is not concerned with fantasizing about catastrophe. It is concerned with being honest about reality; something which most of us, as human beings, find painfully hard.
>
> (Dark Mountain, 2010: 3–4)

This idea that they, unlike the rest of us, are facing reality is a recurring motif in what, following Christopher Lasch, I will call survivalist writing.

Bomb Culture

Bomb Culture, the book Jeff Nuttall published in 1968, is an anarchical study of the aesthetic of protest in the shadow of the bomb, from the teddy boys and the beatniks of the 1950s to the emergence of the underground and psychedelia in the mid-1960s. For Nuttall, despite the existence of movements such as the Aldermaston Marches, bomb culture was a culture of despair: "no single solitary one among us had the slightest spark of hope or gave a damn about a thing except the crackling certainty of Now" (p. 24). The casual sex and violence, the obsession with speed and danger, the constant search for new highs, were expressions of a "new affectlessness"—"excitement was set in the place where emotion had formerly been" (p. 27), "it was impossible to live with the bomb and the cold war and retain sympathetic faculties" (p. 35). The whole business of empathizing with other peoples had to be dissolved in humour—sick humour was the humour of a culture that was ill. Lenny Bruce, the king of sick, developed a style of self-destructive humour which "became increasingly a flagellation of himself and his audience, as every single sacred, serious thing, every single thing held in love and reverence was revealed as lost" (p. 107).

There were few heroes in this culture, and those there were tended to be tragically creative figures bent on self-destruction—Charlie Parker, James Dean, Billie Holiday, Jackson Pollock. Those experiencing the worst forms of mental suffering also became idealized, for if living with the bomb was normal, then perhaps it was the mad who were truly sane. Thus R. D. Laing in his book *The Politics of Experience* could say, "we can no longer assume that such a voyage (schizophrenia) is an illness that has to be treated … . Can we not see that this voyage is not what we need to be cured of, but that it is itself a natural way of healing our own appalling state of alienation called normality" (Laing, 1967, p. 136). The so-called voyage of the mad became the theme of Doris Lessing's *Briefing for a Descent into Hell*, and I can remember, as an enthralled but puzzled teenager, seeing Laing and Lessing share the same platform at the Conway Hall in London.

Psychic survival in troubled times

Move us on a bit to the late 1970s, and the bomb is still here alongside the first glimmerings of other potential disasters, including the ecological. These are themes of Christopher Lasch's two books *The Culture of Narcissism* and *The Minimal Self*. Lasch argues that there was an ongoing retreat into the self, the origins of which he traces to much of the so-called radicalism of the 1960s generation. For this was the generation which threw off the chains of repression to seek pleasure in the moment, this was the "me generation". For Lasch, the celebration of self-exploration, one of the virtues of hippydom, was simply a turn towards the self. And whilst for some, there was a genuine spiritual depth to this turn, for the majority, in the grip of powerful cultural forces, the turn to the self was not a turn towards depth but towards shallowness. In an other-directed and consumerist culture, "the self" becomes a skin, an outward appearance, an object constantly subject to the gaze of the other. "Personality" displaces "character", we adopt a "theatrical view" (1984, p. 30) of our own performances on and off the job. So paradoxically, the turn to the self conceals its opposite, the disappearance of a secure sense of selfhood. Echoing the object relations and self-psychology traditions in psychoanalysis, Lasch sees narcissism as a defence against the loss of selfhood: "Every day life has begun to pattern itself on the survival strategies forced on those exposed to extreme adversity. Selective apathy, emotional disengagement from others, renunciation of the past and the future, a determination to live one day at a time" (p. 57). In a brilliant chapter in the *Minimal Self* called "The Survival Mentality", Lasch then proceeds to lay out the parameters of the minimal self, the psychic survivor.

Survivalism

Christopher Lasch wrote his book *The Minimal Self* after the Iranian hostage crisis and during the Reagan/Thatcher years. Lasch's thesis was that, at an unconscious level, people were already preparing for the worst, "sometimes by building fallout shelters and laying in provisions, more commonly by executing a kind of emotional retreat from the long-term commitments that presuppose a stable, secure and orderly world" (p. 16). His book examined the ordinary and not so ordinary forms that this survivalism was taking, one of which was the retreat into the self. But one of the less ordinary forms of survivalism that he explored he referred to as the "apocalyptic imagination". This was exemplified by writers of the time such as Doris Lessing (*Briefing for a Descent into Hell*; *Martha Quest*), who regarded civilization as already effectively finished and whose passing could be regarded "on the whole, without regret" (Lasch, 1984, p. 82). Reading Lasch twenty-five years later, I'm surprised by the precise way in which history seems to repeat itself, how powerful the apocalyptic imagination has already become in response to climate change.

I was working with a team recently who provide therapeutic support to those with terminal or life-threatening illnesses. We were thinking about the sources of strength people found when faced with the uncertainty of death (for example, not knowing whether you have two months or twelve months to live) when one of the team mentioned the opposite: how some people would humiliate and embarrass themselves in their desperation to live at any cost. This is what Lasch means by "survivalism". Indeed, he uses the words of Lewis Mumford who, in his critique of appeasement at the time of Munich in 1938, said, "a meaningful world is one that holds a future that extends beyond the incomplete personal life of the individual; so that a life sacrificed at the right moment is a life well spent, while a life too carefully hoarded, too ignominiously preserved, is a life utterly wasted" (cited by Lasch, 1984, p. 75).

Applied to the world of politics, or to the life of a group or an organization, the question is not what must we do in order to survive, but what must we do in order to continue to live life with value and purpose? The survivalist individual or group has become demoralized and questions of value have been rendered meaningless, destroyed. The survivalist has lost their love of the world; instead of a secure attachment to life, there is a desperate clinging.

Faced with social catastrophe, the survivalist group does what it must do in order to survive. In the landscape of Cormac McCarthy's *The Road*, this is a vigilant and predatory group whose brutality is fired not so much by sadism but by a cold resolve to live. Where the choices are seen as victim or predator, it is better to prey than be preyed upon. What distinguishes man from animal steadily disappears. It is a survival of the fittest.

Apocalyptic survivalism

This is a bleak future governed by the mob where elites seem to have no place. Apocalyptic survivalism provides that place. According to Lasch, "the apocalyptic vision appears in its purest form not in the contention that the nuclear arms race or uninhibited technological development might lead to the end of the world but in the contention that a saving remnant will survive the end of the world and build a better one" (1984, p. 83). The select few, or what Cohn (1993) calls the "chosen people", will therefore survive. There is what Lasch calls a "pseudo-realism"

(1984, p. 86) about this way of thinking, one which is contemptuous of what it sees as the myopia of those (in peace or environmental movements) who believe that it is never too late to act. Such beliefs are seen as consolatory illusions, the resort of the weak. Tough-mindedness (as we have seen from the Dark Mountain Project) means being able to think the unthinkable, have the foresight to prepare for the worst, and the moral fibre to prevail (1984, p. 81). The conceit and superiority in this stance is not hard to spot. Interestingly enough, Lasch notices the influential role of Social Darwinism in such positions and adds that, far from being a property of the right, one can observe liberal and leftist variations, the latter promoting "a lifeboat ethic" under which scientists and intellectuals claim the right to pronounce on the survival value of different social phenomena in the benign authoritarian state of the future (p. 70).

The idea of a "lifeboat ethic" had already been propounded by the influential Texan ecologist Garrett Hardin (1974). Hardin invites the reader to imagine a rich nation as a lifeboat in an ocean full of more numerous poor people who would dearly like to climb aboard. Offering a "consequentialist" form of ethics in which the value of an act is judged by its consequences, Hardin argues that it would be wrong to help the poor in this way because "the boat swamps, everyone drowns. Complete justice, complete catastrophe" (1974, p. 36). For Hardin, "survival" is the criterion with which the consequences of such actions should be measured. Hardin's work has been very influential within environmentalism, particularly his idea of the tragedy of the commons (Hardin, 1968), that is, the idea that resources that we hold in common such as the oceans will ultimately become depleted by individuals acting rationally in their own short-term interests. However, it is puzzling why Lasch connects "lifeboat ethics" to the political left because Hardin's stance, informed by Darwinist and Malthusian assumptions, generally leads him to quite reactionary conclusions regarding population control, food aid, and other policies. Not surprisingly, Hardin's ideas have had some influence over the new generation of climate change scientists and policy-makers, and this can be seen particularly clearly in the work of James Lovelock.

Climate change, James Lovelock, and lifeboat politics

The starting point for Lovelock is simply this—the game is up. He speaks of "the lush and comfortable world that once we knew is departing forever" (Lovelock, 2009, p. 19), and of that "lush, comfortable and beautiful Earth we left behind some time in the twentieth century" (p. 44). *The Vanishing Face of Gaia* is Lovelock's briefing for the descent into hell, "the troubled times ahead when the climate changes and there are shortages of food and fuel and major demographic changes" (p. 68, my emphasis). Don't be under any illusion, that last phrase is barely concealed code for massive extermination. So this is thinking the unthinkable, but thinking it in an emotionally and morally disconnected way. This is where Gaia and Social Darwinism come in. Take Gaia, for example. He invests in Gaia living qualities, so that "it" (that is, Gaia) disapproves (p. 4), reacts, regulates, and so on. I also noticed that in a couple of decades' time, "*it* will save itself as *it* dispatches all but a few of those who now live in what will become the barren regions" (p. 55, my emphases). His Darwinian pseudo-realism pops up all over the place. For example, in his belief that we are Earth's most intelligent species so we have a "duty to survive"; or in his belief that, as a species, we are "unusually tough" (p. 52) and hence, whilst our chances of personal survival may be slim, we can "take hope" that our species is likely to survive climate catastrophe; or again in his belief that in the future we will need to defend ourselves not from climate change "but indirectly from starvation, competition for space and resources, and tribal war" (p. 20). It also strongly inflects (infects?) a disturbing authoritarianism. Some of the passages made my jaw drop. Take this, for example:

> To the refugees we are their lifeboat, but the captain and officers of the ship have to decide how many we can take—who can be allowed to board and who must remain and take their chances? Fairness suggests a lottery, but common sense rules out so simple a selection. The sick, the lame and the old would have to stay behind and take their chances along with passengers who felt called upon to help them. On ships it used to be women and children first, but some men would be needed—what would be the right ration of the sexes? I suspect that it would not be far from equal, for that is the proportion that natural selection has chosen.
>
> (Lovelock, 2009, p. 56)

Sounds a bit like Martin Bormann? Clearly, given the many references to Churchill, what Lovelock has in mind is some kind of enlightened despotism. As he says, "Orderly survival requires an unusual degree of understanding and leadership and may require, as in war, the suspension of democratic government for the duration of the survival emergency" (p. 61).

Picking up where Garrett Hardin left off, a constant theme in Lovelock's book is a call to "man the lifeboats" by making those temperate islands such as ours (which he believes to be the only parts of the Earth likely to survive the heating) self-sufficient in food and energy as quickly as possible (pp. 16, 20, 22, 59ff, 86ff). The "proper" term for this is "autarky", that is, the philosophy of economic or political self-sufficiency. It has long been an element of English conservatism, sometimes referred to as "Little Englandism". At the opposite pole is what we might call "cosmopolitanism"—the idea that we are inextricably bound up with the rest of the world, and that this is something to be welcomed rather than feared. For political writers like David Held, we need to embrace cosmopolitan governance if globalization is to be subordinated to human purposes (Archibugi, Held & Kohler, 1998). It is interesting to note, therefore, that Lovelock has nothing but scorn for what might otherwise be thought of as one of the finest achievements of the trend towards cosmopolitan governance. In Chapter Two, he damns the Intergovernmental Panel on Climate Change for being compromised politically, methodologically, and conceptually; indeed, he has the conceit to argue in the introduction to this chapter that a single "independent scientist" such as himself is more to be relied upon than the thousands who contribute to the IPCC.

In short, Lovelock epitomizes the apocalyptic imagination. His world is a world in which all but a few are already doomed (and where the "captains and officers" will decide who stays and who goes, not "the gullible multitude" (p. 53)). His pseudo-realism offers nothing but contempt for those who believe it is not too late to act, and in particular for advocates of wind farms (pp. 17–59), renewables (p. 12), and for "greens" in general (p. 55). Lovelock already inhabits McCarthy's landscape, the landscape of the paranoid group, the Hobbesian world were life is nasty, brutish, and short. And as those in the lifeboats push away the drowning with their oars, they can in good conscience do so, knowing they have a duty to ensure this intelligent species of ours must survive.

Between alarmism and complacency

The apocalyptic survivalism of Lovelock could be dismissed if it weren't for the fact that it is already a detectable element in our culture and within the "green movement" itself. I have contrasted this form of survivalism to the "redemptive" response to perceived disaster of Adorno and, in relation to climate change, of the Dark Mountain Project. Both responses are catastrophist, announcing the end of the world as we know it. Clinically, catastrophism is a familiar phenomenon both in its normal and extreme forms. Regarding the latter, delusional belief systems referring to the coming "end of the world" have been a noted feature of some forms of psychosis since Freud's observations on the "Schreber case" (Freud, 1911). Considered as a more normal feature of the psychic landscape of the Western individual, catastrophism denotes a temporary or sometimes recurring difficulty in getting things in perspective or proportion. The individual has no firm ground or sense of self on which to stand, and as a consequence slights, setbacks, problems, and so on are perceived as overwhelming, and threatening catastrophe. As a consequence, the individual is plunged back into an underlying despair and often needs to undertake painstaking work to climb back out again and put the event into perspective. Within the Kleinian tradition, such individuals are seen as being in the grip of depressive anxieties characterized by an unconscious belief that the internal resources they require to face reality have been destroyed or are simply lacking. The common response to such anxiety is the "manic defence" in which phantasies of omnipotence act as a cover for the opposite, a bleak sense of helplessness and uselessness (Riviere, 1936).

The point of this brief clinical diversion is this, as I noted with Adorno: catastrophism is intimately connected to despair. Politically, this despair is manifest simultaneously in an exaggeration of the forces against us and an underestimation of the resources we have to face them. In the case of climate change, many who take this catastrophist view adhere to a totalizing vision in which the Earth is perceived to be threatened by "progress" or "civilization". The nuances, contradictions, ambivalences, and conflicts inherent to society are abolished so that "civilization" becomes a psychical object devoid of differentiation—almost a reverse image of the idealization of progress and civilization that is sometimes associated with Enlightenment thought. In a fascinating debate with George Monbiot, Paul Kingsnorth, the inspiration behind the Dark Mountain Project, articulated this totalizing view, one which leads him, like Lovelock but for different reasons, to oppose many possible technical responses (such as wind farms and tidal barrages) to the challenge of climate change. Their discussion, and the online debate that then followed it, is well worth tapping into (*Guardian*, 18 August 2009), not least for the way in which Monbiot articulates an alternative to the politics of despair of Kingsnorth and other apparent radicals.

In his provocative book *Why We Disagree About Climate Change*, Mike Hulme offers a sustained critique of disaster-mongering and alarmism within the climate change community. Within climate science, Hulme links this perspective to the way in which complex systems thinking has been recently incorporated, giving rise to the language of positive feedback loops, "tipping points", abrupt non-linear dynamics, and so on (Hulme, 2009, pp. 60–67). As the title of his book suggests, Hulme seeks to reintroduce the idea of pluralism within climate science, one which recognizes that a variety of perspectives exist, and that disagreement and difference is the soil upon which science flourishes. But Hulme's calm, reasoned, and dispassionate approach (classically "academic" in both its positive and negative meanings) seems to me to be an example of that kind of rationalism which has often sought to manage the problem of excess by disavowing it. Hulme seems to see passion as the enemy of reason rather than its ally. Hulme's many critics suggest that this leads to a position which gives succour to caution and quiescence which, given the failures of Kyoto and Copenhagen, are clearly not the public virtues we need right now. To his credit, Hulme provides a detailed vignette of a recent debate he has had with one of his critics, James Risbey, who argues that it is both possible and necessary to avoid alarmism whilst also insisting that the situation we now face is clearly alarming. I find myself joining with Risbey on this. In his review of the evidence, Risbey (2008) finds considerable grounds for asserting that climate change could well be catastrophic if the Greenland and West Antarctic ice sheets melt, that changes such as extended droughts may be rapid, that the situation is urgent (this is the oil tanker problem— once you are set on a course, the tanker doesn't respond to changes in direction until well after the changes have been put in place), that many changes will be irreversible, and that most incoming evidence suggests that IPCC projections will prove conservative. Risbey concludes by taking a stance that sees climate change as alarming if action is not taken soon:

> In this view, climate change looms large, but there is still time to take actions to avert larger changes. However, the large reductions in carbon emissions required to avert those changes will

require comprehensive responses, small and large. This requires a fundamental restructure in the way in which we generate and use energy. This discourse thus differs from "alarmism" in that the problem is not viewed as out of control or inevitable, and it differs from "small actions" in that responses must be comprehensive. The discourse is "alarming" in that it sounds the alarm to alert the public to the need to change course.

(Risbey, 2008, p. 34)

Climate science being a post-normal science proceeds on a probabilistic basis. The statements of the Intergovernmental Panel on Climate Change are couched in terms of degrees of certainty. So when the IPCC says "it is very likely that anthropogenic greenhouse gas increases caused most of the observed increase in globally averaged temperatures since the mid twentieth century" (IPCC, 2007), it is referring to an established IPCC terminology where "very likely" means more than ninety per cent probable, and "likely" means more than sixty-seven per cent probable. But the "denial lobby" demands certainty, and in its absence insists that climate science is simply opinion dressed up as science, just as creationists argue that evolutionism is just another opinion. These so-called sceptics argue that those outside the consensus are the real bearers of truth; in contrast, the "consensus" is construed as an exclusive group of insiders, a conspiracy against free-thinkers, a "highly politicized scientific circle" according to the Republican populist Sarah Palin.

Meanwhile the UK's Meteorological Office, a key global reference point for climate science, pronounced that 2010 was the second warmest year on record (Met Office, 2011), and recent research suggests that in the absence of global action to tackle climate change, it is now very likely that we will be unable to stabilize emissions in such a way that global temperature increases can be restricted to 2°C (generally recognized as the safety threshold) (Anderson & Bows, 2008).

The situation is alarming, and whilst complacency is no longer an option, nor is a politics of climate catastrophe a viable alternative. For catastrophism is a politics of despair which draws on the same survivalist mentality as previous apocalyptic movements. Survivalism is a demoralized state of mind in which questions of value have been progressively destroyed; its radicalism can so quickly take on the authoritarian cloak of lifeboat ethics. But without passion, a politics of climate change is left disarmed. Given the nature of climate science, we just don't know how bad things are likely to be and, given the uncertainty, all we can do is try our hardest to make sure we avoid the worst. Which brings me to that phrase from Yeats' poem "The Second Coming" (1920), "the best lack all conviction, while the worst are full of passionate intensity". As I suggested at the beginning of this essay, "the best lack all conviction" is the problem of "the depressive position". We need to be thoughtful, generous, concerned, sceptical, and able to manage uncertainty, but we also need to yoke this to a fighting spirit, to anger, hope, and yes, at times, to unreasoned passion.

Note

1. This paper was first published in *Psychoanalysis, Culture and Society, 16(2):* (2011). It is reprinted here with the kind permission of Palgrave Macmillan.

References

Adorno, T. (1951). *Minima Moralia: Reflections from Damaged Life*. Trans. Dennis Redmond, 2005. http://www.efn.org/dredmond (accessed 13/11/2010)

Anderson, K. & Bows, S. (2008). Reframing the climate change challenge in the light of post-2000 emission trends. *Philosophical Transactions of the Royal Society, 366*: 3863–3882.

Archibugi, D., Held, D. & Kohler, M. (1998). *Reimagining Political Community: Studies in Cosmopolitan Democracy*. Stanford: Stanford University Press.

Britton, R. (1998). *Belief and Imagination*. London and New York: Routledge.

Cohn, N. (1993). *The Pursuit of the Millennium*. London: Pimlico.

Dark Mountain (2010) Editorial: It's the end of the world as we know it (and we feel fine), Issue 1, Summer: 3–4.

Diamond, J. (2005). *Collapse: How Societies Choose Either to Survive or Fail*. New York: Viking Penguin.

Fonagy, P. (1999). The transmission of holocaust trauma: lessons learned from the analysis of an adolescent with obsessive-compulsive disorder. *Attachment and Human Development, 1(1)*: 92–114.

Freud, S. (1911). *Psycho-Analytic Notes on an Autobiographical Account of a Case of Paranoia*. SE, 12 (pp. 9–79). London: Hogarth.

Freud, S. (1920). *Beyond the Pleasure Principle*. SE, 18 (pp. 3–64). London: Hogarth.

Gray, J. (2010). Uncivilization: The Dark Mountain Manifesto. *New Statesman*, 10 September.

Greer, J. (2008). *The Long Descent: A User's Guide to the End of the Industrial Age*. Philadelphia, PA: New Society.
Hardin, G. (1968). The tragedy of the commons. *Science, 162, 3859*: 1243–1248.
Hardin, G. (1974). Lifeboat ethics: the case against helping the poor. *Psychology Today, 8*: 38–43.
Hoggett, P. (1998). The internal establishment. In: P. B. Talamo, F. Borgogno & S. Merciai (Eds.), *Bion's Legacy to Groups* (pp. 9–24). London: Karnac Books.
Hoggett, P. (2009). *Politics, Identity and Emotion*. Boulder, CO: Paradigm.
Hulme, M. (2009). *Why We Disagree About Climate Change: Understanding Controversy, Inaction and Opportunity*. Cambridge: Cambridge University Press.
Laing, R. D. (1967). *The Politics of Experience and the Bird of Paradise*. London: Penguin.
Lasch, C. (1978). *The Culture of Narcissism*. New York: W. W. Norton.
Lasch, C. (1984). *The Minimal Self: Psychic Survival in Troubled Times*. New York: W. W. Norton.
Lovelock, J. (2009). *The Vanishing Face of Gaia: A Final Warning*. London: Allen Lane.
Meltzer, D., Bremmer, J., Hoxster, S., Weddell, D. & Wittenberg, I. (1975). *Explorations in Autism*. Perthshire: Clunie.
Met Office (2011). 2010—a near record year. http://www.metoffice.gov.uk/news/releases/archive/2011/2010-global-temperature accessed 15/09/2011
Nuttall, J. (1970). *Bomb Culture*. London: Paladin.
Risby, J. (2008). New climate discourse: alarmist or alarming? *Global Environmental Change, 18*: 26–37.
Riviere, J. (1936). A contribution to the analysis of the negative therapeutic reaction. *International Journal of Psycho-Analysis, 75*: 304–320.
Volkan, V., Ast, G. & Greer, W. (2002). *The Third Reich in the Unconscious: Transgenerational Transmission and its Consequences*. New York: Brunner Routledge.
Whitebook, J. (1997). *Perversion and Utopia: A Study in Psychoanalysis and Critical Social Theory*. Boston: MIT Press.
Yeats, W. B. (1920). *Michael Robartes and the Dancer*. Churchtown, Dundrum, Ireland: The Chuala Press.
Yusoff, K. (2009). Excess, catastrophe and climate change. *Environment and Planning D: Society and Space, 27*: 1010–1029.

CONCLUDING REMARKS

The past and present as a mirror of the future

James Krantz

It is a great pleasure to read these wonderful chapters and a daunting task to write the final commentary. So many themes and ideas are woven together in each chapter, and then again to create the larger tapestry of the volume. At the broadest level, this book unequivocally demonstrates how the psycho-social underpinnings of social, economic, and technological phenomena are basic drivers of what so often seems incomprehensible at the surface level. The conceptual machinery of psychodynamic thinking, refreshed by Eisold here, renders the impact of anxiety, primitive mechanisms, and defensive strategies so clearly visible in the issues taken up in these chapters. They also demonstrate how much damage is created when unconscious suffering is transferred from the self, and then vicariously projected onto others. And, as with all deeply reasoned thinking about the psychodynamics of social life, the discussions throw us back onto ourselves, pointing us towards recognizing our own complicity in these phenomena.

The volume highlights both the novel and the enduring. Several chapters are cast in light of historical, cyclical inevitability. Epidemic, apocalyptic fear and the unconscious meaning of money are grounded in dynamics that appear and reappear in different guises, taking on the particular cast of the historical moment in which they manifest, but nevertheless reflecting inherent, recurrent themes of human affairs. Others speak to the socio-emotional meaning of phenomena that are uniquely characteristic of the contemporary moment, including toxicity in service relationships, unconscious dynamics unleashed by mergers, the psychodynamics of fashion, celebrity worship, the insurance industry, and workplace burnout.

To the largely retrospective focus on this volume, I think it fitting here to also raise questions about the future and, in particular, what these extraordinarily rich discussions might suggest about it. In this regard, I am mindful of ideas linked with two of the founding spirits of the systems psychodynamic tradition. Both underscore the importance of not only looking, so to speak, in the rear-view mirror to achieve understanding, but also looking through the windshield, as Philip Boxer so ably does in his discussion of the paradigm shift represented by Twitter.

First, the comment attributed to Bion that anxiety is the shadow of the future (1994). Object relations and systems psychodynamics provide tools for understanding that anxieties and phantasy reflect the immediate social context. Bion's suggestion opens up an important line of inquiry, one that can utilize anxiety as a window, of sorts, into the future as well. It provides an avenue to deciphering as-of-yet tacit, unspoken changes in the context of work that, if decoded, could provide invaluable information about emergent issues, preoccupations, and forces.

The second observation, from the work of Eric Trist & Fred Emery (1975), is best encapsulated by the title of Emery's book: *Futures We Are In* (1977). In this phase of their work, they were interested in how "leading elements" of the future already exist in the present, which make it possible to discern the outlines of emerging systems. Early detection of emergent processes that lie concealed in existing systems, with which they share parts, creates opportunities to adapt and even shape the future. These emergent processes may also stimulate primitive anxieties associated with invasion and, as a result, debilitate existing systems.

With post-industrialism in the latter part of the twentieth century, the world moved towards a constant change gradient, and as a result, we entered a state of continuous transition. Now we are entering what I believe to be another state, one in which the gradient of change, largely due to information technology, is shifting from linear to one that is exponential. The changes we are now facing and will continue to face much more ferociously are of such magnitude that survival will depend on the ability of people to work through the effects at the deepest levels of their personalities.

Whether we have the resilience to cope with these changes is, itself, a source of anxiety. There is certainly ample evidence for concern about the degree of social fragmentation. There is abundant evidence that our reliable containers, which have been vital to human development, are dissolving: familiar family structures, community, social institutions, stable groups and organizations, accepted norms, and so on. Without transformative containers, the cycle of projection and introjection that allows us to stay in contact with the reality of others can no longer do its integrative work. Psychotic anxieties and primitive rages and yearnings are unmediated and unmodified by containers that can no longer help to transform them into tolerable experience or reparative impulse. The recognizable sources of development of depressive integration (Klein, 1957) appear to be scarcer as the social environment fragments.

Threats to stability, community, and personal development in this new phase are profound and only beginning to be understood. Deterioration in their containing functions releases frightening aggression and disorientation which, in turn, elicits primitive defences that foster hostile projection or alienated withdrawal. The threats to identity and primitive mechanisms alluded to in many of these chapters bring the current manifestations of the death instinct and social nihilism into focus, as poignantly described in Khaleelee's introductory comments.

Perhaps we are not resilient enough, psychologically and sociologically, to cope with the enormous ambivalence and anxiety accompanying these changes, dooming us to live in the polarized, rigid world of fundamentalism, moralism, political correctness, and denigration that seems increasingly to define our public spaces. Such dynamics can readily evoke an "apocalyptic-trajectory-in-the-mind": the idea that unleashed hostility and aggression mixed with disassociative technological advances will lead us towards massive destruction.

My motivation for bringing this perspective forward stems partly from concern about the ongoing relevance of psychoanalytic thinking to emergent organizational realities, and questions about whether the field is defending itself against the conceptual realignment necessary to keep the tradition relevant into the twenty-first century. Hopefully, we will be able to adapt our tools to the information world where our relatedness is profoundly shaped by computer-mediated interaction and where so much is disembodied and immaterial. Clinging to ideas of social defence that are rooted in twentieth-century organizations becomes a social defence in itself. It functions as an ideology that binds the insecurity of "not-knowing" at the expense of relinquishing our ability to learn new ways of bringing enduring truths forward into novel circumstances.

To adapt our ideas, I believe we will have to relinquish one *leitmotif* which makes fleeting appearance in this volume and appears quite prominently in many other psychodynamically grounded discussions of contemporary life, namely, the narrative of decline and decay. Even *prima facie*, the idea that human civilization advanced up to our generation and then declined thereafter must be questioned as self-idealizing and grandiose. I would suggest that the idea that we are heading towards destruction is another "apocalyptic mindset", of the type discussed by Hoggett in this volume. While it accentuates the legitimate areas of concern, it eradicates the vast potential for innovation and growth that are also embedded in the present.

Instead, I want to suggest that we are at a specific developmental moment. The transition to our information society is, and will continue to be, traumatic. There are both great gains and great losses involved in crossing this divide. How the psychodynamic perspective can join with creativity and development in this new emerging order remains to be seen.

I believe we have a great deal to contribute to the development and deployment of information technology and computer-mediated work. On one level, the source codes and algorithms that enable computers to function are themselves symbolic representations of the world. Computer programs are a form of relatedness. On another level, the Internet is about connection. Yet the quality of those connections, the quality of the information that passes through them, and the quality of the relationship that the connections permit is of concern. So much of the social networking software encourages people to make weak, adolescent, superficial connections. It too can function as a social defence by helping co-workers escape the anxieties elicited through interdependence at a distance, with limited knowledge of the "other", and with the great vulnerability that permeates modern global organizations.

The potential regressive effects of Internet-based activity seem vast. Does a technology that creates the illusion of actual, immediate proximity in time and space distort how we relate to others and to ourselves?

Could it impact upon our ability to tolerate the necessary frustrations of reality? Does being able to "know" things instantaneously, instead of having to tolerate the discomfort of not knowing, impair the development of thinking? Does this perhaps constitute a breakdown of the authority of reality, resulting in less repression, diminished ability to cope with reality, and reduced sublimation?

Approaches to the application of psychoanalytic thinking about organizational life puts the highest premium on reflection, and emphasizes the creation of reflective space as the critical path to depressive-position functioning. The speed at which life unfolds seems to work against reflective capacity. Concentrated thought takes time for the patterns to emerge and for connections and interactions to form new patterns in our minds. We seem to lose the chance to reflect, to analyse, and perhaps even the ability to form moral judgements in the new organizational forms. Without reflective underpinning, interrelationships seem increasingly glib and formulaic. It is essential that we find new possibilities for reflective integration and reflective space in the context of the new forms. My working hypothesis is that if they seem invisible, it is because we have not yet adapted our concepts sufficiently to the new configurations.

The systems psychodynamic tradition has helped twentieth-century organizations productively incorporate reflective activity. Could we do the same with the more network-oriented organizations in which team composition is constantly shifting like sand dunes? One critical step is in understanding about group process in unbounded networks, as Boxer suggests with his discussion of "affective networks". This point is being vividly illustrated at the time when this volume is being produced, Spring 2011, when we are in a moment of *statu nascendi* in which the geopolitics of the world are being redrawn with the help of new technology in the hands of the new generation, leading and initiating revolutions in the Middle East, itself a revolutionary process.

These, and many similar, questions are beginning to emerge. I hope those of us who work from the psychodynamic perspective will join with others who are discerning the outlines of the emergent social and economic systems. As my colleague Larry Hirschhorn pointed out (2006): one critical analytic task is to disentangle the trauma of the transition from the tasks of creating new social and work systems, befitting the new order. This volume, and others like it that further our understanding of the unconscious background of social and organizational life, play an important role in supporting our efforts to reframe and adapt our concepts to be relevant to the emerging world.

References

Bion, W. R. (1994). On a quotation from Freud. In: his *Clinical Seminars and Four Papers* (pp. 306–311). London: Karnac Books. [The quote from which this idea is derived is: "I could say that this meeting itself can be regarded as an expression, as a revision of such experience and knowledge as we have managed to pick up in the course of our lifetime, but it can also be regarded as showing the shadow of a future we don't know any more than we know the past, a shadow which it projects or casts before" (p. 309).]

Emery, F. (1977). Futures we are in. Leiden: Martinus Nijhoff.

Emery, F. E. & Trist, E. L. (1975). Towards a Social Ecology. New York: Plenum Publishing.

Hirschhorn, L. (2006). personal communication.

Klein, M. (1957). *Envy and Gratitude*. London: Tavistock Publications.

INDEX

activism, paradoxes of 233–235
Adorno, Theodore 236
    facing the Holocaust 237–238
aggressive impulses 11, 13, 15
    projection of 14–15
AI (Artificial Intelligence) 180
AIDS 216–217
Aladdin 71
    magic lamp 88
Alexander, Cecil
    Irish poet 161
Al Qaeda market 138
Alvarez, Anne 163
American Federalism 151
Andersson & Pearson 43
annihilation, fears of 3
Anzieu, D. 33, 42, 166, 168
apathy 54, 198, 240
apocalyptic imagination 233, 240, 244
apocalyptic survivalism 241–242, 244

apocalyptic-trajectory-in-the-mind 253
Australia-New Zealand (A-NZ)
    business units 6
    empty land mass 8
    operations 10
    radical downsizing of 8

baby-boomer generation 117
Baez, Joan 169
Bain, Alistair 101
Band Aid movement 170
Barsade, S. B. 33
Barthes, Roland 114, 125
    The Fashion System 127
Bate, David 124
BBC
    EastEnders 173
Beckham, David 167, 174–175
Belafonte, Harry 169
Bentham, Jeremy 30

Berlin, Heather 182
Biblical criticism 143
Bick, E. 42
Bierut, Bolesław 199, 207
Bion, Wilfred 167
    catastrophic change 9
    protomentality 169
    proto-mental levels 169
    use of the concept of "desire" 110
Bomb Culture 236, 238–239
borrowed ego 84, 89
Boulding, K. E. 28
Boultwood & Jerrard 123
Bourdin, Guy 125
Bowe, J. 28, 30, 35–37, 39–41
Bowe, M. 28, 30, 35–37, 39–41
Boxer, Philip 127, 133, 137, 139, 188, 252, 255
brain activity 190
Brand W campaign merchandise174
    Texan Southern American drawling speech 174
Brazilian music and drama 170
Brazilian television network *Rede Globo de Televisio* 170
British Imperium 151
Britton, Ron 172, 234
Brown & Starkey 34
Bruce, Lenny 239
Bruner, Jerome 180
burnout 51
    case of 52–54
    definition 53–54
    different types 51
    five phases of 54
    organizational risk factors 56–57
    personal risk factors 55–56
    prevention and treatment of 59–63
    prevention in emotionally demanding organizations in health/social care and education 63
    prevention in formalized-bureaucratic type of organization 62
    prevention in unrestricted-informal type of organization 62–63
    prevention measures at organizational level 61–63
    risk factors for 55–57
    risk factors in different types of organizations 58–59
    treatment of 60
burnout syndrome
    effects of 54–55
    five phases of 54
    loss of motivation 54
    result of 54

Captain Ahab, *Pequot* 83
Cartesian Theatre 181
Cartesian theory 181
casino mentality 88
cathectic energy 202, 204
CDS (credit default swaps) 87
celebrating in celebrities 159–176
celebrity and celebration down the ages 161–162
celebrity as a group phenomenon 164–167
    Diana at a palace garden party 164–167
celebrity attitude scale 164
celebrity phenomenon 161
celebrity worship, a pathology 164
    contributory dynamics of 172
celebrity worship syndrome, cult or religion 162–163
censorship 185
Cherns, A. 44

child psychoanalytic psychotherapy 163
Chinese censors 137
Christianity 77, 82
    Zoroastrians 82
Civilization and Its Discontents 200
classical psychoanalytical theory 75
climate change 242–244
Coelho, Maria 170–171
Cohn, Norman 234
    chosen people 241
collective trauma 235–237
collective unconscious 115–119
collisions 203
common-sense points 227
competitive identity 134
compulsive personality structure 56
computer-mediated interaction 254
congruent and ego-syntonic 59
conscious fantasies 38
consciousness 181, 203, 210
    traumatized 206
consumer of sexuality 30
containment 17–22
    process 21
contemporary fashion imagery 126
contemporary fashion industry 125
conviction politics 233
Cornelissen, J. P. 28–29
corporate consumerism 119
"cosmopolitanism" 244
counselling families 14
"crying wolf" 234
Csikszentmihalyi, M. 62
Cuban Missile Crisis 235
customer–employee interchange 35
customers and toxicity 34–36
customer-service situations 32
cynicism 54

Damasio, Antonio 180–181
Dark Mountain Project 238, 245

DARPA 190
Darwin, *The Descent of Man* 187
Darwinian pseudo-realism 243
Daum, Matthieu 95
Dean, James 239
decision-making processes 227
default network 189
default system 189
Dennett, Daniel 180
depressive personality structure 55
Derrida, Jacques 90
desired ego 84
Desmonde, W. H. 75
destructive capacity 15
destructive impulses 10–14, 18–22
developmental injury 38
Dialectic of Enlightenment 237
Disneyland 39
disorganization 54, 225
divine transformation, hope for 78–79
Douglas, Mary 33
Dylan, Bob 169
dynamic unconscious, coherent
    theory of 179

early warning signals 17
Edelman, Gerald 180, 184
egalitarian utopia 117
ego 5, 13
    aggrandizement of 206
Eisold, Kenneth 179, 181, 251
emergent infections 214
Emery, Fred 252
emotional
    "amplifiers" 220
    connectedness 5, 13, 17
    experiences 4, 17, 22–23
    forces 4
    link 4
    retirement are predominant 54
emotionally demanding type of
    organization 59

employee–boss boundary 43
employee–customer
 boundary 43
 interface 27, 31, 44
 relationship 27, 29–32
employee–customer interface 27, 29
 images illuminating 29–31
employee–external employee
 boundary 43
employee–team boundary 43
Enron scandal 5
 Andersen Consulting 5
epidemic psychology 218
epidemics as psychosocial processes
 216–219
Erasmian
 equivalent 143
 perspective on truth 148
Erikson, Erik 188
Eskimos 186
Ettinger, Bracha 123
 fascinance 124
 mother–daughter relations 124
Evans, Caroline 115
excessive boundary permeability
 33
excessive miserliness 76
exhibitionism 174
external and psychic realities 10–11

Facebook 126
face-to-face meetings of work groups
 18
fashion
 conscious individual 126
 magazines 123, 127
 photography 124–125
 writing 115, 127–128
fashion archetypes 115–119
 women, men, and children
  119–122
fast fashion 122

Faust 77
 psychology analysis of 77
Festinger, Leon 185
Flugel, J. C. 114
Folgero & Fjeldstad 31
Fonagy, Peter 188
Foucault, M. 28, 30, 186, 224
Frankel, Viktor 62
free-floating attention 189
Freeman, Walter 180
Freud, S. 76, 115, 166, 179, 199, 205
 analysis of Schreber case 204
 experience of the First World War
  235
 formula 205
 *Group Psychology and Analysis of
  the Ego* 221
 imaginary identification 148
 keenest sexual pleasures 165
 primary process 183
 repression 182
 Rome 201
 sexual sublimation 165
 symbolic identification 148
 "terrible war" 236
 unconscious 182
 view of the unconscious 180
Freudian idea of phantasies 90
front-line workers and customers 42
Frost & Robinson 32
frustration 11, 54, 58, 225
Fry, Stephen 169
Fuery, Kelli 126
Fuss, Diana 124

Gardner, Howard 180
Geldof, Bob 169–170
General Jaruzelski 199
geographic distance, complications
 of 18
Gerloff 73
global warming 143

Goethe 76–77
Gollini, Silvia 95
Gomulka-period 209
good container 17
good-enough container 18
good-enough containment 21
Google 136
Gooijr, Jinette de 3
Gray, John 238
Great Mother 72–73, 75
Great Recession 139
Greek mythology 37
Greek thinking 82
Grimm's fairy tale "Star Coin" 79
group behaviour 134
group ego-skin 42
Gucci family dynasty 37
Gutenberg 134, 140, 144

H1N1 A influenza 214
hallucinatory experience 118–119
Hammurabi 37, 97
Hardin, Garrett 242, 244
Hauff, Wilhelm, collection *The Caravan* 79
hedonism 117–118
Held, David 244
helper syndrome 59
Helplessness 56, 87, 203, 220, 245
Hexensabbat 82
Higgitt, Anna 188
Hillman, J. 72, 82–83
Hirschhorn & Gilmore 32
Hobbesian nightmare 218
Hobbesian world 244
Hochschild, A. R. 28–29, 38, 56
Hockett, Jeremy 173–174
Hoggett, Paul 143, 233–234, 254
Holiday, Billie 6, 82, 100, 239
Hong-Kong influenza 216
Hopfl, H. 29, 31, 37
Hopper, Earl 147, 168, 171

Horkheimer, Max 237
Hotter than my Daughter 121
Huddart, Stephen 169
Hulme, Mike 235, 246
   Why We Disagree About Climate Change 246
hyper-sexualized imagery 125
hypnotic fascination 159
Hyppokrates 216

idealistic enthusiasm 54
idealization of autonomy 12–14
identity and identification 163–164
Images of Organizations 28
imaginary identification 148
individualism 117
individual–society interface 217
infantile sexuality in *Three Essays* 179
influenza viruses 216
inner performance script 55
in-patient psychotherapy 60–61
In Pursuit of the Millennium 234
insurance and anxiety 98–99
insurance industry function in the world 95
   creating our own unwanted future 103–105
   inner origin of the desire for 101
   "Roaring Thirties" 101
   role in transforming this situation 108–110
   with a long history 96–98
insurance, leadership, and management 106–108
Intergovernmental Panel on Climate Change (IPCC) 244
   projections 246
   terminology 247
internal catastrophe 10
intra-organizational mergers 3
Iran Hostage Crisis 235

Irigaray, Luce 124
ISPSO Symposium in Philadelphia 64

Japan-China incident 136
Jared Diamond 236
Jewish Combat Organisation 198
Judaeo-Christian discourse 238
Jung, C. G. 115
    collective unconscious 115–116
    fashion industry 119
Jung-Beeman, Mark 190
Jungian psychoanalyst 69

Kaiser Family Foundation 135
Kandel, Eric 180
Kingsnorth, Paul 245–246
Klein, Melanie 4–5, 10–11, 32, 35, 42, 165, 171, 234, 245
known dangers and unconscious anxieties 10–13
Korczynski, M. 28, 35, 41
Kounios & Jung-Beeman 190
Kounios, John 189–190
Krantz, James 32, 251
Kurtzman
    Harvard Business Review 89
    The New York Times 89

Lacan's
    fascinum 125
    formulation of "fascinum" 124
    identification 148–149
    psychoanalysis 202
Laing, R. D. 110
    The Politics of Experience 239
Lakoff, George 186
    Democratic and Republican parties in America 186
    theory 190
Lasch, Christopher 126, 238
    pseudo-realism 241

    The Culture of Narcissism and *The Minimal Self* 239–240
leadership, insurance 106–108
Leder, Andrzej 197, 212
LeDoux, Joseph 180, 185
Lessing, Doris, *Briefing for a Descent into Hell* 239–240
Levinas, Emmanuel 101
libidinal cathexis 207
lifeboat politics 242–244
Lipman-Blumen, J. 32
"Little Englandism" 244
Lockhart, R. A. 83
Lohmer, Mathias 51, 57
Lovelock, James 242–244
    The Vanishing Face of Gaia 243
Luther, Martin 142–143, 145–146
Lyth, Menzies 171–172

mainstream fashion 119
Maitlis & Ozcelik 32
Maltby, John 164
management
    insurance 106–108
    neurotic anxieties 16
    thinking 16
Mangham & Overington 29
Manichaeism 82
Marches, Aldermaston 239
mass-circulation media images 123
mass-market consumer goods 117
mass-produce pamphlets 142
mass-produced consumer goods 118
media-consuming society 126
Meltzer, Donald 233–234
Melville's *Moby Dick* 83
memory and desire 95
Mephistopheles 76–78
merger
    as foreign invasion 8
    catastrophic change 9–10
    destructive power 9
    murderous mergers 3

meta-traumatic reflexion on the
    process of reparation 206–208
metonymic movement 202
mind–body duality 81–83
*Minima Moralia: Reflections from
    Damaged Life* 237–238
Minimal Self 240
minimalism 117
Minogue, Kylie 169
Mitchell, Juliet 129
Mnemosyne 72
Monbiot, George 245
money 80
    alienation of 89–90
    archetypal dialectics of 71–73
    as a fetish 87–89
    as a mirror 83–84
    as phantastic object 69
    as transitional object 84–87
    assess oneself/as self-worth 92
    complex 89
    divine power of 73–76
    embodies the mind–body duality
        81–83
    fantastic possibilities of 91
    fundamental archetype of 87
    in Europe 73
    mirroring quality of 84
    money = love/eros 91
    negative transformative character
        of 81
    phantastic or fantastic object?
        90–91
    phantastic quality of 84–87
    projection function of 88
monopolization of knowledge 141
monotonous oscillation 203
Morgan-Jones, Richard 16, 28, 127,
    159, 168–169, 176, 189
motivated neural activity 184
Mourning and Melancholia 203
multidimensional matrix of
    plurality 118

multi-matrix structure 13
multi-modal therapy 60
multiple organizational structures
    13
    social defence of 13–14
Mundle, G. 59
Munk, Peter 79, 81
murderous rage, primitive
    destructive impulses of 19
Mutually Assured (Nuclear)
    Destruction 236
mutualness 207

Nagel, Claudia 69
narcissistic decay 226
narcissistic injury 38
narcissistic personalities 80, 126
narcissistic personality structure
    56
narcissistic personality traits 59
Narcissus 84
    myth 84
natural and social sciences 28
natural philosophy 141
Nazi occupation 198
negative capability 228
Neumann, E. 72
"new affectlessness" 239
new unconscious
    opening wider perspectives on
        society 179–193
    primary process 179
No-Go-For-Metro Bolesław Bierut
    207
Nuttall, Jeff 238–239

Obama, Barack, in the US
    presidential election 137
Obholzer, Anton 45
obsessive-compulsive individual 76
Oedipal phantasy 172
Offerman 32
Organization Studies 45

organizational
    burnout 51
    container 18
    containment, practice of 22
    development, primary process of 22
    dynamics 43, 220
    object 4
    phenomena 28
    realities 18
    risk factors 51
    structure 51
organizational merger 4–5, 11, 18
    as foreign invasion 8
    catastrophic change of 19
    container–contained in 21
    destructive power 9
    primary processes of 23
    unconscious anxieties in 5
organization-in-the-mind 4, 146

Palace of Culture 206
Palin, Sarah 247
panic and pandemics
    from fear of contagion to contagion of fear 213
paper dolls 122–123
paradoxes of activism 233–235
paranoid-schizoid position 234
Paris Match 174
Parker, Charlie 239
Pasini, Walter 213
Pearson, C. M. 37, 43
"People's Autumn" 199
perceptual identity 146
persecutory
    anxieties 5, 13, 17, 21–22
    defence mechanisms against 22
    feelings 12
persecutory anxieties 5, 13
    scapegoat for 15

Perini, Mario 213
permeable boundary regions 32
personal identity 147
personality
    disorder 61
    pattern and organizational structure 51
    styles 61
phallocentric psychoanalytic theory 129
phantastic object 69–71
phantasy 90
physical and psychological health 51
Polish Communist leaders 199
Polish Lithuanian Commonwealth 197
Polish resistance army 198
political activism 233
    paradoxes of 233
Pollock, Jackson 239
post-industrial economy 27
postmodernism, theories 118
"post-normal science" 235
post-traumatic stress disorder 197, 199
potential markets 139
potential space 85
potty training 76
powerlessness sense 202
pre-economic sites of exchanges 74
prevention and treatment of risk factors
    on personal level 59–60
printing revolution, technology's impact on the social 140–141
prions illness 214
problematic theory, "primary process" 182
projective identification 42–43
projective processes of splitting 3
Protestant movement 142

protomentality 169
psyche 60, 71, 90–91, 116, 119, 124, 167, 236
psychic
    dangers 17, 20, 22
    reality of organization 4, 14
    survival in troubled times 239–240
psychoanalysis 34, 43, 86, 114, 133–134, 163, 179, 200
    of a cityscape 197, 199
    of urban space 200
    unsubstantiated assertions of 180
psychoanalysis of a cityscape 197
    Warsaw 199–200
psychoanalytic
    sectarian battles 180
    sense 9
psychoanalytic reflections 159
    on the fantastic objects of desire 67
    on the world around us 195
    on the world of interconnectivity 131
    on the world of work 1
psychoanalytical
    case study 197
    pathomorphology 208
    processes 3, 5
    psychodynamic alteration 60
    reflections on fashion system 113
    thought 128, 251
psychodynamic theory 113–115, 122
    and the fashion image 123–127
psychological "poisoning", metaphorical idea of 32
psychological notion of protection and security 75
psycho-physical experience of succour 166
psycho-physical-social experience 169

psycho-physiological phenomena 168
psycho-social
    analysis 170
    epidemic 218
    functions 217
psychosocial roots of fear 220
psycho-social underpinnings of social 251
psychotherapeutic process 129
psychotherapy patients 52
psychotic anxieties and primitive rages 253
psychotic thinking 160, 162

Raptus Melancholicus 203
Reaganomics 117
Real identification 149
realistic anxiety 16
    capacity to tolerate 19
regression by managers from their role 16–17
reification trap 56
revenge 33
Richard Normann Prize 45
Riviere, Joan 120–121, 245
"role analysis" 63
role-holders 16, 18
Roosevelt, Theodore 137
ruined walls and apartment blocks 200–202
Rycroft, Charles 90

sado-masochistic imagery 124
SARS 214, 216
Satan 77
Schatzhauser 79
Schneider, S. C. 32, 43
"Schreber case" 245
Seabright & Schminke 37
Searle, John 180
Searles, Robert 180

Second World War 116, 207
Segal, Hanna 162
Self symbol (Jungian) 83, 87
self-reliant individuals 7
self-representation, practice 126
sentient group 14
sexual component 30
sexual desirability 122
sexual harassment, breeding-grounds for 31
sexuality 3, 77, 82, 118, 121, 179, 183, 185
shame, shamelessness, and the skin game 167–170
skin ego 42
Social Darwinism 242–243
social defence systems 17
social defences 13, 217, 221
social issues, unveiling hidden 226–227
socio-emotional meaning of phenomena 252
socio-technical
  design 43
  systems 43
Solidarity movement 199
"Sorry-I-did-not-see-your-hand" tactic 39
SRI, Socially Responsible Investment 110
Stalin, "Real Socialism" 199
Stein, Mark 27, 37, 45
stimulus-independent thoughts (SITs) 189
Strong, Philip 218
Sullivan, Harry Stack 185
superego and the id 127–128
supra-individual collective experiences 72
survivalism 240–241
swine flu 214

symbolic identification 148
systemic inter-relatedness 43

Terkel, S. 28–29, 35–36
Thatcherism 117
The Cold Heart 81
The Economist 135
The Estate Behind The Iron Gate 205
The Fashion System 127
The Gold Fish 81
The Nielsen Company 135
thought identity 146
Torres, Nuno 168
totalitarian government 220
toxic
  decision processes 32
  environment 39–41
  experiences 43
  retaliation 39
toxicity
  and revenge 36–39
  image 31–34
  manifestations of 34
toxin handler 32
traffic jams as the symptom of melancholia 202–204
transgenerational transmission of trauma 236
transitional object 85
  functions 85
trauma's concealed memory 206
traumatic neurosis 199
Traumdeutung 200
Treblinka 198
Trist, Eric 252
Tsoukas, H. 28, 42, 44
Tucket & Taffler 70–71, 87–88, 192–193
Turner, Terence 168
Turquet, Pierre 168, 170
  theory of basic assumption oneness 171

TV fandom in Brazil 170–171
Twitter revolution 133–134, 144, 150
   attitude toward the real 148–149
   effects of 151
   identifying truths, recognizing what we want 145–146
   matter of attitude 147–148
   recognizing a beyond 149–150
   social consequences 150–152
   social network is something more than the network itself 136–137
   something more than an information revolution 135–136
   today's 142

ultra-radicalism 238
unconscious
   conflict patterns 60–61
   dynamics and social learning processes 219
   fantasies 38, 119, 219
   fantasy of retribution 38
   new 179
   phantasy as defence against social anxiety 171–172
   processes 123
United States Environmental Protection Agency 2010 143
unprocessed anxieties 17
unrestricted-informal type of organization 58–59
Uprising Monument 210
uselessness 245

Vera & Crossan 29
Volkan, Vamik 187, 236

voluntary-sector organizations 28
voyeurism 165, 174

waitresses' lexicon 34
Warsaw ego 204
Warsaw's heavy industry 198
Warsaw-the-Brave for dead 201
Warsaw through a kaleidoscope of history 197
   blow, the dream, and the bucolic green 204–206
   metaphor of the postmodern world 210–211
   non-continuity and artefacts 210
   severe mechanical concussions 199
Wax, Ruby 169
weak thinking 228
Weick, K. 28
Westen, Drew 191
Whitebook, Joel 238
WikiLeaks 137, 146
Wilkinson, Jonny 167, 174
   England Rugby 175
Wilson, Elizabeth 118–119
Wilson, Timothy 184
Winnicott, D. W. 85, 133–134, 160
work enterprisers 57
work–life balance 55, 61
World of Warcraft, role-playing games 136

XYZ company 6, 10, 12–13, 17
   A-NZ regional operations 12

YouTube video 137

Zen monk 190